The Metamorphosi.

The Metamorphosis of Ovid

From Chaucer to Ted Hughes

Sarah Annes Brown

Duckworth

First paperback edition 2002
First published in 1999 by
Gerald Duckworth & Co. Ltd.
61 Frith Street, London W1D 3JL
Tel: 0171 434 4242
Fax: 0171 434 4420
inquiries@duckworth-publishers.co.uk
www.ducknet.co.uk

A catalogue record for this book is available
from the British Library

ISBN 0 7156 3177 2

Typeset by Ray Davies
Printed in Great Britain by
Bookcraft (Bath) Ltd, Midsomer Norton, Avon

Contents

Credits

The author and publisher are grateful to all who have given permission for the use of copyright material in this book, including the following:

Excerpts from the creative writings of James Joyce are reproduced with the permission of his Estate, © The Estate of James Joyce.

Quotations from Virginia Woolf, *Orlando*, are reproduced by permission of the Society of Authors as the literary representative of the Estate of Virginia Woolf, and by permission of Harcourt Brace & Company Ltd.

Quotations from Ted Hughes, *Tales From Ovid*, are reproduced by permission of Faber & Faber, and Farrar, Straus & Giroux.

Quotations from T.S. Eliot, *The Waste Land*, are reproduced by permission of Faber & Faber.

Acknowledgements

I would like to acknowledge the help and advice of the following people, all of whom have provided me with useful ideas and suggestions for my research: Denis Feeney, Stuart Gillespie, Debbie Johnson, Ian Johnson, Duncan Kennedy, Robert King, John Lee, Raphael Lyne, Michael Liversidge, Rachel Lynch, Lesley MacDowell (for her generous help with my chapter on Joyce), Neil Rhodes, Nick Roe, Susan Sellers and Myra Stokes.

I would also particularly like to thank Alex Brown and David Hopkins for their many valuable suggestions, and my Ph.D. supervisors, Tom Mason and Charles Martindale, whose criticism, encouragement and time helped me greatly.

Prefatory note

Except where I have indicated otherwise, Miller's translation of the *Metamorphoses* from the Loeb edition of the text is used throughout. Other translations have been used where, for example in the case of Shakespeare and Golding, they made an important contribution to a writer's reception of Ovid.

I have silently modernised punctuation and spelling for ease of reading. However in the case of authors such as Golding and Spenser, where a number of problematic issues are raised by complete modernisation, I have retained the original spelling but normalised certain other aspects of the text.

Although this study is only lightly annotated it is indebted to the work of numerous critics and scholars whose works are listed in the bibliography rather than cited in individual notes. The bibliography is selective, and the emphasis is on authors, such as Shakespeare, whose relationship with Ovid has been well documented rather than on those texts, such as *Orlando*, whose debt to the *Metamorphoses* has not been discussed extensively elsewhere.

To my parents

1

Ovid and Ovidianism: influence, reception, transformation

parte tamen meliore mei super alta perennis
astra ferar, nomenque erit indelebile nostrum,
quaque patet domitis Romana potentia terris,
ore legar populi, perque omnia saecula fama,
siquid habent veri vatum praesagia, vivam.

Still in my better part I shall be borne immortal far beyond the lofty stars
and I shall have an undying name. Wherever Rome's power extends over
the conquered world, I shall have mention on men's lips, and, if the
prophecies of bards have any truth, through all the ages shall I live in
fame. (XV 875-9)

Naso [Ovid] had escaped every control for good and all. Naso was
unassailable, invulnerable. And anyone could make use of his memory
as he or she pleased without fear of ever being contradicted by a note
passed from the prison of his exile, by his return or pardon. (Rans-
mayr, p. 82)

Ovid's *Metamorphoses* is one of the cornerstones of Western culture. It
contains versions of many of the most famous myths of Greece and
Rome, and has proved a continuing inspiration for poets, composers and
painters alike. The title of Ovid's poem is self-explanatory; each of the
tales contains a transformation of some kind, whether a god assumes a
disguise in order to seduce a beautiful nymph, or a mortal turns into
some plant or animal, perhaps as a punishment for wrongdoing, per-
haps as a means of escape from a still more dreadful fate. In some tales
the metamorphosis is almost tangential – the description of Phaethon's
sisters' transformation into trees (II 340-66) is hardly more than a coda
to the main narrative – but more often it forms the tale's climax. Typical
is the well known metamorphosis of Daphne into a laurel as she flees
in terror from Apollo:

mollia cinguntur tenui praecordia libro,
in frondem crines, in ramos bracchia crescunt,
pes modo tam velox pigris radicibus haeret,
ora cacumen habet: remanet nitor unus in illa. (I 549-52)

1

A filmy rind about her body grows;
Her hair to leaves, her arms extend to boughs:
The nymph is all into a laurel gone:
The smoothness of her skin remains alone (Dryden, II, p. 819)

The attention to detail, the careful itemisation of each feature's before and after state, the identification of some characteristic which remains unchanged, all these can be seen again and again in the poem's many metamorphoses. We are forced to perceive an affinity where there might at first seem only to be a bizarre incongruence. The transformation of fierce Tereus into a hoopoe (VI 671-4) may appear arbitrary, but we are told that the crest on his head and his long beak suggest a soldier's helmet and sword. We might be reminded of Dr Johnson's often-quoted strictures on the metaphysicals' fondness for 'occult resemblances in things apparently unlike' and 'heterogeneous ideas ... yoked by violence together' (Johnson 1905, vol. 1, p. 21). And Ovid's transformations are conceits of a kind – metamorphoses could be described as metaphors made flesh.

The poem's title connotes more than mere physical transformation. The *Metamorphoses* itself is metamorphic, slipping out of one genre or mood into another, eluding the reader just as the shape-shifting Thetis eludes the amorous advances of Peleus (XI 243-6). Written in the metre of epic, it embraces a range of modes including elegy, panegyric, history and philosophy. One story merges into another, changing form as radically as Daphne or Actaeon. We think we are on familiar territory when Ovid begins to narrate the famous history of Rome's founding hero Aeneas, only for the narrative to swerve away from Aeneas, and indeed from epic, and into the pastoral world of Acis and Galatea. (This episode is discussed at length in Chapter 4.) As we shall see in Chapter 2, Homer as well as Virgil is subjected to Ovidian metamorphosis – and Ovid does not forget to transform himself in the poem's final apotheosis, quoted at the very beginning of this chapter. Although audacious, Ovid's claim that he will live forever has certainly (so far) stood the test of time.

*

In English literature, Ovid's influence is most obviously apparent in the later Middle Ages and the Renaissance, when direct retellings of his work flourished and allusions to his poems became a pervasive literary presence. The *Metamorphoses* is only one of the many works for which he is celebrated. Nearly as well known and admired are the *Ars Amatoria*, a mock-didactic handbook containing racy advice to young lovers of both sexes, and the *Amores*, a collection of sophisticated love elegies addressed to 'Corinna' – part of the tradition which lies behind the erotic poetry of Renaissance poets such as Donne. Also influential were the

Heroides, a series of 'letters' by such legendary women as Dido and Ariadne. Their pathos and apparent empathy with their female subjects are tempered, perhaps undercut, by wit and irony. Among the later works influenced by the *Heroides* are Chaucer's *Legend of Good Women* and Pope's 'Eloisa to Abelard'. Ovid also wrote the *Fasti*, a poetical calendar of Roman legends and festivals, and during his exile he composed the *Tristia* and *Epistulae ex Ponto* which, although not among his most popular works, contain a number of interesting reflections on the earlier *Metamorphoses*.

One reason for perceiving the *Metamorphoses* as the pinnacle of Ovid's achievement is its permeation into so many revered literary texts. The fact that it is a more visible presence than, say, the *Amores* is partly due to the nature of its subject matter. We do not immediately start wondering about the source of an Elizabethan poem describing a man's ardent wooing of his mistress; such situations are felt to be universal, and thus we may assume that the poet's inspiration was entirely personal and autobiographical, ignoring the long and complex heritage lying behind his achievement. By contrast it is immediately apparent that a work such as Shakespeare's *Venus and Adonis* is derived from an earlier mythological tradition, so we are more likely to become aware of its precise source in *Metamorphoses* X.

So why were so many poets drawn to the *Metamorphoses*? What features of Ovid's work attracted them so irresistibly? This book is partly concerned with answering these questions, defining Ovidianism as a set of characteristics identifiable in Ovid, in particular the Ovid of the *Metamorphoses*. But it is a cause as well as a sign of the poem's importance that so many later writers turned to it for inspiration. Although its intrinsic richness and complexity provided the original impetus behind its popularity, its permeation into so much of English literature has in turn shaped each generation's response to Ovid and lent still more resonance to his voice. As the quotation from Ransmayr at the beginning of the chapter suggests, Ovid's immortality is bound up in his capacity for endless change, continual reappropriation. Each of the Ovidians I discuss could be said to have constructed their own 'Ovid' and our reception of the poem is complexly intertwined with our reception of Milton, Shakespeare and the many others who form part of the Ovidian line. A modern assessment of the *Metamorphoses* will be infected by our conscious and unconscious knowledge of what earlier writers valued in Ovid, as well as by the particular preoccupations of our own era. It is difficult, for example, for a modern reading of the poem to be uninfluenced by previous preferences for certain stories over others – we are likely to dwell with particular interest on those narratives which have been most imitated by later writers. It is of course also true that our judgement as to what features in Ovid most fascinated

3

Shakespeare will be swayed by our own tastes and preferences within both Ovid and Shakespeare.

*

All too often the unprejudiced reader comes away with the uneasy feeling that the poem that Ovid said was a better likeness of himself than any portrait has been metamorphosed into a creation of the critic's own private imagining. Each critic becomes a Pygmalion. (Curran 1972, p. 71)

I do not seek to absolve myself from Curran's charge – all my readings, both of Ovid himself and of his imitators – are determined by my own tastes and interests, themselves the products of various contingent circumstances. The same could of course be said of Curran himself – in the same article he refers to the way Ovid was 'used – and misused – in the Middle Ages and in the Renaissance'. This suggestion that a range of responses to Ovid may easily be divided into sheep and goats is problematic. It may be hard for us to engage with the medieval commentators' contributions to Ovid's reception, but to recontextualise the *Metamorphoses* within, say, a Christian context is surely no more nor less justifiable than siting the text within a feminist or post-Freudian framework. And the impulse behind these different moves – to make Ovid more 'relevant', more acceptable – is surely analogous.

Because of the importance of Ovid and the complexity of his influence many different kinds of books might be (and have been) written about his presence in English literature. Among those I have found most useful are *Ovid Renewed*, a wide-ranging collection of essays edited by Charles Martindale, Leonard Barkan's impressive study of the Renaissance Ovid, *The Gods Made Flesh*, and Charles Tomlinson's account of Ovid's influence on Modernism, *Poetry and Metamorphosis*. The scope and range of *Ovid Renewed* is similar to my own, although it necessarily lacks the emphasis on particular developments and continuities within the tradition that I have tried to include in this study. However, I do not attempt to present an account of each period's encounter with Ovid from a rigorously historicist perceptive – such as Michael Calabrese offers in his excellent *Chaucer's Ovidian Arts of Love*. I aim to establish a continuous 'Ovidian' tradition and explore the reception of Ovid and 'Ovidianism' rather than provide an exhaustive account, or even an overview, of any one poet's debt to Ovid. Whole books have of course been devoted to Ovid's influence on a single author – notably Jonathan Bate's *Shakespeare and Ovid*, Richard DuRocher's *Milton and Ovid* and John Fyler's *Chaucer and Ovid*. The discussions which follow focus on specific points of contact between each writer and the *Metamorphoses*, a series of snapshots, as it were, of English Ovidianism.

With a few exceptions – Beddoes, H.D. and some of the writers discussed in Chapters 7 and 12 – this study focusses on the canonical mainstream. This conservative stance reflects my own perception of English Ovidianism as a phenomenon. The writers of each age go back, not just to Ovid, but to his earlier imitators; therefore each age's most renowned writers help shape the development of Ovid's reception for future generations.

Various patterns of affinity between the writers I discuss have long been recognised and in some cases acknowledged by those concerned: Spenser was well aware of his indebtedness to Chaucer and was in turn a major influence on Keats; Joyce and Woolf look back to Shakespeare – as does just about everybody else. No one has disputed this complex network of continuities, but it seems possible to posit an extra Ovidian connection running as a distinct, if not perfectly neat or continuous, strand through their work. They have gone back to Ovid himself, but they have also gone back to the Ovid of their fellow countrymen. Here it is perhaps worth mentioning two poets who had a great influence on English Ovidianism despite being outside the canon, Arthur Golding and George Sandys, whose very different translations of the *Metamorphoses* were to have a major impact on the reception of Ovid by many more esteemed writers. (Golding's translation appeared in 1567, Sandys' in 1626.)

The intensity and depth of someone's influence is too nebulous a quantity to be evaluated with ease or certainty. It cannot be gauged, for example, simply by the number of allusions to the *Metamorphoses* in a writer's works. In fact this is an area where the very familiarity of Ovid's great poem has done him a disservice in terms of our assessment of its importance, causing his influence to be underestimated; important debts have either been overlooked or attributed to a general classical tradition rather than to the direct impact of the *Metamorphoses*. For although the *Metamorphoses* is far more than a 'myth kitty', it is undeniable that Ovid is the source for some of the most memorable and resonant stories ever to fire the Western imagination. Ovid was not a great originator of narratives, but the tales are still every bit his own – just as the characters of Lear and Hamlet are now inseparable from Shakespeare. We might think of Narcissus and Echo or Pygmalion's statue as 'Greek myths', but in fact the familiar versions of these stories can only be traced back as far as the *Metamorphoses*. Ovid was the first to associate Echo and Narcissus together, and previously Pygmalion had merely fallen in love with a statue, not sculpted it himself. Clearly the nymph who can only echo the words of others is the perfect counterpart for the youth who falls in love with his own reflection, and the reinvention of Pygmalion as an artist of genius transforms an originally prurient narrative into a tender and miraculous affirmation of the power of love combined with art. Or does it? We might resist this interpretation if we remember the tale of Narcissus and reflect that

5

Pygmalion is similarly obsessed with a projection of himself rather than with an independent woman. And if we do not make this connection – six books separate the two tales – Ovid prods us again by telling the story of Pygmalion's grandson Cinyras who followed the sculptor's example by falling in love with his own creation – his daughter Myrrha. Endlessly supple and subtle, the *Metamorphoses* encourages us to make these and many other connections, inviting us to judge and interpret, while at the same time warning us that it is easier to look for a solution than to find one:

> Rumor in ambiguo est; aliis violentior aequo
> visa dea est, alii laudant dignamque severa
> virginitate vocant: pars invenit utraque causas.

> Common talk wavered this way and that: to some the goddess seemed more cruel than was just; others called her act worthy of her austere virginity; both sides found good reasons for their judgement. (III 253-5)

In these lines Ovid ostensibly refuses to guide our response to the punishment of Actaeon, metamorphosed into a stag to be slaughtered by his hounds following his inadvertent glimpse of Diana bathing. Modern readers tend to be on Actaeon's side: Ted Hughes affirms that 'It is no crime/ To lose your way in a dark wood' (p.105), thus aligning the hunter with Dante, and David Slavitt, in his 'translation' of the tale, suggests that even Diana's nymphs are against her:

> The naked nymphs
> have seen him, are horrified, and throng about their mistress
> to hide her body with theirs (*or perhaps the youth from Diana's
> wrath?*), but it's too late. (III 171-4)

It seems that Ovid also sympathised with Actaeon, for in his exile poetry he identifies his own mysterious *error* with Actaeon's inadvertent crime:

> cur aliquid vid? cur noxia lumina feci?
>   cur imprudenti cognita culpa mihi?
> inscius Actaeon vidit sine veste Dianam:
>   praeda fuit canibus non minus ille suis.
> scilicet in superis etiam fortuna luenda est,
>   nec veniam laeso numine casus habet.

> Why did I see anything? Why did I make my eyes guilty? Why was I so thoughtless as to harbour the knowledge of a fault? Unwitting was Actaeon when he beheld Diana unclothed; none the less he became the prey of his own hounds. Clearly, among the gods, even ill-fortune must be atoned for, nor is mischance an excuse when a deity is wronged. (*Tristia* II 103-8)

1. Ovid and Ovidianism

Part of the poem's resilience lies in the fact that individual stories can be appropriated for so many different purposes. I have mentioned just a handful of the tales which have been invested with new layers of significance – through excavation as much as through accretion – in the two thousand years which have passed since the *Metamorphoses* was written. Ovid's many imitators have been drawn to some of his tales far more frequently and urgently than to others. Often the explanation for such preferences is not difficult to find – the story of Daphne's transformation into a laurel is told at length, whereas the similar fate of Syrinx, turned into reeds, is barely touched on. This imbalance is reflected in later poets' allusions to the two tales.[1] In some cases a striking reinvention of Ovid – such as Shakespeare's *Venus and Adonis* – can ensure that a particular story retains prominence in readers' minds. But not all tales enjoy a consistently glorious afterlife. The moving story of 'Ceyx and Alcyone' – and particularly its set piece description of the Cave of Sleep – was once widely admired. Among the writers who drew on it for inspiration were Chaucer, Spenser and Shakespeare, and it was memorably translated by Dryden. But no version is included in the two most recent anthologies of Ovidian translation, Ted Hughes' *Tales from Ovid* and Hofmann and Lasdun's *After Ovid*. The latter's editors are anxious to remind us of the poem's 'relevance', its preoccupation with 'holocaust, plague, sexual harassment, rape, incest, seduction, pollution, sex-change ...' (p. xi). The faithful wedded love of Ceyx and Alcyone certainly cannot be easily assimilated into such a view of the *Metamorphoses*, yet it is one of the poem's highlights, nonetheless. The stars of some tales, on the other hand, have risen. Pygmalion's artistry has always been well known – the tale lies behind Hermione's miraculous reanimation in *The Winter's Tale* – but it seems to acquire new (or renewed) resonances over the course of its complex *Nachleben*, and thus becomes an increasingly persistent presence in the latter half of this study. My focus on this myth is just one example of the way I have consciously privileged certain aspects of Ovid's art, carefully unwinding a few Ovidian strands, in order to demonstrate more clearly how Ovidianism develops. The 'darkening' of Pygmalion, the effect of other cultural developments on the tale's reception, is just one facet of the way the wider Ovidian discourse has evolved.

Ovid's stories are the most easily visible signs of his influence upon later works. Other elements of Ovidianism are more elusive to pin down, yet it is possible to identify a set of characteristics, patterns and procedures, none of which is the exclusive prerogative of Ovid, but which may yet, when taken as a whole, be styled 'Ovidian'. When we

---

[1]The comparative fame of these two stories is not easy to assess scientifically. However it is significant that the first two discs of the Chadwyck-Healey English Poetry Full-Text Database (600-1800) contain 373 references to Daphne and only 48 references to Syrinx. (The English Poetry Full-text Database, Copyright © [1992-1994] Chadwyck-Healey Ltd.)

examine the influence of Ovid on the works of his followers we gain a fresh insight, not only into their own poems, but into the poetry of Ovid himself, for we are encouraged to reflect on those qualities in the *Metamorphoses* which proved so unfailingly fascinating to generations of future readers and writers. As well as developing a narrative of English Ovidianism each of the chapters in this book develops one or more aspects of Ovid's peculiar genius as manifested both in his own work and in that of his imitators. Through the use of very specific moments within each writer's dialogue with Ovid, I attempt to build up a kind of mosaic in which a single feature is taken from each different work or author in order to construct a portrait, as it were, of English Ovidianism. Because each chapter contributes to this larger project, my particular subjects and texts are not necessarily the most immediately obvious ones. The Romantic Ovid, for example, is represented by Keats' 'Ode on a Grecian Urn' (which contains no overt Ovidian allusions) rather than, say, Shelley's 'Arethusa'. However its inclusion here may be justified because Ovid's very absence – or absent presence – itself typifies Ovid's reception in the nineteenth century (and in any case it might be argued that the Ode is a more Ovidian poem than 'Arethusa').

The world of the *Metamorphoses* has its own peculiar atmosphere. Although pathos is not quite absent, the overriding impression is of a kind of aesthetic detachment, rather than a deep involvement with any of the characters. This may partly be accounted for by the lack of a single focus as there is in the *Aeneid*. This dispassionate quality in Ovid's work seems to have affected the reception of the *Metamorphoses* by many of the poets I discuss, perhaps none so intensely as Shakespeare. Although Ovid does not always invite debate so obviously as at the end of the Actaeon narrative, his imitators' engagement with him often manifests unease as well as fascination. The detachment of the *Metamorphoses* is simultaneously rejected and confirmed in *A Midsummer Night's Dream*, and a later Ovidian, Keats, evinces a similarly troubled response to this quality in the poem. Perhaps only Marvell appears to have felt quite at home in the Ovidian universe. His contemporary, Milton, certainly had an uneasy relationship with Ovid; on the surface *Paradise Lost* appears to possess a vision of the universe consistent with the moral absolutes of Christianity, yet if we examine it in the context of its Ovidian borrowings a rather different picture emerges. Milton reconfigures Ovid's stories in order to make them more palatable, but the fissures are still apparent. Woolf uses the same procedures to further a very different project, manipulating Ovid's tale of Daphne and Apollo for an unexpected purpose, the establishment of good and equal relations between the sexes.

Although Ovid's perspective often seems cool and remote he is also well known as a documenter of human passion. Love – or rather sex – is the topic with which he has often been most readily associated, particularly at times when his reputation has been in decline. This subject is most prominent in his earlier works – notably the *Ars Amatoria* and the *Amores* – but the *Metamorphoses* does not lack eroticism, often of a rather suspect kind. Sexual feeling is frequently both violent and unreciprocated; typical is the passion felt for Callisto by Jove which burns like a fire in his marrow (II 410), a line thus rendered by Ted Hughes:

> Lust bristled up his thighs
> And poured into the roots of his teeth. (p. 46)

It is Callisto who must suffer metamorphosis into a bear as a punishment for her quite involuntary pregnancy – Diana's anger against the nymph anticipates her harsh treatment of Actaeon – but for Hughes it is the rapist who is most bestial. Indeed on many notorious occasions Jove *does* transform himself into an animal – a bull to carry away Europa, for example, or a swan to seduce Leda. In fact perverse – or at least non-standard – sexuality seems almost to be the norm in the *Metamorphoses* which features homosexual and incestuous liaisons, in addition to a variety of cross species couplings. Predictably Ovid's depiction of sexuality receives most attention from twentieth-century writers, although Dryden and Marvell were also apparently attracted by Ovid's treatment of unconventional sexual responses.

Ovid depicts violence as vividly as sex, often with a kind of gruesome wit, as during the battle between the Lapiths and the Centaurs when the blood of drunken Aphidas, who has been speared through the throat, drips into his goblet like wine (XII 316-26). Particularly grisly is the punishment of Tereus, the rapist who is fed the flesh of his own son. When he asks for the child his wife replies gleefully: 'intus habes, quem poscis', 'you have, within, him whom you want' (VI 655). Such touches might seem especially congenial in the age of Tarantino, but Shakespeare had already topped Ovid's mannered violence in *Titus Andronicus*, and even in the 'elegant' Augustan age Ovid's description of Philomela's severed tongue, squirming like a snake, had been singled out for approval by Sir Samuel Garth (1661-1719; his contribution to English Ovidianism is discussed in Chapter 7).

Ovid is justly famous for his wit – a quality difficult to define, and discussed in more detail in Chapters 5 and 7. Linguistic play – including puns and zeugma – is one aspect of this facility, as is a love of the incongruous, particularly when used to depress pretention or overturn expectations. A typical example of Ovid's verbal wit is his description of Narcissus; the very shape of the language suggests the youth's self-reflexive obsession:

se cupit inprudens, et, qui probat, ipse probatur,
dumque petit, petitur, pariterque accendit et ardet.

Unwittingly he desires himself; he praises, and is himself what he
praises; and while he seeks, is sought; equally he kindles love and burns
with love. (III 425-6)

Both Shakespeare and Milton assimilate this chiastic effect into their
own reception of the legend, illustrating the dual significance of style
and story for followers of the *Metamorphoses*. In *Venus and Adonis*
Shakespeare writes that 'Narcissus so himself himself forsook,/ and
died to kiss his shadow in the brook' (161-2), and in *Paradise Lost* Milton
invokes Narcissus when he describes Eve's glimpse of herself in a pool:

> I started back,
> It started back; but pleased I soon returned,
> Pleased it returned as soon with answering looks
> Of sympathy and love ... (IV 462-5)

Such elements of Ovidian style have often been perceived as no more
than a trivial, if attractive, veneer. However recent criticism – particu-
larly Garth Tissol's excellent *The Face of Nature* – has highlighted the
interpretative importance of wit in the *Metamorphoses*, its embedded-
ness in Ovid's metamorphic vision.

More abstract preoccupations such as an interest in art's relationship
with reality and in the nature of fiction itself also seem to have struck
his poetic successors as forcibly as his lively tales. Those aspects of Ovid
which might cause him to be seen as a precursor of postmodernism – in
particular his alertness to the mechanisms of textuality – have been
appreciated by every generation of Ovidians, not just by those at work
this century. Indeed the very first English poet discussed in this study,
Chaucer, perhaps responds to this aspect of Ovid's work with most
confidence and least anxiety. Ovid's fascination with artists, his aware-
ness of his affinity with their creative power, generates some of the most
powerful moments in the poem, such as the stories of Arachne and
Pygmalion. Both the weaver and the sculptor are ambiguous figures
who elicit praise from some readers and suspicion from others. The
influence of Ovid's artists is apparent in *The Tempest* and *The Faerie
Queene* – Spenser in particular appears troubled as well as fascinated
by this aspect of Ovid's art. Although he shares Ovid's tendency to
identify with artists, he is repelled by the moral ambiguity which taints
their skill.

The fascination Ovid exerted upon his imitators sometimes resem-
bles the attraction of a snake whose gaze its frightened prey seeks to
avoid, yet cannot resist. A turning point in this study comes in Chapter
7, which deals with the Augustan reception of Ovid, with particular

reference to the translation by several hands edited by Garth. Tacit unease now gives way to overt disapproval; as Ovid's reputation began to wane his poetry was seen as frivolous. But too many of the greatest English writers had entered into a profound engagement with Ovid for his influence to lessen greatly; the *Metamorphoses* had received re-newed force and vitality through imitation. Although many writers and critics in the eighteenth and nineteenth centuries were scornful of Ovid, their hostility or indifference to his works is belied by the increasingly internalised – sometimes unacknowledged – Ovidianism in the poetry of the time. Browning for example briefly evokes Ovid as a symbol of licentiousness yet his poetry is full of allusions to the *Metamorphoses*, and, more significant, these allusions function in a way which might itself be described as Ovidian.

Indeed by this point Ovidianism was so potent, so thoroughly synthe-sised into the whole tradition of English poetry, that it eventually became possible for a non-classicist such as Keats to write in a way which is profoundly 'Ovidian' even though his knowledge of the *Meta-morphoses* was nothing like so rigorous as that of Spenser or Milton. Ovidianism has thus developed into a semi-autonomous phenomenon which we might term 'embedded' Ovidianism; a modern writer who has never read Ovid might well produce a poem or a novel which seems unmistakably Ovidian if he has read a number of the texts discussed in this study (not counting translations). In 'Ovid and the nineteenth century' Norman Vance describes the same phenomenon, but sees Ovidianism as diluted rather than enriched by his imitators' role in Ovid's later reception:

> Part of the difficulty in assessing the significance of Ovid in the nine-teenth century is that one can never see him on his own. His influence is nearly always mediated, sometimes by old paintings on Ovidian subjects such as Polidoro da Caravaggio's *Andromeda* which haunted the young Browning or Piero di Cosimo's *Death of Procris* which inspired a poem by Austin Dobson. Even without the painters, other poets, translators, com-mentators and compilers constantly interpose themselves between Ovid and the nineteenth-century reader. Chaucer, Shakespeare and Milton, Natalis Comes, George Sandys and the Revd John Lemprière all cluster round holding up a bewildering array of coloured lenses and more or less distorting mirrors. (p. 215)

It is certainly true that by the time we come towards the end of a strand of Ovidianism such as the reception of Pygmalion it is almost impossible to establish what writers such as H.D. and Joyce owe to Ovid and what to Ovidian intermediaries – H.D. for example explicitly alludes to a celebrated Ovidian text, *The Winter's Tale*. But whether direct or indirect it is clear that these later Ovidians' works share the original preoccupations of the *Metamorphoses* – Joyce's awareness of the connections between himself and his Pygmalion-like characters is particularly Ovidian. But although Ovid's version of this tale survives the effect of numerous retellings, there has been a metamorphosis of the original none the less. Over the course of the three hundred years which separate Dryden from Ted Hughes the hints of darker meanings lying behind an ostensibly 'happy' story have been taken up more and more vigorously, a gradual change which seems to possess its own momentum independent of external influence, but which may partly be connected with the influence of the powerful Frankenstein narrative, as well as the emergence of feminism as a potent discourse. Clearly the (potential) separation of Ovidianism from Ovid himself can become problematic. How far might we want to push the adjective? When is something *really* Ovidian? Consider the case of a poem which is partly concerned with a woman who is one of Ovid's Heroides, which plays with ideas of literary authority and history and treats a great Greek hero subversively, which presents its characters with pathos but also with detachment, which shows the mortals as victims of the dispassionate gods and, most significantly, is so consummately ecphrastic that its most memorable character is woven on a coverlet – this poem would surely merit the label 'Ovidian'. Unfortunately, if 'Ovidian' is defined as 'profoundly influenced by Ovid' this poem, Catullus LXIV, would be out of the running as it was composed before Ovid was born.

Metamorphosis is a helpful metaphor to use of the process of translation or imitation. Although the original is transformed, some quality remains, allowing the relationship to be identified, just as Daphne retains her *nitor*, 'beauty' (I 552), even as a laurel. Seneca, writing in the same period as Ovid, compared the processes of imitation and mellification; bees transform nectar into honey in the same way as 'we should so blend those several flavors into one delicious compound that, even though it betrays its origin, yet it nevertheless is clearly a different thing from that whence it came' (Seneca, epistle 84.5). The history of Ovid's reception may be seen as a series of individual metamorphoses, not simply of Ovid's masterpiece itself, but of the productions of all the intervening artists who have helped shape our own conception of the poem – artists, composers and novelists as well as poets.

Ted Hughes subtly acknowledges that his translator's art is also a metamorphosis at the beginning of his 'Creation; Four Ages; Flood; Lycaon':

> Now I am ready to tell how bodies are changed
> Into different bodies.
>
> I summon the supernatural beings
> Who first contrived
> These transmogrifications
> In the stuff of life.

1. Ovid and Ovidianism

You did it for your own amusement.
Descend again, be pleased to reanimate
This revival of those marvels.
Reveal, now, exactly
How they were performed
From the beginning
Up to this moment. (Hughes, p. 3)

At first this might seem to be a reasonably faithful rendition of the
Metamorphoses' famous opening lines:

In nova fert animus mutatas dicere formas
corpora; di, coeptis (nam vos mutastis et illas)
adspirate meis primaque ab origine mundi
ad mea perpetuum deducite tempora carmen!

My mind is bent to tell of bodies changed into new forms. Ye gods, for you
yourselves have wrought the changes, breathe on these my undertakings,
and bring down my song in unbroken strains from the world's very
beginning even unto the present time. (I 1-4)

Two words, reanimate and revival, hint that the 'marvels' are not simply
metamorphoses but the *Metamorphoses*. This modification of the origi-
nal opens up the possibility in the next four lines that Hughes' poem will
in some sense be a summation of the poem's whole reception – 'from the
beginning/ Up to this moment' – rather than an isolated response,
separated from the original by a two thousand year gulf. It is certainly
true that Hughes is indebted to earlier Ovidians, and particularly to
Shakespeare, but one of the clearest examples of an intertextual nexus
of Ovidianism can be found in the piece which follows Hughes' earlier
version of this translation in *After Ovid*, Jorie Graham's 'Flood' which
ends:

These are not pearls nor are they eyes –
(like a bored salesgirl, current gnaws the banks) –
and all whom the water has spared will now begin

to starve. (Hofmann and Lasdun, p. 26)

The echo of Ariel's song in *The Tempest* (which I discuss in more detail
in Chapter 4) is instantly recognisable, and its evocation of metamor-
phic decay is decidedly Ovidian. But the next two lines reveal that
Graham is not simply reading Ovid through Shakespeare. A twentieth-
century reader is as likely first to encounter 'Those are pearls that were
his eyes' in *The Waste Land* as in *The Tempest* itself; the body's mutation
now also figures the processes of change undergone by the Shakespear-
ean phrase as it is recontextualised first by Eliot, then by Graham. The
references to the bored salesgirl and the gnawing current recall the

typist's indifferent acquiescence to the 'young man carbuncular' and the opening decayed riverbank scene in 'The Fire Sermon'. The image of gnawing may incline us to read 'bored' rather differently – as suggestive either of sexual penetration or (as in 'Full Fathom Five') corrosive decay. It is fitting that Eliot should have appropriated Ariel's metamorphic song, for *The Waste Land* is perhaps his most Ovidian work. So Graham is not merely reading Ovid refracted through Shakespeare and Eliot as discrete Ovidian voices; she is reading him through Eliot reading Shakespeare reading Ovid.

A further suggestive gloss on the complexities of literary influence is provided by Keats' sonnet 'How many bards gild the lapses of time', a striking attestation to the importance of a poetic lineage:

> How many bards gild the lapses of time!
>   A few of them have ever been the food
>   Of my delighted fancy – I could brood
> Over their beauties, earthly, or sublime;
> And often, when I sit me down to rhyme,
>   These will in throngs before my mind intrude:
>   But no confusion, no disturbance rude
> Do they occasion; 'tis a pleasing chime.
> So the unnumbered sounds that evening store:
>   The songs of birds, the whispering of the leaves,
>   The voice of waters, the great bell that heaves
> With solemn sound, and thousand others more
>   That distance of recognizance bereaves,
> Make pleasing music, and not wild uproar.

Keats sketches the outline of a methodology for tracing connections between Ovid and the poets who followed him. The selectivity implied by the phrase 'a few' suggests that there may be particular lines of connection between poets, that certain poetic lineages and traditions, such as the Ovidian, may be identified. By referring to his own favourite poets as 'the food/ Of my delighted fancy', Keats acknowledges his indebtedness to their productions which have fuelled his own poetic creativity. The nature of this indebtedness is apprehended consciously, at least in part, as can be seen in the word 'brood' and in the very existence of such a poem in the first place. After disclaiming any 'anxiety of influence' Keats modulates the phenomenon he describes, suggesting, in those 'unnumbered sounds ... that distance of recognizance bereaves', the larger intertextual picture as well as more specific, conscious connections between poets.

Identifying a relationship between two poets, pinpointing verbal echoes or the provenance of a plot motif, does not necessarily enhance our appreciation of a text, or affect the way we interpret it. We have to perceive a dynamic interplay of some kind between the two works if source hunting is to become an interpretative tool and not just a

14

footnote opportunity. An introductory example of how our under-
standing of a work of art may be illuminated by acknowledging the
presence of an earlier work lying behind it – as well as some indication
of the problems involved simply in establishing such a relationship –
may be found in Bernini's celebrated sculpture, *Apollo and Daphne*. Did
Bernini read Ovid? It is unwise to underestimate the scholarship and
sophistication of artists of this period and, even though we should not
be surprised to find quite independent presentations of a woman turn-
ing into a tree following the same predictable pattern, Bernini's
depiction of Daphne's metamorphosis is remarkably similar to *Meta-
morphoses* I. Her hair changes to leaves and her feet become roots
(Bernini shows her toenails grotesquely extended, pinning her to the
ground just as in Ovid). One element the two metamorphoses have in
common is the emphasis on the fact that the bark surrounds Daphne
and grows around her body, as opposed to an alternative mode of
transformation, equally feasible, whereby her skin actually turns into
bark, and her legs join together. This identification of an apparently
strong link between Bernini and Ovid suggests the *Metamorphoses* was
a direct influence on the statue. John Pope-Henessy's description of
Bernini's sculpture certainly assumes a conscious and sophisticated
debt to Ovid:

> By temperament he was an illustrator: the form and subjects of his early
> groups may vary, but the intention behind all of them is uniform, to
> provide a visual embodiment of a literary text. Ovid's Pluto, like Bernini's,
> has been pierced by Cupid's dart, and is inspired by love, not lust. It is
> Ovid who describes the wind baring the limbs of Daphne and Apollo's
> hand feeling her pulse beneath the bark, and Ovid who pictures Triton
> rising from the water to sound his echoing conch as Neptune stills the
> flood. In the seventeenth century it was popularly held that painting was
> mute poetry. Bernini transfuses this conception to the sister art of sculp-
> ture. In France he expressed his admiration for Poussin with the words
> 'o il grande favoleggiatore', and Poussin alone rivals the mythopoeic
> faculty, the gift for supremely sensitive narration, evident in his early
> groups. (Pope-Hennessy, p. 108).

An awareness that Bernini was directly inspired by Ovid's *Metamor-
phoses* may alter the way we perceive the figures. A number of critics
have commented on Apollo's expression as he beholds the transforma-
tion of Daphne. Nigel Llewellyn says that 'the god is shown chasing still
but amazed at the transformation only he, as yet, has noticed' (p. 160).
This astonishment troubled John Moore as did the expression of terror
on Daphne's face:

> The face and figure of Apollo are deficient in simplicity; the noble simplic-
> ity of the best antique statues: he runs with affected graces, and his
> astonishment at the beginning transformation of his mistress is not, in

15

my opinion, naturally expressed, but seems rather the exaggerated astonishment of an actor. The form and shape of Daphne are delicately executed; but in her face, beauty is, in some degree, sacrificed to the expression of terror; her features are too much distorted by fear. (Bauer, p. 58)

Wittkower ascribes an acute, non-classical, 'psychological complication', as he terms it, to the figures:

Daphne turns back horror-stricken because she feels the hand of the pursuer, but is not aware of the simultaneous transformation of her body. Apollo, however, notices with amazement the transformation at the very moment when he seemed to be sure of his victim; but his body has not had time to react and he is still chasing what he suddenly sees to be unattainable. Similar psycho-physical subtleties, unknown in antiquity, were to gain even greater importance in Bernini's later work. (Wittkower, p. 7)

But it is possible to perceive the figure of Apollo in a quite different way, exhibiting, not amazement, but rather a calm, even vacuous, serenity which offers a shocking contrast to the undoubted horror on Daphne's face. This disparity is entirely apt if we accept the sculpture's direct debt to the *Metamorphoses*, whose gods, for all the ostensible 'humanity' of their passions, are rendered remote and largely indifferent to mortals because of their own power and immortality. Ovid's Apollo is only briefly thrown by Daphne's metamorphosis. He places his hand on the bark, tries to kiss her although she still shrinks from him, and declares, with measured aplomb, that if she cannot be his bride she will be his tree. Bernini's Apollo also has his hand on the bark and perhaps his lips are slightly parted, not in an expression of amazement, but because he is in the middle of describing the laurel's future role. John Moore – whose account of the statue's effect seems to me the most perceptive of the descriptions quoted above – was understandably perturbed by the contrast between the mannered god and the agonized nymph. But Bernini may just as well have been imitating the tone of the *Metamorphoses* as guilty of an artistic blunder. This incongruity, even indecorum, is itself very Ovidian. In the *Metamorphoses* Daphne's experience of Apollo's pursuit is very different from the god's. *She* is a desperate hunted animal. *He* can give expression to facetious pleas for her to slow down lest she hurt herself, promising to match his own speed to hers; the emotions of both participants are given equal weight by Ovid allowing us to choose with whom to identify, and the story's reception by later writers is correspondingly troubled and ambivalent as we shall see in later chapters. The gulf between Apollonian remoteness and human vulnerability can be traced in another of Bernini's most celebrated works, the statue of St Theresa. Leaving aside the vexed question of the exact nature of the saint's rapture, there is something unsettling in the contrast between her expression of sublimely intense and all-encompassing emotion and the icy sweetness of the angel's blank smile. We might almost imagine him saying, with Puck, 'Lord, what fools these mortals be!'

So an understanding of the way one text lies behind another text (or image) may radically alter our perception of that later text, offering new interpretative possibilities. The moment of fusion between Shakespeare and Ovid or between Bernini and Ovid is dependent for some of its impact upon a knowledge of the *Metamorphoses*, just as the moment of fusion between nymph and laurel seems more effective to the onlooker if he realises that Daphne is neither a permanent cross between a tree and a woman nor a laurel who is turning into a nymph.

*

If we try to establish the very earliest example of a poetic reception of the *Metamorphoses* it would be difficult (indeed impossible) to find a better starting point than one within the *Metamorphoses* itself. Stephen Hinds notes that when Orpheus alludes to the rape of Proserpina in Book X the reader will inevitably think back to Ovid's own retelling of this story in the fifth book:

> And if *we* recall the Persephone myth most sharply from the hexameters of *Metamorphoses* 5.341-661, Orpheus too, interestingly, can be thought of as having precisely this version in *his* mind. Orpheus' mother, remember (Ovid himself draws our attention to the fact below at *Metamorphoses* 10.148), at whose knee he will first have learnt the great stories of the world, is the muse Calliope; and Calliope it was who sang for us in the fifth book of the *Metamorphoses* ... The story of the rape has not yet left Ovid's study; but the story of its reception has already begun. (Hinds, 1987a, p. 135)

A slightly less extreme case of self-reflexivity may be identified in Ovid's *Tristia*, the collection of poems he wrote from exile, whose highly self-conscious, crafted literariness belies the apparent – and presumably real – sorrow and depravation attendant upon banishment in Tomi.[2] Here Ovid appears to echo one of the most memorable passages from the *Metamorphoses*, the description of the flood with which Jupiter punishes mankind. As this episode was to influence many of Ovid's later imitators, it is worth quoting at some length:

> Occupat hic collem, cumba sedet alter adunca
> et ducit remos illic, ubi nuper arabat:

[2] The Emperor Augustus exiled Ovid to Tomi, now part of Rumania, in AD 8. One reason for the Emperor's decision was the licentious character of Ovid's *Ars Amatoria*, another is some unspecified 'error' which Ovid committed, the nature of which has never been established.

ille supra segetes aut mersae culmina villae
navigat, hic summa piscem deprendit in ulmo.
figitur in viridi, si fors tulit, ancora prato,
aut subiecta terunt curvae vineta carinae;
et, modo qua graciles gramen carpsere capellae,
nunc ibi deformes ponunt sua corpora phocae.
mirantur sub aqua lucos urbesque domosque
Nereides, silvasque tenent delphines et altis
incursant ramis agitataque robora pulsant.

Here one man seeks a hill-top in his flight; another sits in his curved skiff, plying the oars where lately he has plowed; one sails over his fields of grain or the roof of his buried farmhouse, and one takes fish caught in the elm-tree's top. And sometimes it chanced that an anchor was embedded in a grassy meadow, or the curving keels brushed over the vineyard tops. And where but now the slender goats had browsed, the ugly sea-calves rested. The Nereids are amazed to see beneath the waters groves and cities and the haunts of men. The dolphins invade the woods, brushing against the high branches, and shake the oak-trees as they knock against them in their course. (I 293-303)

Ovid's evocation of the effects of winter upon Tomi has a similarly surreal, alien quality:

quaque rates ierant, pedibus nunc itur, et undas
    frigore concretas ungula pulsat equi; ...
vix equidem credar, sed, cum sint praemia falsi
    nulla, ratam debet testis habere fidem:
vidimus ingentem glacie consistere pontum,
    lubricaque inmotas testa premebat aquas.
nec vidisse sat est; durum calcavimus aequor,
    undaque non udo sub pede summa fuit ...
tum neque se pandi possunt delphines in auras
    tollere; conantes dura coercet hiems ...
inclusaeque gelu stabunt in marmore puppes,
    nec poterit rigidas findere remus aquas.
vidimus in glacie pisces haerere ligatos,
    sed pars ex illis tum quoque viva fuit.

Where ships had gone before now men go on foot and the waters congealed with cold feel the hoof-beat of the horse ... I may scarce hope for credence, but since there is no reward for a falsehood, the witness ought to be believed – I have seen the vast sea stiff with ice, a slippery shell holding the water motionless. And seeing is not enough; I have trodden the frozen sea, and the surface lay beneath an unwetted foot ... At such times the curving dolphins cannot launch themselves into the air; if they try, stern winter checks them ... shut in by the cold the ships will stand fast in the marble surface nor will any oar be able to cleave the stiffened waters. I have seen fish clinging fast bound in the ice, yet some even then still lived. (III x 31-49)

In both of these accounts of natural upheaval Ovid places such an extravagant emphasis on the instability of the dissolving boundaries that we might almost think some magical metamorphosis was taking place. In the *Metamorphoses* this breakdown prefigures the more profound reversals which lie at the heart of the poem. These are of course absent in the *Tristia*, yet echoes of the earlier poem haunt his descriptions of life in Tomi, hinting that even in the 'real' world the potential for miraculous metamorphosis can never be discounted. The barbarity of the Getae recalls metamorphoses such as Lycaon's into a wolf. He says of them 'vix sunt homines hoc nomine digni,/ quamque lupi, saevae plus feritatis habent', 'They are men scarce worthy of the name; they have more of cruel savagery than wolves' (V vii 45-6). After his transformation Lycaon is also 'feritatis imago' (I 239). The very appearance of the Getae is animalistic, 'oraque sunt longis horrida tecta comis', 'and their shaggy faces are protected with long locks' (50), and by a process of degeneration they have forgotten Greek, 'in paucis extant Graecae vestigia linguae;/ haec quoque iam Getico barbara facta sono', 'A few retain traces of the Greek tongue, but even this is rendered barbarous by a Getic twang' (51-2). This is analogous both to Lycaon's inability to speak, 'exululat frustraque loqui conatur', '[He] howls aloud, attempting in vain to speak' (233) and to the way his essential character survives metamorphosis, just as the Getae retain something of their former civilisation, 'veteris servat vestiga formae', 'and yet retains some traces of his former shape' (237). By imitating his own account of a literal, bodily transformation to accentuate his portrayal of moral disintegration, Ovid anticipates the methods of many of his Christian imitators, such as Spenser and Milton, for whom the moral resonances of such 'downwards' metamorphoses are more urgent than for Ovid. The currency of such views may be seen in the following passage by Sir John Hayward:

> And as every kind of beast is principally inclined to one sensuality more than to any other; so man transformeth himself into that beast, to whose sensuality he principally declines ... This did the ancient wisemen shadow forth by their fables of certain persons changed into such beasts, whose cruelty, or sottery, or other brutish nature they did express. (Hayward, 251)

In the following account of his own physical deterioration, natural bodily changes are evoked by Ovid in words which recall the dramatic alterations undergone by characters in the *Metamorphoses*, 'nam neque sunt vires, nec qui color esse solebat/ vix habeo tenuem, quae tegat ossa, cutem', 'For I have neither the strength nor the colour I used to have; my thin skin scarce covers my bones' (IV vi 41-2). He also describes himself fading away like a leaf in autumn:

19

vexant insomnia, vixque
ossa tegit macies nec iuvat ora cibus;
quique per autumnum percussis frigore primo
est color in foliis, quae nova laesit hiems,
is mea membra tenet, nec viribus adlevor ullis,
et numquam queruli causa doloris abest.

I am harassed by sleeplessness, scarce does the lean flesh cover my bones,
food pleases not my lips, and such a hue as in autumn, when the first chill
has smitten them, shows on the leaves that young winter has marred,
o'erspreads my body; no strength brings relief, and I never lack cause for
plaintive pain. (III viii 27-32)

Even though this image is no more than a comparison it may recall the
way more spectacular transformations are described in the *Metamor-
phoses*. Ovid's description of the flesh hardly covering his bones might
put the reader in mind of transformations, such as that of Anaxarete
into stone, where the flesh completely disappeared. The colour change
may be natural, but by using the image of a tree he allows us to think
perhaps of Daphne or Baucis and Philemon. Although it is not equiva-
lent in any precise way, the metamorphosis of Echo may be adduced as
an approximate analogue to Ovid's account of his deterioration, particu-
larly as her transformation seems at first to be only a natural decline:

extenuant vigiles corpus miserabile curae
adducitque cutem macies et in aera sucus
corporis omnis abit; vox tantum atque ossa supersunt:
vox manet, ossa ferunt lapidis traxisse figuram.

Her sleepless cares waste away her wretched form; she becomes gaunt
and wrinkled and all moisture fades from her body into the air. Only her
voice and her bones remain: then, only voice; for they say that her bones
were turned to stone. (III 396-9)

But this was not the first time that Ovid had imitated himself in this
way, using his readers' memories of his poetry of metamorphosis to
make natural phenomena seem extraordinary. At the very end of the
Metamorphoses, in Pythagoras' speech, the distinctions between natu-
ral and unnatural metamorphoses are collapsed and the miraculous
workings of nature that we take for granted are defamiliarised by
association with the impossible metamorphoses that Pythagoras de-
scribes:

in scrobe deiecto mactatos obrue tauros
(cognita res usu): de putri viscere passim
florilegae nascuntur apes, quae more parentum
rura colunt operique favent in spemque laborant.
pressus humo bellator equus crabronis origo est;

concava litoreo si demas bracchia cancro,
cetera supponas terrae, de parte sepulta
scorpius exibit caudaque minabitur unca;
quaeque solent canis frondes intexere filis
agrestes tineae (res observata colonis)
ferali mutant cum papilione figuram.

Dig a ditch and bury the carcases of bulls after they have been offered in sacrifice (it is a well-known experiment), and from the putrid entrails everywhere will spring flower-culling bees which, after the fashion of their progenitors, frequent the country fields, are fond of work, and toil in hope of their reward. A horse, which is a warlike animal, buried in the ground will produce hornets. If you cut off the hollow claws of a sea-crab and bury the rest in the ground, from the buried part a scorpion will come forth threatening with his hooked tail. And worms that weave their white cocoons on the leaves of trees (a fact well known to country-folk) change into funereal butterflies. (XV 364-74)

*

In the light of Ovid's imitation of himself, it could be argued that this book's starting point comes some fourteen centuries too late. One justification for selecting Chaucer as the first example of Ovidian influence might be that, although he is not the first poet to imitate the *Metamorphoses*, he is in another important sense the originator of a tradition. A number of talented poets were at work in the latter half of the fourteenth century, including Langland and the *Gawain*-poet, yet it was Chaucer who, in matters of style, language, poetic forms and sophisticated use of European and Classical influences, was to prove so influential on succeeding generations that he might justly be described as 'the father of English poetry'. If we think again of Keats' sonnet 'How many bards gild the lapses of time', the first poet writing in English who would have contributed to the 'unnumbered sounds' would almost certainly have been Chaucer.

2

Rumour, authority and the literary text: Chaucer's *House of Fame*

The choice of Chaucer's *House of Fame* as the starting point for a discussion of English Ovidianism might be seen as a reflection of the circumstances in which this study is written, its situation in a postmodern moment and my own absorption in 'the late twentieth-century aesthetic which privileges metaliterary self-consciousness as its master-term' (Hinds 1998, p. 90). Yet our own preoccupation with the processes of literary production and the nature of textuality is easily matched by both Chaucer and Ovid. Ovid's description of Fama in Book XII of the *Metamorphoses* may be read as a comment on the production and dissemination of literary works as well as an evocation of the more general phenomenon of rumour. The operations of the goddess adumbrate the processes of reception, assimilation and transmission at work in the formation of a literary tradition. This episode thus provides an apt introduction to any discussion of Ovid's influence on the poets who succeeded him.

The House of Fama itself may be seen as a melting pot where texts and literary reputations are established, altered or destroyed – a 'universe of discourse' (Hanning, 141). The description of her house throws suggestive lights on questions of canonicity, authority and reception. An apparently simple statement, 'Fama tenet summaque domum sibi legit in arce', 'Rumour dwells here, having chosen her house upon a high mountain-top' (XII 43), reveals on closer inspection a telling ambiguity. *Lego* might imply that Fama has chosen her stronghold, or, since *lego* may mean to read as well as to choose, that she is a passive peruser. Boitani depicts a similarly double-edged Fame:

> On the one hand it acts as a mysterious, fickle, chance-inspired, fortune-like choice of the tidings that come from fame-rumour; on the other, it imposes on them the order and the sanction of the few who use the written word – the opinion-makers and the depositories of tradition. (Boitani, p. 6)

Yet it could be said that the apparent disjuncture between reading and

23

choosing does not really exist – to read is never a purely passive activity for it always involves interpretation, as when we hover between two different connotations of an ambiguous word. To shift the frame of reference slightly, the two readings of *lego* might figure two opposed views of the idea of a 'canon' of literary texts, one that sees it as historically contingent, one that sees it as having created itself.

The House of Fama is a place where continual sound and movement make it difficult to tell what is going on. One aspect of this confusion is the problem the reader faces in establishing to what degree the 'rumours' are meant to be seen as autonomous personifications or as the passive currency of human agents. As with the ambiguity of *lego*, sorting out this particular indeterminacy also has a bearing upon the way texts are imitated and transmitted:

> atria turba tenet: veniunt, leve vulgus, euntque
> mixtaque cum veris passim commenta vagantur
> milia rumorum confusaque verba volutant.

> Crowds fill the hall, shifting throngs come and go, and everywhere wander thousands of rumours, falsehoods mingled with the truth, and confused reports flit about. (XII 53-5)

It is not clear whether the *turba* is identical with the *milia rumorum*, or whether Ovid is describing actual people hearing and spreading rumours. The verb *vagantur* (54) may mean no more than 'to be diffused', a reading consistent with the incorporeal, purely verbal character of rumours, but it could also be translated 'to roam, to wander', thus allowing for the possibility that the rumours have an actual physical reality, that they are being semi-personified by Ovid. Here again the text hovers between passivity and activity. The phrase 'confusaque verba volutant' (55) may be understood in two distinct ways, compounding the ambiguity. The subject may be the *verba* themselves and the phrase translated as it is in the Loeb edition, 'confused reports flit about'. The immediate context undoubtedly favours this reading. But the uncertainties described above in our perception of what is going on in the House of Fama, the suggestion that it contains people processing and acting upon the rumours, might encourage a reader to translate *volutant* as 'to ponder', 'to consider', with an unspecified subject acting upon the 'milia rumorum confusaque verba' which, being neuter, may be either subject or object. The rumours grow and develop like a game of Chinese whispers, 'mensura ficti/ crescit, et auditis aliquid novus adicit auctor', 'the story grows in size, and each new teller makes contribution to what he has heard' (57-8), a statement which looks forward to the *Nachleben* of the *Metamorphoses* itself, which was to undergo all kinds of accretions, sometimes as part of the process of imitation and reception, sometimes more directly as a result of the commentary tradition (Medieval and Renaissance texts of the poem included copious marginalia). The *Metamorphoses* may be seen simultaneously as a passive and an active agent in this process; what might seem to be a startling innovation on the part of a later imitator may, for example, turn out to have been an embedded possibility in Ovid's text all along.

The significance of Fama only becomes apparent if we examine the context in which she is placed by Ovid. She is described in the middle of an account of the Trojan war where Ovid retells, in an unexpected way, material that was extremely familiar to his audience through the work of Homer and Virgil. This makes it possible to read what is an ostensibly self-contained description of the workings of Fama as a tacit · commentary on this entire movement of the poem. The particular characteristics of the goddess clearly have a bearing on the way texts are changed when, like Homer's *Iliad* in this section of the *Metamorphoses*, they are transmitted or retold. Due (p. 148) complains of the inordinate length of the ecphrasis, which he views simply as a contrivance to explain how the Trojans knew the Greeks were coming, and Bennet claims that 'the whole of Ovid's description could be detached from its context in the *Metamorphoses* without the slightest loss to the central narrative' (Bennett, p. 72). Neither critic recognises how skilfully Ovid has integrated Fama into the *Metamorphoses*. Due notes that she has become principally a place rather than a goddess as in Virgil. This observation might have helped him find a justification for the length of Ovid's description. Because all poets become, as it were, Fama, when they retell famous stories such as the Trojan war, it is appropriate that she should not be individualised too strongly. Due also suggests, somewhat oversubtly, that Ovid says Fama is unreliable and yet shows her telling the truth to show up the illogicality of her presentation in Virgil.

> In the *Aeneid* Fama blends true and false, we are told, when she disseminates the news about Dido and Aeneas; but her actual report is strictly in accordance with truth. Ovid on the one hand stresses Fama's unreliability and on the other the actual veracity of her message. By being in this respect more awkward than Vergil he draws attention to the fact that there *is* an awkwardness – in Vergil. So it seems that here the traditional form of a classic predecessor is used to direct a good-humoured criticism against the form itself. (Due, p. 148)

Yet if we realise that she lies behind Ovid's entire retelling of Homer and Virgil and is not just the bearer of one simple piece of information, then it becomes clear that Ovid's Fama *is* wayward and variable.

Because of its curious emphases and omissions – the best known events are ignored while the adventures of such obscure characters as Cycnus are told at length – this account of the Trojan war is calculated to engage the reader with one of Ovid's favourite preoccupations, the questioning of literary authorities. The *Heroides*, with their imaginative reconstructions of the oft-neglected feelings of the women of antiquity and their sly discrepancies with the 'received versions' of Homer and Virgil, comprise Ovid's most sustained engagement with this issue, but the *Metamorphoses* also contains oblique criticisms of the supremacy of these revered texts. Ovid's approach is similar to that of many modern writers. His emphasis on very minor incidents in the Trojan war is comparable to Stoppard's treatment of *Hamlet* in *Rosencrantz and Guildenstern are Dead*. In the *Heroides*, when he attempts to portray the feelings of Briseis who only makes a brief appearance in the *Iliad* despite her importance as a catalyst to the plot, Ovid is making the same kind of imaginative reconstruction as Jean Rhys does when she makes the first Mrs Rochester the subject of her novel *Wide Sargasso Sea*.

This aspect of Ovid's creativity is clearly in tune with modern preoccupations. But although the gap between today's modernists and the super-sophisticated writers of Ovid's generation seems relatively easy to bridge, a poet like Chaucer, firmly rooted in the Middle Ages, may not at first seem to fit in to this self-referential context. Yet Chaucer's *Legend of Good Women* is modelled on the *Heroides*, and its wit is equally dependent upon its readers being familiar with the original versions of the lives of these 'good women'. A reader who did not know Ovid's version of the story of Procne and Philomela would not understand the importance of Chaucer's self-conscious omission of the tale's grisly climax. After recounting how Procne discovered that Tereus had raped and mutilated her sister Chaucer continues evasively:

The remenaunt is no charge for to telle,
For this is al and som: thus was she served,
That nevere harm agilte ne deserved
Unto this crewel man, that she of wiste.
Ye may be war of men, if that yow liste. (2383-7)

Our perception of Philomela as a hapless victim would have been substantially modified had Chaucer related how she and Procne served up Tereus' son Itys to his unwitting father. He changes a celebrated story to fit in with his theme of good women, apparently intending that the audience should appreciate his alteration of the text, and thus perhaps perceive that the compliment he is paying to women is very backhanded. Chaucer's capacity for appreciating and imitating Ovid's subtle distortions of earlier texts is as apparent in *The House of Fame* as in *The Legend of Good Women*.

The House of Fame is the most apparently inchoate of the dream visions, embracing a gallimaufry of topics ranging from the interpretation of dreams to the theory of sound. It is episodic in structure: the narrator considers the different types of dreams, invokes the god of sleep and recounts a dream that he had 'of Decembre the tenthe day' (111). First of all he dreams that he is in a temple of Venus where he looks at a representation of the story of Aeneas. Then in Book II he is taken up into the sky by an eagle with whom he discourses on a variety of subjects. In Book III he arrives at the House of Fame itself where he sees, among other things, statues of famous poets of antiquity, before witnessing the goddess decide whether or not to award the prize of fame to various companies of people who have performed either good or evil deeds. Then he goes to the House of Rumour, a whirling wicker cage whence come true and false rumours. All are waiting for 'a man of gret auctorite' (2158) to speak, but the poem ends abruptly and we are left uncertain as to what he signifies.

On a cursory reading one might think that Chaucer's use of Ovid was somewhat incoherent. There are strong verbal reminiscences, and the central idea is still intact, but Chaucer has described two separate houses – those of Fame and Rumour – as opposed to Ovid's one, has placed his imitation within the very Medieval category of dream vision, has scrambled together allusions to other works such as the *Paradiso* and has introduced a long digression on the story of Dido. The diffuse nature of Chaucer's borrowing from the *Metamorphoses* might suggest that he has used Ovid opportunistically rather than engaged with the text at any deeper level. But it is in his metamorphosis of Fama, and of Ovid, that he shows his understanding of his source most sharply.

Helen Cooper, writing in *Ovid Renewed*, recognises the centrality of the idea of literary authority in *The House of Fame* but does not fully acknowledge Chaucer's indebtedness to Ovid in this respect, 'His description of the dwelling of Fame shows his inspiration by Ovid at its fullest; but even that paradoxically underlines his independence, for he includes within the province of this most untrustworthy of personifications not only rumour and reputation but the telling of tall stories, story-telling in general, and, deriving from all those, literature and historiography' (Cooper, p. 72). This analysis of Chaucer's use of Fama is accurate, but it is equally applicable to his Ovidian source:

e quibus hi vacuas inplent sermonibus aures,
hi narrata ferunt alio, mensuraque ficti
crescit, et auditis aliquid novus adicit auctor.

some of these fill their idle ears with talk, and others go and tell elsewhere what they have heard; while the story grows in size, and each new teller makes contribution to what he has heard. (XII 56-8)

This could just as well be a description of the dissemination of texts or the development of a literary tradition (such as Ovidianism) as of

27

gossip. The 'mensura ficti' might mean either 'the extent of the lie' or 'the length of the story'. The occurrence of the word *auctor* is significant, and is again used at line 61 when Ovid describes 'dubioque auctore Susurri', 'inauthentic Whisperings'. The Latin form of the word (rather than the modern 'author') was still in use during the fourteenth century, and Chaucer often talks about *auctors* and *auctoritee*. Ovid's repeated use of the word could have encouraged Chaucer to see Fama as an essentially literary phenomenon, a comment on the way writers expand and modify their sources. Chaucer, like Ovid, exploited the tensions between himself and his *auctors* with subtlety and wit.

In his essay on *The House of Fame* Fry writes:

> Among Medieval authors, Geoffrey Chaucer paid the most ostensible homage to *auctoritees*, but he also distorted these sources, combined them, mistranslated them, and even invented 'Lollius' ... The skeptical Geoffrey Chaucer mistrusted his *auctoritees*, mistrusted the distortions of transmitted knowledge, trusted only his own art. (Fry, 39)

His fake *auctor* Lollius is invoked with particular emphasis in the following stanza from Book I of *Troilus and Criseyde*. The 'Canticus Troili' which follows is in fact a close imitation of a Petrarchan sonnet:

> And of his song naught only the sentence,
> As writ myn auctour called Lollius,
> But pleinly, save oure tonges difference,
> I dar wel seyn, in al, that Troilus
> Seyde in his song, loo, every word right thus
> As I shal seyn; and whoso list it here,
> Loo, next this vers he may it fynden here. (I 393-9)

Bella Millet says of Chaucer's constructed source, 'his emphasis on the authenticity of Troilus's song is more explicable if we take it as a half-private joke, directed to those members of the audience who would have recognized its actual source' (Millet, p. 102). His sophisticated alertness to this question would have made him more receptive to the possible literary ramifications of Ovid's Fama. Millet goes on to ask an important question which she answers only in the most general terms:

> But this still leaves open the question why Chaucer should have reacted against the 'medieval theory of authorship' in the first place. The most likely explanation is that he was also influenced by a tradition of secular entertainment, outside the range of scholastic commentary and incorporating rather different assumptions about the uses of literature. (p. 102)

The most satisfactorily specific answer, I would argue, is that Chaucer's reaction against the medieval theory of authorship was spurred by his

enthusiastic engagement with that eminently secular, eminently enter-
taining overturner of *auctoritees*, Ovid himself.

Instead of following Ovid's example of using an unusual retelling of
material from Homer to illustrate the workings of Fama, Chaucer turns
to the ever popular Book IV of the *Aeneid* to fulfil the same purpose.
This is a clever choice of foil for the description of the House of Fame
itself. As well as having a ready made rewriting of Virgil to draw on in
the shape of *Heroides* VII, Chaucer has also selected a text far more
familiar to Medieval audiences than Homer. The *Iliad* had acquired a
great deal of excess baggage in the shape of various versions of the
'matter of Troy', and Greek scholarship was still floundering in a
pre-Renaissance slump. Chaucer's readers would have been far more
alert to the differences between Virgil's version of the story of Dido and
the account given by Geoffrey in *The House of Fame*, than they would
to a similar treatment of the *Iliad*. An additional edge is given to the
use of Dido's story if we remember that the inspiration for Ovid's Fama
was also taken from Book IV of the *Aeneid*. The gap between the
Virgilian and Ovidian Famas complements the gap between the Vir-
gilian and Ovidian Didos.

Chaucer's dreamer in *The House of Fame* retells the story of the
Aeneid which he purports to have seen narrated in a series of paintings.
This interlude might at first seem to contribute to the ostensibly
episodic and incoherent character of the poem. But a more considered
reading reveals the underlying thematic integrity of *The House of Fame*.
The tensions between the two meanings of *lego* may be perceived in the
contradictions between the dreamer's alleged faithful adherence to
Virgil and his actual partiality. He is a selective rather than a passive
peruser.

The dreamer finds himself in a 'temple ymad of glas' (120), which he
realises must be dedicated to Venus because he sees a picture of her
'Naked fletynge in a see' (133). In the light of his initial description of
what meets his eyes it is tempting to question the dreamer's assump-
tion, for he has already informed us that he sees:

>   moo ymages
> Of gold, stondyne in sondry stages,
> And moo ryche tabernacles,
> And with perre more pynacles,
> And moo curiouse portreytures,
> And queynte maner of figures
> Of olde werk, then I saugh ever. (121-7)

The dreamer takes for granted what his own disingenuous description
calls into question. When surrounded by such a clutter of contradictory
images why does the figure of Venus stand out for him so prominently?
It would seem that Chaucer's habitual characterisation of himself as a

poet of love, albeit an unlucky lover, might explain this bias. The clumsy switch from 'nyste', to 'wyste' in the following quotation, even though the two statements are not inherently contradictory, helps to suggest that Chaucer may be jumping to conclusions:

> For certeynly, I nyste never
> Wher that I was, but wel wyste I
> Hyt was of Venus redely,
> The temple; for in portreyture
> I sawgh anoon-ryght hir figure ... (128-32)

It could be argued that the dreamer might know that he is in a temple of Venus and yet not know his exact geographical location, just as one might know that one is in a church but not what country one is in through the generic similarities of such buildings. Yet the repetition of the rhyme portreyture/figure at lines 131-2 might take us back to the previous use of the rhyme (125-6) and remind us that there are many 'portreytures', emphasising that the dreamer seems to have made his own choice of which one to pick out for particular attention.

The glass of the temple, like the twigs of Rumour's house and the ice of Fame's, may denote insubstantiality (Bennett, p. 11). It is also tempting to adduce the reflective quality of glass. Chaucer's dreamer sees as though through a mirror, not his own portly person, but a reflection of his solipsistic concern with love, recalling his mention of the idea that 'folkys complexions/ Make hem dreme of reflexions' (21-2). This is a tangible example of the elusive double-edged word *lego* in practice. The dreamer thinks he is a dutifully passive vessel, merely reporting what he saw in his dream, but he betrays his own concerns and his own inevitable choices.

> I wol now synge, yif I kan,
> The armes and also the man
> That first cam, thurgh his destinee,
> Fugityf of Troy contree ... (143-6)

The cautioning, qualifying phrase 'yif I kan' immediately alerts the reader to possible problems in Chaucer's retelling of the *Aeneid*. As a modesty tag this phrase would be quite in place in a Medieval romance such as those Chaucer parodies in *Sir Thopas*. However its interpolation into an otherwise pretty literal translation of the opening lines of the *Aeneid* suggests the difficulty of telling the story from the correct perspective, rather than a simple lack of eloquence or poetic skill, and, as Fyler says, 'implies in general terms the uncertain ability of art to be true to the facts' (Fyler, p. 33). The equally uncertain ability of one work of art to be true to another is also exemplified in what follows. Fama's Chinese whispers (or the operations of différance) have plenty of scope

in this narration of a dream about a series of paintings based on the
Aeneid. As many have noted, Chaucer's version of Dido owes at least as
much to *Heroides* VII as it does to Virgil. Any nascent doubts about
Chaucer's objectivity aroused in the reader's mind by his apparently
arbitrary selection of Venus as the temple's dedicatee are upheld by the
prominence of that goddess and her attendant preoccupations in the
version of Aeneas' story that is given here.

Unlike Virgil, the dreamer appears far more moved by the sorrows of
Dido than by Aeneas' destiny, and becomes more shameless in his
partisanship as his description progresses. At the beginning he dili-
gently punctuated his account with repetitions of the phrase 'ther saugh
I', as if to assure the reader that he is reporting what he saw faithfully.
The different, more personal and confidential formula with which he
opens the following passage is at one with the judgmental criticism he
makes of Aeneas:

> But let us speke of Eneas,
> How he betrayed hir, allas,
> And lefte hir ful unkyndely.
> So when she saw al utterly
> That he wolde hir of trouthe fayle,
> And wende from hir to Italye,
> She gan to wringe hir hondes two. (293-9)

The scornful speech Dido proceeds to make upon the faithlessness of
men is capped by the following assurance from the dreamer:

> In suche wordes gan to pleyne
> Dydo of hir grete peyne,
> As me mette redely –
> Non other auctor alegge I. (311-14)

Because he styles himself an *auctor*, the reader may not immediately
realise that Chaucer is assuring him that his narrative is completely
subjective. The subversiveness of anyone's reliance on himself as an
auctoritee can be seen more clearly in The Wife of Bath's Prologue where
Chaucer wanted to draw our attention to the speaker's unconventional-
ity, 'Experience, though noon auctoritee/ Were in this world is right
ynogh for me' (1-2).

Dream visions more usually include accounts of literary works
within the external framework surrounding the presentation of the
dream rather than within the substance of the dream itself, as in *The
Parliament of Foules* and *The Book of the Duchess*. One might think
there was an essential incompatibility between a genre which, unusu-
ally for the Middle Ages, depends upon at least a pretence of subjectivity
for all the learned matter it might contain, and the very different

31

process involved in retelling another poet's works where a controlled response, free from the vagaries of dreaming, is required. Another point at which a similar admission of subjectivity appears to be cloaked beneath a construction better suited to the acknowledgement of an exterior source is the end of the proem to Book II:

> O Thought, that wrot al that I mette,
> And in the tresorye hyt shette
> Of my brayn, now shal men se
> Yf any vertu in the be
> To tellen al my drem aryght. (523-7)

These lines have been compared to the following lines from the *Inferno*, but Dante uses the word 'mente' (memory) rather than 'thought'. Dante's dream has the status of a divine vision and it is therefore quite appropriate that his memory should be referred to as though it were an *auctoritee*:

> O muse, o alto ingegno, or m'aiutate;
> O mente che scrivesti ciò ch'io vidi,
> Qui si parrà la tua nobilitate.

> O muses! O profound inclination, help me!
> O memory, which recorded what I saw,
> Here will be shown what there is noble in you. (II 7-9)

But the passage is perhaps even more like part of an invocation to Apollo from the *Paradiso*:

> O divina virtù, se mi ti presti
> tanto che l'ombra del beato regno
> segnata nel mio capo io manifesti.

> O divine power, if you lend yourself to me
> So that the ghost of the blessed kingdom
> Traced in my brain, is made manifest. (I 22-4)

Once again, we might ignore the implication of Chaucer's invocation because it is couched in phraseology more appropriate to an allusion to an *auctor*; Virgil or Dante could be substituted for 'Thought' and 'write' for 'mette'. Similarly the invocation at the beginning of Book III expresses a wish that he might be aided to show 'That in myn hed ymarked ys' (1103). The dreamer seems to be treating his imagination as a source text; simultaneously its writer and its reader. We may compare the way Ovid's many imitators read and responded to Ovid and then helped construct him anew for later generations.

32

The dreamer's presence is allowed to make itself felt in a speech which is ostensibly spoken by Dido:

> O wel-awey that I was born!
> For thorgh yow is my name lorn,
> And alle myn actes red and songe
> Over al thys lond, on every tonge.
> O wikke Fame! – for ther nys
> Nothing so swift, lo, as she is! (345-50)

In Book IV of the *Aeneid* Fama does indeed spread malicious reports of Dido's affair with Aeneas. But Fame, as she is described here, like Ovid's own Fama, seems to have as much to do with the transmission of literature as with scandal-mongering – mere gossip is not generally 'red and songe'. Yet again, as we perceived in the increasingly partial way he championed Dido's cause, the dreamer's own mind has infiltrated his retelling of the story as he ascribes an awareness of her future literary reputation to Dido that she cannot possibly have possessed. We are reminded of Dido's words when the eagle gives Geoffrey a description of the House of Fame as he carries him through the air; his account of its location is identical to that given by Ovid:

> Hir paleys stant, as I shal seye,
> Ryght even in myddes of the weye
> Betwixen hevene and erthe and see. (713-15)

> Orbe locus medio est inter terrasque fretumque
> caelestesque plagas, triplicis confinia mundi;

> There is a place in the middle of the world, 'twixt land and sea and sky, the meeting-point of the threefold universe. (39-40)

The description continues in a way which shows that Chaucer has chosen to give emphasis to Ovid's hints connecting the activities of Fama with the characteristics of literature, and to do so in a way which also echoes Dido's anachronistic plaint. Ovid's description continues, 'unde quod est usquam, quamvis regionibus absit,/ inspicitur, penetratque cavas vox omnis ad aures:', 'From this place, whatever is, however far away, is seen, and every word penetrates to these hollow ears' (41-2). In *The House of Fame* the 'vox omnis' of the *Metamorphoses* has been extended and made more specific:

> Or what so cometh from any tonge,
> Be hyt rouned, red, or songe,
> Or spoke in suerte or in drede,
> Certeyn, hyt moste thider nede. (721-4)

Thus Chaucer helps us to perceive the integrity of the Dido 'digression' with the rest of the poem through the verbal echo of the tonge/songe rhyme, at the same time emphasising the House of Fame's connections with the process of poetic imitation. Because Ovid's description of Fama is a comment on the production of literature, Chaucer's *House of Fame* illustrates the processes of Fama not only in his version of the *Aeneid*, but in the writing of the entire poem. It stands in a similar relationship to Book XII of the *Metamorphoses* (and to other authorities such as Dante) as Geoffrey's account of Dido does to Virgil, except that there is no suggestion that Chaucer is undercutting Ovid.

We have already seen that Ovid makes it difficult to establish whether Fama's stronghold is filled with people spreading rumours, or simply with the rumours themselves, creating a shifting impressionistic effect, difficult for the reader to visualise in a concrete or definitive way, and reflecting the problematic balance between autonomy, and dependence on those by whom they are read and transmitted, possessed by works of literature. The same ambiguity in Ovid seems to have struck Chaucer, for he makes his dreamer question the eagle on this very point. He answers:

> Whan any speche ycomen ys
> Up to the paleys, anon-ryght
> Hyt wexeth lyk the same wight
> Which that the word in erthe spak ... (1074-7)

But this definition is not borne out by what follows in *The House of Fame* which seems full of historical individuals, not embodied speeches. Far closer to the eagle's statement, and clearly derived from the *Metamorphoses*, is Chaucer's evocation of the House of Rumour, although even here Chaucer's presentation of the rumours is not quite consistent with the eagle's explanation, and the uncertainties of the *Metamorphoses* are not resolved. Our first impression of the House of Rumour is that it is filled with a crowd of people, like the *turba* in the *Metamorphoses*, 'But which a congregacioun/ Of folk, as I saugh rome aboute/ Some wythin and some wythoute' (2034-6). Their apparent autonomy seems confirmed when Chaucer makes it clear that they are acting upon the rumours, and thus cannot be mere embodied rumours themselves:

> Whan oon had herd a thing, ywis,
> He com forth ryght to another wight,
> And gan him tellen anon-ryght
> The same that to him was told,
> Or hyt a forlong way was old,
> But gan somewhat for to eche
> To this tydynge in this speche
> More than hit ever was ...
> Were the tydynge soth or fals,

34

Yit wolde he telle hyt natheles,
And evermo with more encres
Than yt was erst. (2060-7, 2072-5)

This passage both translates and, because it is so much amplified,
exemplifies the line 'et auditis aliquid novus adicit auctor', 'and each
new teller makes contribution to what he has heard' (58). The prolifera-
tion of meanings generated among the readers of a text, as well as the
metamorphosis of a text through imitation, could be signalled. But the
description continues in a way which introduces the contrary idea of the
rumours' independence from human intervention:

And that encresing ever moo,
As fyr ys wont to quyke and goo
From a sparke spronge amys
Til al a citee brent up ys. (2077-80)

The image of fire which may be started by human agency but which
grows by means of its own momentum is an appropriate image for
Chaucer to use within the context of an intermediate state for the
rumours between autonomy and passivity. From this suggestion of the
rumours' self-sufficiency Chaucer moves on to full blooded and amusing
personification:

And somtyme saugh I thoo at ones
A lesyng and a sad soth sawe,
That gonne of aventure drawe
Out at a wyndowe for to pace;
And, when they metten in that place,
They were achekked bothe two,
And neyther of hem moste out goo
For other, so they gonne crowde,
Til ech of hem gan crien lowde,
'Lat me go first!' 'Nay, but let me!
And here I wol ensuren the,
Wyth the nones that thou wolt do so,
That I shal never fro the go,
But be thyn owne sworen brother!
We will medle us ech with other,
That no man, be they never so wrothe,
Shal han on [of us] two, but bothe
At ones, al besyde his leve,
Come we a-morwe or on eve,
Be we cried or stille yrouned.'
Thus saugh I fals and soth compouned
Togeder fle for oo tydynge. (2088-109)

This little episode suggests something of the complexity of literary
reception, and imitates the ambiguities of Ovid's Fama – Ovid's original

two line spark (lines 53-4 quoted above) has increased tenfold. Chaucer replicates the effect created by Ovid's confused syntax; by showing the rumours apparent escape from human agency as they self-assertively elect to be compounded together, Chaucer implies that those who repeat or write down something they have heard or read cannot make wholly independent decisions about the way they do so, but must to some extent be acting, if not precisely subconsciously, at least without complete awareness of the preoccupations and assumptions which govern their methods. The passage might also suggest the role of readers in constructing a text's meaning, which, like Chaucer's rumours, is not dependent upon authorial intention. After the account of the liaison between truth and falsehood Chaucer offers a thumbnail sketch of the kind of people who are spreading news and rumours:

> And, Lord, this hous in alle tymes
> Was ful of shipmen and pilgrimes,
> With scrippes bret-ful of lesinges,
> Entremedled with tydynges,
> And eek allone be hemselve.
> O, many a thousand tymes twelve
> Saugh I eke of these pardoners,
> Currours, and eke messagers,
> With boystes crammed ful of lyes
> As ever vessel was with lyes. (2121-30)

These seem to be 'real' people, in charge of the stories they tell, yet they also look forward to the pilgrims of Chaucer's later *Canterbury Tales*, themselves simultaneously literary constructs and tellers of tales. A final indication of the House of Rumour's textuality is its fabric – it is wicker and therefore woven – *textum*.

In a sense Ovid did not have to complement his description of Fama with a skewed account of the Trojan war in order to exemplify her workings. She is herself an example of the way a story can be altered or added to, for her presentation inevitably recalls and distances itself from Virgil's Fama. In addition, the ambiguities in Ovid's description of her house force the reader to make choices about its precise nature, leading to the potential for divergent readings, and reinforcing the notion of textual instability. Chaucer's readers are given a still more open invitation to invest the text with meaning, because they are offered, in addition to local ambiguities, a final space which we can fill in any way we like, or not at all.

The poem concludes:

> Atte laste y saugh a man,
> Which that y [nevene] nat ne kan;
> But he semed for to be
> A man of gret auctorite ... (2155-8)

36

2. Chaucer's House of Fame

In the light of the dreamer's cavalier treatment of the other *auctoritees* that he makes use of in *The House of Fame* we perhaps should not be surprised that this final unnamed *auctoritee* does not even begin to speak. It would be dangerous to assert confidently that the poem is left unfinished deliberately or that the speech or identification of the 'man of greet auctoritee' is as inconceivable as the appearance of Godot. Yet it is clear from 'The Tale of Sir Thopas' that Chaucer was capable of designing a story whose unfinished state is determined by the very structure of the text as well as being more obviously the result of the host's interruption.[1] The lack of closure in *The House of Fame*, whether deliberate or not, is an appropriate reflection of the way both Chaucer's dreamer and Ovid demonstrate the ease with which an apparently closed work like the *Aeneid* or the *Iliad* may be opened up. Barthes' description of an ideal textuality in *S/Z* throws some suggestive light upon Fama's significance within the story of Ovid's reception, for it seems simultaneously to invoke the goddess's dwelling place and the *Metamorphoses* as a whole:

> In this ideal text the networks are many and interact, without any one of them being able to surpass the rest; this text is a galaxy of signifiers, not a structure of signifieds; it has no beginning; it is reversible; we gain access to it by several entrances, none of which can be authoritatively declared to be the main one ... the systems of meaning can take over this absolutely plural text, but their number is never closed, based as it is on the infinity of language. (Barthes, pp. 5-6)

[1]See Burrow 1991 for an account of this tale's entropic structure.

37

3

The equivocal morality of artifice: Spenser's *Faerie Queene*

Spenser was drawn to an aspect of the *Metamorphoses*, Ovid's depiction of the visual arts, which was to exert a powerful influence on many later Ovidians, including all the writers whose response to Pygmalion will be discussed later in this book. Although Arachne is the more prominent presence in *The Faerie Queene*, Spenser's response to Ovidian ecphrasis rehearses many of the problematic features of Pygmalion's reception. Both weaver and sculptor have a dubious status within Ovid's text, being both privileged and rendered suspect by their genius. Behind Spenser's responsiveness to Arachne's equivocal position as a creator of illusions is an implicit uneasiness about his own artistry.

In the fourth book of *The Faerie Queene* Spenser reveals that his inspiration for the tale of Cambell and Triamond came from the works of 'Dan Chaucer, well of English undefyled,/ On Fame's eternall beadroll worthie to be fyled' (IV ii 32). Spenser expresses his regret that his source, *The Squire's Tale*, was left unfinished through an image which recalls Chaucer's own evocation of transitory Fame, both in *The House of Fame* (1114-17) itself and in *Anelide and Arcite* (6-9):

> But wicked Time that all good thoughts doth waste,
>   And workes of noblest wits to nought out weare,
>   That famous moniment hath quite defaste,
>   And robd the world of threasure endlesse deare,
>   The which mote haue enriched all us heare.
>   O cursed Eld the cankerworme of writs,
>   How may these rimes, so rude as doth appeare,
>   Hope to endure, sith workes of heauenly wits
> Are quite devourd, and brought to nought by little bits? (IV ii 33)

It is eloquent of the pervasiveness of Ovid's influence that this passage might equally well be traced back to Pythagoras' speech in Book XV of the *Metamorphoses*.[1] *The Faerie Queene* is full of Ovidian motifs, includ-

---

[1] Lines 176-85 are particularly pertinent and were also an important influence on Shakespeare's Sonnet 60.

ing many metamorphoses, but it is perhaps through his use of ecphrasis that Spenser reveals his most telling debt to the *Metamorphoses*, betraying a greater affinity with Ovid than his reputation as a sage and serious poet might suggest.

Although any extended description – such as that of Fama in Book XII – may be described as an ecphrasis, the term is most commonly used to denote an account of an artefact within a literary work. The most famous example is probably the shield of Achilles in Homer's *Iliad*. Another celebrated ecphrasis is the depiction of the Trojan war on the walls of Juno's temple, described by Virgil in the second book of the *Aeneid*. Ecphrasis has a special resonance within Ovid's work, for one of the hallmarks of the *Metamorphoses* is its preoccupation with various kinds of artists and with the nature of the art they produce. The idea of the artist includes the gods – both as creators and as shapeshifters – as well as the poet himself, and Ovid exploits the potential ambiguities involved when writing about artistic creativity within something which is itself an artistic creation.

Two locations in *The Faerie Queene* owe a particular debt to Ovidian ecphrasis, the house of Busirane in Book III, and the Bower of Bliss at the end of Book II. Busirane's tapestry is clearly derived from Ovid's account of the competition between Arachne and Minerva, and, although there is no single source for the Bower, it has marked affinities with two of Ovid's ecphraseis: Diana's grotto (III 155-64) and the doors of the Palace of the Sun (II 1-18).

It seems as though Ovid wished to emphasise the connections between his own skill as a poet and that of certain of his characters. He describes the subtle artistry of Arachne's almost imperceptible employment of minute gradations of colour to create a rainbow-like effect as proof of her consummate skill:

> qualis ab imbre solent percussis solibus arcus
> inficere ingenti longum curvamine caelum;
> in quo diversi niteant cum mille colores,
> transitus ipse tamen spectantia lumina fallit:
> usque adeo, quod tangit, idem est; tamen ultima distant.

> As when after a storm of rain the sun's rays strike through, and a rainbow, with its huge curve, stains the wide sky, though a thousand different colours shine in it, the eye cannot detect the change from each one to the next; so like appear the adjacent colours, but the extremes are plainly different. (VI 63-7)

Earlier we learnt how her embarrassed anger at Minerva's appearance makes her blush:

sed tamen erubuit, subitusque invita notavit
ora rubor rursusque evanuit, ut solet aer
purpureus fieri, cum primum Aurora movetur,
et breve post tempus candescere solis ab ortu.

... though she did turn red, for a sudden flush marked her unwilling
cheeks and again faded: as when the sky grows crimson when the dawn
first appears, and after a little while when the sun is up it pales again.
(VI 46-9)

The phenomenon is a different one but both descriptions evoke gradual
changes of colour. The connection between Arachne and her tapestry is
strengthened by the fact that the blushing woman is such a conven-
tional topos, emphasising woman as aestheticised object. She is a
spectacle, a work of art to be admired:

nec factas solum vestes, spectare iuvabat
tum quoque, cum fierent: tantus decor adfuit arti ...

And 'twas a pleasure not alone to see her finished work, but to watch her
as she worked; so graceful and deft was she. (17-18)

By making us perceive the similarity between weaver and web Ovid
draws attention to his own status as a creative artist, and thus to his
affinity with his fellow artist Arachne. Spenser's relationship with art,
on the other hand, appears to be more problematic. After making an
exception for the description of Alma's house in *The Faerie Queene*, C.S.
Lewis asserts that 'everywhere else Spenser uses art to suggest the
artificial in its bad sense – the sham or imitation' (p. 327). But reading
Spenser's ecphraseis through Ovid casts a somewhat different light on
the matter.

The description of the tapestry in Busirane's castle and the account
of the weaving competition between Minerva and Arachne are both
ecphrastic tours de force. Ovid's tale of the mortal girl who claimed to
weave more skilfully than Minerva, only to be defeated and metamor-
phosed into a spider, includes lengthy descriptions of the tapestries
woven by both goddess and woman. Whereas Minerva depicts the
triumphs of the gods and the punishments they confer on presumptuous
humankind, Arachne implicitly criticises the gods by portraying them
in the various guises they assume in order to seduce mortals such as
Europa and Leda. In Book II of *The Faerie Queene* the warrior maiden,
Britomart, is sent to rescue Amoret from Busirane, an evil enchanter.
After passing through a wall of fire Britomart comes to three chambers,
the first of which contains a series of sinister tapestries. Spenser follows
his predecessor's subject matter closely in this unusually extended debt
to the *Metamorphoses*, often expanding and embellishing Ovid's brief

41

retellings of the gods' amours, and sometimes adding stories from other books of the *Metamorphoses*, such as that of Phaethon.

Although she will eventually become a victim of the gods, Arachne is connected with the idea of a creative and powerful divinity by a verbal allusion to the very beginning of the *Metamorphoses*. The creator of the world – 'quisquis fuit ille deorum', 'whoever of the gods it was' (I 32) – moulds the form of the earth just as Arachne rolls her balls of wool, 'magni speciem glomeravit in orbis', 'moulded the earth into the form of a mighty ball' (I 35), 'sive rudem primos lanam glomerabat in orbes', 'whether she was winding the rough yarn into a new ball' (VI 19). Such a reference makes her seem to be a more than mortal craftswoman, and prepares the reader for the tacit connections Ovid makes between her and the shapeshifting gods.

Within the fabric of Arachne's tapestry, art and metamorphosis are linked by their shared reliance on imitative skill. The theme of metamorphosis as subterfuge is common to all the stories Arachne represents, and this paves the way for Ovid to draw attention to the similarly deceptive character of pictorial representation. This connection between the tapestry's subject matter and the medium in which it is rendered is emphasised in the *Metamorphoses* by Ovid's ambiguous use of language, as are other problematic aspects of describing a work of art by means of narrative.

Ovid's admiration for Arachne's skill is not diminished by his realisation that its misleading verisimilitude places it in an uneasy association with the disguises assumed by Jove to ensnare his victims. Yet although Arachne's creative skill may link her with Jove the shapeshifter, the reader is bound to identify her with all the wronged women that she represents, particularly considering the subject matter of Minerva's tapestry and the fate the goddess metes out to Arachne. It is typical of the tenor of the entire *Metamorphoses*, of Ovid's involvement with the shifting instability of boundaries and categories, that Arachne can be connected both with the gods and the women they deceive in the tapestry.

The peculiar affinities between the stories she is portraying and the actual fabric of the tapestry are highlighted in the following lines:

illic et lentum filis inmittitur aurum
et vetus in tela deducitur argumentum.

There too, they weave in pliant threads of gold, and trace in the weft some ancient tale. (VI 68-9)

The verb *deduco* has many shades of meaning. Within the context of the first line, which describes the weaving of golden threads into the design, a concrete interpretation of the word seems most likely, in its sense of drawing and spinning out fabric. But the conclusion of the second line tells us that *deducitur* denotes another kind of 'spinning out' (even in translation English idiom allows the wordplay to remain) and that Ovid is in fact referring to the representation of stories on the tapestry. The word which makes this interpretation certain is *argumentum*, a tale. It is significant that this is the final word of the line, and that the final word of the preceding line was *aurum*. The one word which might be expected in the place of *argumentum* is *argentum*, to balance *aurum*. This slippage from weaving to writing strengthens the bond between Arachne's project and Ovid's; at the very opening of the *Metamorphoses* Ovid uses *deduco* in his invocation to the gods when he begs for inspiration, 'adspirate meis primaque ab origine mundi/ ad mea perpetuum deducite tempora carmen!', 'Breathe on these my undertakings, and bring down my song in unbroken strains from the world's very beginning even unto the present time' (I 3-4).

Spenser sees an equally intimate yet rather more disturbing connection between the fabric and the subject matter of the tapestries. He does not inform us who the artist was, but creates the impression that the tapestries are a spontaneous manifestation of evil. Here too the interweaving of gold thread is dwelt upon:

> Woven with gold and silke so close and nere,
> That the rich metall lurked privily,
> As faining to be hid from envious eye;
> Yet here, and there, and every where unwares
> It shewd it selfe, and shone unwillingly;
> Like a discolourd snake, whose hidden snares
> Through the greene gras his long bright burnisht backe declares.
>
> (III xi 28)

The tapestry itself takes on the negative attributes of the gods it depicts. 'Close and nere' suggests the fineness of the weaving, but also has connotations of secretiveness, and this effect is compounded in the next line, when we learn that the gold thread 'lurked privily'. Spenser goes on to describe the way the metal wishes to conceal itself. This is a curious idea which recalls the doubtful beauty of the addition of art to nature in the Bower of Bliss (see below, pp. 48-56). But as this is a tapestry, not a garden, the gold threads are no less natural than any other colour. We might instead look for an explanation of their negative portrayal in the parallels Spenser seems to want to draw between the tapestry itself and the stories it represents. The image of gold trying to conceal itself, but revealing its brightness unwittingly, recalls the idea of a god who has assumed human or animal form, but cannot completely hide his divinity. The personification of the thread as a snake reinforces this association. The phrase 'hidden snares' could be used of Jove's disguise as a bull, luring Europa by his beauty, or indeed of his trans-

formation into a 'varius serpens', 'a spotted snake' (VI 114) to deceive
Proserpina, and any reference to a deceitful snake is bound to recall
Satan's own use of metamorphosis to ensnare a mortal woman. Thus
the sinister skill of the artist is aligned with that of the shapeshifting
gods. A third factor could be brought into the equation, Spenser
himself, who partakes of the same transformative power through
poetic mimesis, making the last line of the stanza take on the quality
of a serpent. So although Spenser, unlike Ovid, does not draw atten-
tion to the links between weaving and writing through etymological
wordplay, it is not difficult for the reader to perceive that the poet
and the tapestry maker are both spinners of yarns, both equally
skilful masters of illusion.

Ovid similarly encourages his readers to perceive the link between
metamorphosis and representative art. The first story Arachne depicts
is that of Europa:

> Maeonis elusam designat imagine tauri
> Europam: verum taurum, freta vera putares ...

> Arachne pictures Europa cheated by the disguise of the bull: a real bull
> and real waves you would think them. (VI 103-4)

Because *imago* can signify a picture the reader may be tricked into
thinking, after having only read the first line, that the idea of deception
contained in the word *elusam* is somehow connected with the mislead-
ingly lifelike nature of the representation. But in fact Ovid is talking
about the events of the story, as becomes clear when we reach the
opening of the second line. The significance of the name *Europam* is
heightened by its prominent position at the beginning of the line,
distanced from the words that follow. *Elusam* describes the reader of the
poem herself, for yet another shift of meaning immediately follows. It
is perhaps fanciful to apply *elusam* to the reader when only the female
portion of Ovid's readership could possibly be implicated. Yet this
episode of the *Metamorphoses* is firmly tied to the idea of an admiring,
wondering *female* audience – the 'nymphae Pactolides' (16) come to
watch Arachne work, Arachne and Minerva are locked in hostile con-
templation of each other's work and within the tapestry itself Europa is
seen watching first Jove, then her companions. The words *verum tau-
rum*, coming straight after *Europam*, at first seem to refer to Jove's
disguise. But *freta vera* must refer to the tapestry, and the reader's
confusion has come full circle.

With Spenser's tapestries, as with Ovid's, the boundaries between art
and metamorphosis are blurred:

> And in those tapets weren fashioned
>   Many faire pourtraicts, and many a faire feate,

44

3. Spenser's Faerie Queene

And all of love, and all of lusty-hed,
As seemed by their semblaunt did entreat ... (III xi 29)

If we understand 'entreat' in its sense of 'treat, discuss' then the final
line refers to artistic representation. The last two lines could be para-
phrased 'the nature of the pictures suggests that they illustrate stories
about love'. But if 'entreat' is taken in its sense of to beg or implore, a
usage current in Spenser's time, then, just like Ovid when he talks of
Europa and the bull, we have slipped out of ecphrasis into narrative.
Spenser could be describing the disguises – 'semblaunts' – assumed by
the gods in order to seduce – 'entreat' – their victims. Here too Spenser
seems to be sucked into the discourse of deception, for we as readers
hover confusedly between these different possible readings, ourselves
the victims of literary metamorphosis.

In his description of Leda's seduction Spenser once again creates an
unexpected Ovidian link between himself, the artist and Jove:

Then was he turned into a snowy swan,
　To win faire Leda to his lovely trade:
　O wondrous skill, and sweet wit of the man,
　That her in daffadillies sleeping made,
　From scorching heat her daintie limbes to shade:
　Whiles the proud bird ruffing his fethers wyde,
　And brushing his faire brest, did her invade;
　She slept, yet twixt her eyelids closely spyde,
How towards her he rusht, and smiled at his pryde. (III 32)

When he praises the weaver's skill he is really praising his own inven-
tion, for the *Metamorphoses* gives only the barest sketch of the story –
'fecit olorinis Ledam recubare sub alis', 'she wrought Leda, beneath the
swan's wings' (VI 109). The bird's 'invasion' of Leda is shared by Spenser
(and the reader), for we are taken behind her closed eyelids and into her
mind, to be told more than we could expect to learn from a woven image.

Critics are divided as to the precise location of Ovid's sympathies in
the weaving contest. Traditionally Arachne's fate has been seen as a
justly deserved punishment for over-reaching, but many recent read-
ings favour the rebel mortal, suggesting that the exiled Ovid might have
felt an affinity with her own clash against a higher authority and
identifying her brand of artistry with the poet's own – both spin the
same kind of yarns. Not surprisingly, critics have also suggested a
compromise solution whereby the poet's sympathies are equally di-
vided. Ovid's narrating voice is sufficiently elusive to allow for such
multiple readings, and there is little sense of an absolute standard
against which we can measure the two participants. There is some
condemnation implied in Arachne's delineation of the gods' amours, but
it is partisan and political, rather than moral. As the challenger to

Minerva's supremacy among weavers, she represents the opposition of human forces to divine power, and her subject matter reflects this. In so far as she is stubborn and foolhardy, we cannot necessarily give her total sympathy or approval. Whether we do or not will depend upon our own ideological position and our reading of the poem as a whole. Similarly Minerva's tapestry, with its depictions of punishment and suffering, is sufficiently ambiguous to make her final border of 'peaceful' olives seem a little ironic.

Ostensibly the function of the tapestry in *The Faerie Queene* is quite different from that of Arachne's web and seems to allow less room for critical manoeuvre. Whereas the dynamic of Ovid's story encourages us to choose between gods and mortals, or between rapists and their victims, Spenser dissolves these oppositions, making both parties to the various sexual encounters on the tapestry the thralls of Cupid:

> And eke all Cupids warres they did repeate,
> And cruell battels, which he whilome fought
> Gainst all the gods, to make his empire great;
> Besides the huge massacres, which he wrought
> On mighty kings and kesars, into thraldome brought. (III. xi.29)

> Kings queenes, lords ladies, knights & damzels gent
> Were heap'd together with the vulgar sort,
> And mingled with the raskall rablement,
> Without respect of person or of port,
> To shew Dan Cupids powre and great effort ... (III xi 46)

Yet the serious context of the ecphrasis cannot efface the effect of Spenser's Ovidian play – in both Busirane's castle and in the Bower of Bliss he is subtly implicated in the tainted artifice of evil. And although the intervention of Cupid alters the dynamic of power suggested both by Arachne and Minerva, in a sense Spenser's portrayal of both gods and mortals as victims is in harmony with much of the rest of the *Metamorphoses* – Ovid is more even-handed than the two rival weavers. The most pertinent illustration is Cupid's response to Apollo's boasting when he shoots both Daphne and the god with his arrows.

Spenser turns to the weaving contest again in a very different poem, his mock heroic jeu d'esprit *Muiopotmos* which tells of the battle between a butterfly and a spider and includes an account of the weaving contest. Here we can see him responding to the subtleties of Minerva's tapestry which, like Arachne's, plays tricks upon the reader. At one point, after the self-aggrandising goddess has woven herself causing an olive tree to spring up, we learn that 'operis Victoria finis', 'victory crowns her work' (VI 82). As this is a contest, we might assume that Ovid has finished describing her tapestry, and that Minerva has won. But the victory refers to her contest with Neptune, one of the tales she depicts on her tapestry. As this dispute is alluded to only obliquely the reader is encouraged to connect 'victory' with Minerva's present dispute with Arachne rather than her old one with Neptune, as it is the former quarrel which is indisputably emphasised. Significantly, it is with a border of olives that Minerva finally completes her tapestry, and the wording with which Ovid describes this design, 'circuit extremas oleis pacalibus oras/ (is modus est) operisque sua facit arbore finem', 'The goddess then wove around her work a border of peaceful olive-wreath. This was the end; and so, with her own tree, her task was done' (101-2) harks back to the real olive tree whose miraculous growth is also depicted on the tapestry, 'operis Victoria finis'. The emphasis given by the phrase in brackets 'is modus est' is perhaps a tacit allusion to the earlier false ending, reassuring the reader that closure has finally arrived.

It is strangely appropriate that what we may have taken for victory over Arachne turns out to be Minerva's depiction of another victory on the tapestry, for the goddess's eventual success is a fabrication, an imposition. Although it is effected by a weaving shuttle it is the ordinary and violent meaning of *percutio* – 'to hit' – rather than its more technical meaning as a term in weaving – 'to throw the shuttle' – which the reader must infer, 'utque Cytoriaco radium de monte tenebat/ ter quater Idmoniae frontem percussit Arachnes', 'and, as she held a shuttle of Cytorian boxwood, thrice and again she struck Idmonian Arachne's head' (VI 132-3). However, as so often in the *Metamorphoses*, the 'wrong' interpretation is not entirely irrelevant. It is fitting that Arachne should be identified in our minds, however fleetingly, with a tapestry figure because her metamorphosis at the hands of a wrathful goddess links her with the women on her own and Minerva's tapestries. And if we look more closely at the description of the punishment we learn that Minerva has yet again crowned her success with olives, for *radius*, 'shuttle', also denotes a kind of olive – so this is (perhaps!) the final closure. It is as easy for Minerva to bring about her victory over Arachne as it is for her to depict similar artistic victories, putting her shuttle to more orthodox use. As we have twice been misled by the verb *percutio* we may be encouraged to insert within the gap between *percutio* (to hit) and *percutio* (to throw a shuttle) yet a third meaning of this verb (to deceive).

In *Muiopotmos* too, the weaver fleetingly becomes part of her own composition. Minerva weaves a butterfly on her tapestry as a finishing touch: 'Which when Arachne saw, as overlaid,/ And mastered with workmanship so rare,/ She stood astonied long, ne ought gainesaid,/ And with fast fixed eyes on her did stare' (337-40). The primary meaning of both 'overlaid' and 'mastered' is to be overpowered, as Arachne is by the goddess's superior skill. Yet as 'to master' may also mean 'to execute with skill' and the verb overlay may be applied to decorative gilding, it is possible that the butterfly, implied by the relative pronoun 'which', is the true object of the two verbs. The description of Arachne's eyes as 'fast fixed' hints at a third possibility, suggesting that it is the weaver herself who is the work of art.

Perhaps surprisingly, ecphraseis of a sort may be produced within a visual medium, for a painting of a painting creates its own ambiguities, as we can see in Velazquez's response to Ovid's weaving contest, *Las Hilanderas*, or *The Spinners*. The painting seems to depict different stages of the story: the contest between Arachne and Minerva (still disguised as a crone) dominates the foreground while the tale's denouement is depicted on a more distant plane behind them. There is some doubt as to whether the figure of Arachne whom we see in the background is real or part of her own tapestry – Leonard Barkan notes (1986, p. 7) that she is superimposed onto her fellow victim of the gods, Europa. As she is presented at the very moment when Minerva has raised her hand to strike such an ambiguity is felicitous – although perhaps also fortuitous.

At the end of Book II of *The Faerie Queene*, Guyon, the knight of temperance, destroys the beautiful Bower of Bliss, home of the evil enchantress Acrasia. The range of responses to this episode is polarised rather in the same way as are readers' reactions to Milton's Satan. Some are shocked by the puritanical Guyon's wanton destruction of so much beauty, others point out that Spenser intended the Bower to be enticing in order to implicate the fallen reader in the sin of intemperance – if we are not seduced by its loveliness then why should the far more virtuous Guyon waver? Of course just as we may conjecture that Milton was 'of the Devils party without knowing it' (Blake, p. 107), we may doubt whether Spenser himself resisted the allure of the Bower.

Much discussion has been generated by the intrusion of art into nature in the Bower. One of the most negative responses comes from C.S. Lewis in *The Allegory of Love*, where he compares the Bower unfavourably with the natural spontaneity of the Garden of Adonis:

> Surely all suspicion that the insistence on Acrasia's artificiality is accidental must disappear if we find throughout the description of the garden of Adonis an equal insistence on its natural spontaneity ... The one is artifice, sterility, death: the other, nature, fecundity, life. (pp. 325-6)

Yet many critics see the artifice, not as inherently evil, but rendered so by force of its inappropriate competition with nature. A suggestive Ovidian intertext for this aspect of the Bower is Ovid's description of the grotto where Diana is glimpsed bathing by Actaeon. Both the Bower and the grotto are the dwelling-places of fascinating, dangerous and powerful females and both are invaded by an unwelcome male intruder, although Actaeon's trespass is unwitting whereas Guyon's is deliberate.

The links between these pairings are not at all exact – Diana is far more like Guyon than Acrasia in her unappealingly violent insistence upon her chastity. The diverse responses to Actaeon's grisly end might serve as an articulation of the reader's ambivalent attitude to the destruction of the Bower of Bliss. Guyon's remorseless dismantling of the Bower and Diana's merciless punishment of Actaeon might equally make the reader wonder whether 'austere virginity' is an unmitigated good.

The description of Diana's grotto foregrounds the relationship between nature and art which Ovid treats in a playfully paradoxical way, 'simulaverat artem/ ingenio natura suo', 'Nature by her own cunning had imitated art' (III 158-9). Here the personification of Nature and the reference to her *ingenium* contradict the idea that she merely *simulaverat artem* because Ovid has made Nature herself an artist. *Ingenium* may also mean 'natural disposition', but it is *not* Nature's natural disposition to simulate art. Therefore we must translate *ingenium* as wit or ability, yet this too is an inappropriate way to characterise Nature. Ovid goes on to tell us more about how the grotto was formed: 'nam pumice vivo/ et levibus tofis nativum duxerat arcum', 'for she had shaped a native arch of the living rock and soft tufa' (III 159-60). In applying the active verb *duxerat* to the arch when it is also described as *nativum* (produced by nature, not artificial), and describing the pumex as *vivus* which may signify 'unwrought', Ovid creates an apparent contradiction which can only be resolved by limiting the degree of Nature's personification, or rather by holding two different pictures of nature, that of controlling artist on the one hand, and also that of a blind impersonal force, in our minds simultaneously.

Yet again, one of the most intelligent imitations of Ovid may be seen, not in a poem, but in a painting, Titian's *Actaeon*. Here a slab of rock, on which Diana and her nymphs are resting, rises up from a little pool. The surface of this rock is absolutely sheer and its edges are sharply defined. Looking at the surface alone we are tricked into thinking it a carpet – Diana's chair and her little dog seem to belong in a boudoir rather than a grotto – and the texture of Titian's brushwork contributes to this effect.

As we shall see, Spenser's evocation of the relationship between Art and Nature contains similar tensions. But whereas the received view of Ovid's poetic personality would incline the reader to emphasise the playful wit with which he invests this relationship, critics of Spenser see in the Bower of Bliss a dangerous and unnatural competitiveness between these two forces.

The door to the Bower is decorated with the story of Jason and Medea, and Spenser uses the same techniques to draw the reader into the picture and the same direct invitation to marvel at its verisimilitude as Ovid employed in his description of Arachne's representation of Europa:

verum taurum, freta vera putares (VI 104)

> Ye might have seene the frothy billowes fry
> Under the ship, as thorough them she went ... (II xii 45)

There is also the same uncertainty as to whether Spenser is talking about the story or the carving that Ovid evokes in his account of the bull and the waves. The word 'as' in the phrase 'as thorough them she went' could be glossed 'when', and refer to the story, or 'as though', and refer to the picture. The next two lines, 'That seemd the waves were into yvory/ Or yvory into the waves were sent' play on the relationship between art and nature by implying that it is not only art that imitates nature, but nature that imitates art. In *Spenser and Literary Pictorialism* John Bender emphasises the disquieting qualities of the Bower: 'the purpose of stanza forty-five seems to be to show transformations of natural substances by art and to represent through images the eerie uncertainties and illusions of the Bowre of Blisse' (p. 179). Had Ovid written an identical ecphrasis – in so far as this is possible in a different language and culture – it is unlikely that it would be characterised as 'eerie'.

We are again reminded of the links between poetry and the decorative arts by Spenser's next observation, which refers to Medea's ruthless slaughter of her own brother:

> And other where the snowy substaunce sprent
> With vermell, like the boyes bloud therein shed ... (II xii 45)

The materials used by the artist to create the effect of blood on white skin are also used as metaphors by Spenser himself to achieve the same result. In Book III Britomart is wounded by Gardante:

> yet was the wound not deepe,
> But lightly rased her soft silken skin,
> That drops of purple bloud thereout did weepe,
> Which did her lilly smock with staines of vermeil steepe. (III i 65)

Spenser's description of 'the snowy substance sprent/ With vermell' is thus only confirmed as a description of the carving rather than the reality it represents by the word 'like' which follows. Spenser draws attention to the affinities between poetic and visual art rather as Ovid did by making his own description of Arachne's changing colour so similar to his account of the hues of her web. And yet again we see Spenser employing the same kind of metamorphic ambiguities in his poetry that he appears so distrustful of in his descriptions of Busirane's tapestry and the design of the Bower.

Just as the tapestry in Busirane's castle seemed to be a spontaneous

3. Spenser's Faerie Queene

expression of evil rather than the work of a specific craftsman, the
Bower of Bliss does not leave us with the impression that it was
'designed' in any normal sense; Spenser creates the impression of an
'Art' which is somehow 'natural':

> Thus being entred, they behold around
>   A large and spacious plaine, on every side
>   Strowed with pleasauns, whose faire grassy ground
>   Mantled with greene, and goodly beautifide
>   With all the ornaments of Floraes pride,
>   Wherewith her mother Art, as halfe in scorne
>   Of niggard Nature, like a pompous bride
>   Did decke her, and too lavishly adorne,
> When forth from virgin bowre she comes in th'early morne. (II xii 50)

One would expect Flora, goddess of flowers and Spring-time, to be
associated with Nature. But Spenser curiously refers to 'her mother Art'
who compensates for Nature's shortcomings. Instead of using the word
Art as an abstract noun, encompassing the productions of all artists and
the skill which inspires them, Spenser makes Art a personification who,
because she is female and a mother, strangely resembles Mother Nature
herself. Nature and Art emerge as two opposed but similar principles,
and Art seems closer to Nature than we would normally imagine
because she is depicted as a comparable force who has as little need of
any intermediate human agency as Nature herself. This competitive
parity matches the relationship between the two forces implicit in the
description of Diana's grotto. And similarly a few stanzas later we are
told that:

> One would haue thought, (so cunningly, the rude,
>   And scorned parts were mingled with the fine,)
>   That nature had for wantonesse ensude
>   Art, and that Art at nature did repine ... (II xii 59)

The implications of this unusual passage are supported by the whole
description of the Bower. Spenser's apparent disapproval of the un-
wholesome intrusion of art into natural surroundings has been
contrasted, *ad nauseam*, with the more positive description of the
Garden of Adonis where Nature is pre-eminent, unadulterated by any-
thing suspectly artificial. But the Bower of Bliss does not play off art
against nature in a simple way. Its art, as commentators have long since
observed, imitates nature, but that which appears to be 'natural' also
imitates art. The same is true of the Bower's other Ovidian intertext,
the description of the palace of the sun. Its doors were carved by
Mulciber, and depict the earth and sky with wonderful verisimilitude.
The account of the ocean and its denizens continues so long that the

51

reader might almost think that he were reading a general account of the nature of the sea, rather than a description of a work of art:

> caeruleos habet unda deos, Tritona canorum
> Proteaque ambiguum ballaenarumque prementem
> Aegaeona suis inmania terga lacertis
> Doridaque et natas, quaram pars nare videtur ...

> The sea holds the dark-hued gods: tuneful Triton, changeful Proteus, and Aegaeon, whose strong arms can overpower huge whales; Doris and her daughters, some of whom are shown swimming through the water ... (II 8-11)

Not until the last line does the verb *videtur* remind us that this is only a representation, and even here the passive form of *video* might presumably be translated as 'to be seen' or 'to appear', rather than 'to seem' with its necessary overtones of illusion. We are apparently reminded very firmly that we are reading about doors, not a real landscape, when Ovid describes Mulciber's carving of the Zodiac: 'signaque sex foribus dextris totidemque sinistris', 'six signs of the zodiac on the right-hand doors, and six signs on the left' (18). Yet a further complication is introduced, for the wording strongly echoes the description of the sky's creation at the beginning of Book I, reminding us that the world itself is the work of an artist who creates a symmetrical design just like Mulciber:

> utque duae dextra caelum totidemque sinistra
> parte secant zonae, quinta est ardentior illis,
> sic onus inclusum numero distinxit eodem
> cura dei, totidemque plagae tellure premuntur.

> And as the celestial vault is cut by two zones on the right and two on the left, and there is a fifth zone between, hotter than these, so did the providence of God mark off the enclosed mass with the same number of zones, and the same tracts were stamped upon the earth. (I 45-8)

These shifts into apparent reality are mirrored by the ecphrastic element in the ostensibly real interior that confronts Phaethon once he has entered the palace itself. The figures who surround the sun god seem more emblematic than the supposedly lifeless carvings on the doors. Ovid suggests their affinity with pictorial art by echoing the symmetry of his earlier description of the zodiac:

> a dextra laevaque Dies et Mensis et Annus
> Saeculaque et positae spatiis aequalibus Horae
> Verque novum stabat cinctum florente corona,
> stabat nuda Aestas et spicea serta gerebat,
> stabat et Autumnus calcatis sordidus uvis
> et glacialis Hiems canos hirsuta capillos.

To right and left stood Day and Month and Year and Century, and the Hours set at equal distances. Young Spring was there, wreathed with a floral crown; Summer, all unclad with garland of ripe grain; Autumn was there, stained with the trodden grape, and icy Winter with white and bristly locks. (II 25-30)

Because they are all presented with their minimum identifying attributes and in such a static manner, these figures appear far more inert than the characters depicted by Mulciber; the anaphoric use of *stabat* to open two consecutive lines contributes to this impression. Through being described as 'positae spatiis aequalibus' the hours seem more like allegorical figures in a masque, or even marks on a calendar, than full blooded personifications.

After passing through a clearly man-made ivory portal, Guyon

> came unto another gate;
> No gate, but like one, being goodly dight
> With boughes and braunches, which did broad dilate
> Their clasping armes, in wanton wreathings intricate. (II xii 53)

The branches themselves seem to emulate a work of art by their apparently independent striving towards elaborate design. The opening of the next stanza, 'So fashioned a porch with rare device/ Archt over head with an embracing vine', is obliquely phrased, in that it omits the mention of any subject, implied or stated, and thus leaves the reader wondering whether the gate formed itself spontaneously or was helped along by another agency. The verb 'fashioned' seems to have acquired reflexivity.

The ambiguity continues, for the vine which forms the gate is described as though it were animate:

> Whose bounches hanging downe, seemed to entice
> All passers by, to tast their lushious wine,
> And did themselves into their hands incline,
> As freely offering to be gathered:
> Some deepe empurpled as the Hyacint,
> Some as the rubine, laughing sweetly red,
> Some like faire emeraudes, not yet well ripened. (II xii 54)

One might suppose that this would provide incontrovertible evidence that the branches had shaped themselves picturesquely of their own volition, yet the methods of personification used by Spenser are the common currency of poets. As with the image of snow and vermeil, the conventions of descriptive poetry blur the distinctions between art and nature. The suggestion that art, like nature, is an impersonal force, in that the artificial elements of the garden seem to owe no more to any agent than those parts which are wholly natural, is upheld by Spenser's description of the golden fruits which, like the snakey threads of gold in Busirane's tapestry, are subtly mingled with those which are coloured more naturally:

> And them amongst, some were of burnisht gold,
>   So made by art, to beautifie the rest,
>   Which did themselves emongst the leaves enfold,
>   As lurking from the vew of covetous guest ... (II xii 55)

The apparent conscious will of the golden fruits makes it difficult to imagine an artist producing them, and the boundaries become even more blurred by Spenser's use of jewel imagery to evoke the colours of the 'natural' grapes. It is not such a big jump, when one is reading a poem, from 'as the rubine', 'like faire emeraudes' to 'were of burnisht gold'. (The golden grapes' apparent artifice is complicated by the fact that 'to burnish' may mean 'to grow, to spread out' as well as 'to shine'.) The effect of such pointed references to the status of art in the Bower is to imbue 'innocent' uses of conventional poetic language with an equivocal, two-edged quality, and, as with the tapestry of Busirane, to implicate Spenser's poetic art in the Bower's artifice:

> The painted flowres, the trees upshooting hye,
>   The dales for shade, the hilles for breathing space,
>   The trembling groves, the Christall running by;
>   And that, which all faire workes doth most aggrace,
>   The art, which all that wrought, appeared in no place. (II xii 58)

The adjectives 'painted' and 'chrystal' are commonplace enough in a description of nature's beauties, but within this context they may be taken literally as well as figuratively. Spenser, like the Bower's architect, leads us up the garden path, as it were, by making it difficult for us to distinguish art from nature. If we didn't feel that we knew what Spenser 'meant' we might apply to him an adjective such as 'self-conscious' or even 'tricksy' at this point. Spenser may not have enjoyed or approved of Ovidian play but he certainly participated in it.

Modern readers will perhaps be more accustomed to decoding such layers of ambiguity in film, a medium which lends itself well to metanarrative confusions. In Buñuel's *Belle de Jour*, for example, the heroine, Séverine, experiences strange dreams and fantasies which we see on screen. It is of course easy for a film maker to make use of effects such as light filters to distinguish between reality and fantasy, yet Buñuel increasingly complicates the relationship between the two, transposing motifs which we have learnt to associate with Séverine's dream world into her 'real' life. But of course just as the whole of Velazquez's *Las Hilenderas* is a painting, and the Bower of Bliss is

54

entirely manmade – by Spenser – so is *Belle de Jour* a film, a fiction from start to finish. We try to work out where Severine's fantasies stop and reality begins but the distinction is ultimately meaningless, for the whole film is Buñuel's extended daydream.

As the description of the Bower continues, the boundaries between natural and artificial substances are further obfuscated:

> And in the midst of all, a fountaine stood,
>   Of richest substaunce, that on earth might bee,
>   So pure and shiny, that the silver flood
>   Through every channell running one might see;
>   Most goodly it with curious imageree
>   Was over-wrought, and shapes of naked boyes,
>   Of which some seemd with lively iollitee,
>   To fly about, playing their wanton toyes,
> Whilst others did them selves embay in liquid joyes. (II xii 60)

The first two lines appear to describe the manufacture of the basin, not the water. But the phrase 'silver flood', occurring straight after the fountain has been described as 'pure and shiny', serves to connect the artificial and natural aspects of the fountain together. The carvings too seem to break free of their artistry and come to life. At first they are no more than adumbrations, 'shapes' who only 'seemd with lively iollitee/ To fly about'. But by the last line they appear to have moved into the fountain rather than merely being carved on its surface.

The golden ivy of the next stanza is so exact a copy that not only the leaf's shape but even its colour has been copied precisely:

> And over all, of purest gold was spred,
>   A trayle of yvie in his native hew:
>   For the rich mettall was so coloured,
>   That wight, who did not well avis'd it vew,
>   Would surely deeme it to be yvie trew ... (II xii 61)

Like the golden grapes and Busirane's gold threads, the ivy shares the contradictory characteristics of a sentient being and a totally artificial object:

> Low his lascivious armes adown did creepe,
>   That themselves dipping in the silver dew,
>   Their fleecy flowres they tenderly did steepe,
> Which drops of Christall seemed for wantones to weepe. (61)

The golden plant seems less egregious because the water itself is likened to both silver and crystal; yet again Spenser betrays his own poetry's affinities with the Bower.

The 'naked Damzelles' playing in the fountain, who pose such a threat to Guyon's self control, only *'seemed* to contend,/ And wrestle wantonly' (63), and perhaps have the same tenuous grip on reality as the naked boys described earlier. After all, the damsels, like the carvings on the ivory doors, have 'snowy limbes' (64) and the same combination of gold and ivory which appears on the door, 'And otherwhiles with gold besprinkeled;/ Yt seemd th'enchaunted flame, which did Creüsa wed' (45) reappears to evoke the hair and skin of the bathing girls, 'And th'yvorie in golden mantle gownd' (67).

Acrasia herself is pictorially evoked and the following lines recall the description of the woven Leda on Busirane's tapestry:

> Upon a bed of roses she was layd,
>   As faint through heat, or dight to pleasant sin,
>   And was arayd, or rather disarayd,
>   All in a vele of silke and silver thin,
>   That hid no whit her alabaster skin,
>   But rather shewd more white, if more might bee:
>   More subtile web Arachne can not spin,
>   Nor the fine nets, which oft we woven see
> Of scorched deaw, do not in th'aire more lightly flee. (II xii 77)

It is appropriate that the Bower's creatrix should be just such a compound of Art and Nature as her much discussed surroundings. Spenser's description of the revealing garment – 'More subtile web Arachne cannot spin' – might be applied to the Bower as a whole, for it displays the same confusions between art and reality, the same exploitation of the ambiguities which are liable to surface when a work of art is described by a poet, as we saw in Ovid's description of Arachne's tapestry. The reference to Arachne might also suggest some connection with Busirane's tapestry, and indeed the voluptuous Acrasia, reclining on flowers and overcome by heat, anticipates the sleeping Leda in Book III, and reminds us that it is Spenser rather than Acrasia who has created this alluring spectacle, rather as, in some of the discussions which follow, we shall be reminded that Galatea's true author is the poet, not Pygmalion.[2] *The Faerie Queene* is itself a 'subtile web', and Spenser is just as apt to trap the reader in its ambiguous mazes as Acrasia is to ensnare knights in her dangerous Bower.

---

[2] Ovid's statue has no name, but I refer to her as Galatea (an eighteenth-century invention) throughout for the sake of convenience.

4

The metamorphosis of narrative:
A Midsummer Night's Dream
and *The Tempest*

Shakespeare's works play a particularly vital role in the story of English Ovidianism. His unchallenged canonical supremacy means that our sense of the *Metamorphoses* must necessarily be affected by its treatment at the hands of Shakespeare. Like Chaucer, he was alert to the way the *Metamorphoses* plays with its own constructedness – a feature which he imitates in his own most Ovidian works. But Shakespeare's relationship with Ovid is not without its tensions. Francis Meres suggests a smooth and seamless interaction between the writers: 'the sweet witty soul of Ovid lies in mellifluous honey-tongued *Shakespeare*, witness his *Venus and Adonis*, his *Lucrece*, his sugared sonnets among his private friends, &c.' (Meres, p. 282). But the dialogue between Ovid and Shakespeare was both more troubled and more interesting than this oft quoted remark implies. Although he is a less obviously 'religious' poet than either Spenser or Milton, Shakespeare sometimes seems to share these writers' apparent urge to distance themselves from Ovid's vision of the world – and like them, I would argue, failed in the attempt. The most obvious Ovidian intertexts in these two plays – the tale of Pyramus and Thisbe and Medea's account of her magic powers – operate so as to suggest that Ovid's narrative is being subjected to a benevolent metamorphosis. But, as with Ovid's own transformations, the essence of the original narrative remains intact despite an apparent alteration in form.

Whereas Spenser was Ovidian apparently almost in spite of himself, a great many Elizabethan poets turned to Ovid with unashamed relish. Among the facets of Ovidianism which found favour with his many imitators in this period were an interest in wordplay and paradox, the employment of decorative mythological machinery and a preoccupation with sexuality, particularly non-standard sexuality. Shakespeare too was alive to all that was elegant, witty or erotic in Ovid. The glamour of the *Metamorphoses* casts its spell over the catalogue of delights offered Christopher Sly in *The Taming of the Shrew*:

Dost thou love pictures? We will fetch thee straight
Adonis painted by a running brook,
And Cytherea all in sedges hid,
Which seem to move and wanton with her breath
Even as the waving sedges play wi'th' wind. (Ind.II.47-51)

This face of Ovidianism finds its most luxuriant expression in *Venus and Adonis*. But Shakespeare's perception of Ovid would seem to be more nuanced than Meres' or, for that matter, Holofernes' in *Love's Labour's Lost*:

> ... for the elegancy, facility, and golden cadence of poesy, caret. Ovidius Naso was the man. And why, indeed, 'Naso' but for smelling out the odoriferous flowers of fancy, the jerks of invention? (IV.ii.117-21)

Shakespeare saw further, finding in Ovid something more than a consummately witty and elegant *praeceptor amoris*. The *Metamorphoses* portrays an unstable world where categories are fluid and shifting, all things are subject to flux and the fates of individuals lie in the power of forces whose dictates appear arbitrary and absurd. The following passage from Thomas Mann's *Lotte in Weimar* is an effective evocation of the dark, even absurd, world picture offered in the *Metamorphoses* – though the real subject of the description is Goethe rather than Ovid:

> Poor humanity can only retain and profit by the moral. A man cannot keep by him what is not moral but a-moral, neutral and puckishly misleading, what is, in short, elemental. I said elemental, and let us stick by the word. I mean it to express and characterise something out of a devil-may-care world that has a destructive tolerance for everything, a world without end or aim, where good and evil both have the same ironic right. A human being cannot retain that, because he cannot trust it, except, of course, with that unbounded trustfulness which he does feel towards it too, and which only proves that a man cannot help having an ambiguous attitude towards the ambiguous. (Mann, p. 66)

These thoughts are ascribed to Goethe's secretary who is torn between feelings of hostility and hero worship towards his celebrated patron; his ambivalence resembles the similarly equivocal response to Ovid which we can detect in so many of his imitators. Goethe's 'destructive tolerance' is matched by Ovid, and it is this aspect of the *Metamorphoses* which causes Shakespeare unease in *A Midsummer Night's Dream*.

Any poet's reading of Ovid is likely to be complicated by the work of commentators and translators. The lively and eccentric 1567 translation of Arthur Golding must have lent its own colouring to Shakespeare's reception of the *Metamorphoses*. This is a very 'English' translation, without the Latinisms of later Elizabethan versions of

Ovid, and it seems to have encouraged Shakespeare to look at the *Metamorphoses* in an unconstrained way, comparatively uninhibited by the usual problems faced when reading the product of a very different culture written in an unfamiliar language. Ezra Pound had no doubts about the importance of Golding's translation, calling it the most beautiful book in the English language.

> Can we, for our part, know our Ovid until we find him in Golding? Is there one of us so good at his Latin, and so ready in imagination that Golding will not throw upon his mind shades and glamours inherent in the original text which had for all that escaped him? Is any foreign speech ever our own, ever so full of beauty as our *lingua materna* (whatever *lingua materna* that may be)? Or is not a new beauty created, an old beauty doubled when the overchange is well done? (Pound, 235).[1]

There are a few passages where Shakespeare's wording can be linked to the translation's phrasing in some way. But more important is the tone of Golding's Ovid. The *Metamorphoses* really is 'Englished', and not merely translated. This results in a certain incongruence between the classical subject matter of Ovid and the homely language which Golding often chooses, as for example in his version of Ovid's Bacchic revelry:

> quacumque ingrederis, clamor iuvenalis et una
> femineae voces impulsaque tympana palmis
> concavaque aera sonant longoque foramine buxus. (IV 28-30)

> Thou commest not in any place but that is hearde the noyse
> Of gagling womens tatling tongues and shouting out of boyes.
> With sound of Timbrels, Tabors, Pipes and Brazen pannes and pots ...
> (35-7)

Golding's 'English' language might have helped prompt Shakespeare to make *A Midsummer Night's Dream* a play whose register goes all the way from the formal dignity of Theseus and Hippolyta to the low life humour offered by the mechanicals.

The mechanicals' version of Pyramus and Thisbe mirrors and parodies the main plot, as well as offering a wonderfully comical travesty of the ineptitude of many sixteenth-century versifiers, perhaps including Golding himself. Reading the source in Book IV of the *Metamorphoses* reveals little immediately interesting interplay between Shakespeare and Ovid. But, as with the use of Fama in *The House of Fame*, the context is all important. Although many of Ovid's tales are individually memorable, we should not forget the poem's commitment to continuity.

---

[1]The importance of Sandys' translation of the *Metamorphoses* for that formidable Latinist, Milton, might be adduced to support Pound's assertion.

The Metamorphosis of Ovid

In nova fert animus mutatas dicere formas
corpora; di, coeptis (nam vos mutastis et illas)
adspirate meis primaque ab origine mundi
ad mea *perpetuum* deducite tempora *carmen*!

My mind is bent to tell of bodies changed into new forms. Ye gods, for you
yourselves have wrought the changes, breathe on these my undertakings,
and bring down my song in unbroken strains from the world's very
beginning even unto the present time. (I 1-4)

So we might conclude that the entire poem is the largest unit whose
relationship with *A Midsummer Night's Dream* could be analysed.
There are certainly some similarities between the two poets' enchanted
worlds. The fairies view mortals much as Ovid's gods do, with compas-
sion and even with desire, but ultimately with no real kinship. The
superior powers of gods and fairies prevent them from taking men
entirely seriously – note Puck's telling response to the antics of the
lovers when he exclaims 'Lord, what fools these mortals be!' (III.ii.115).
Even when they wish humans well their compassion is tinged with
amused callousness. Yet despite the fairies' dispassionate stance, the
world of the play seems to fall short of the 'destructive tolerance' that
we find in the *Metamorphoses*.

Of more specific importance for *A Midsummer Night's Dream* is the
first half of *Metamorphoses* IV (lines 1-414). The comic dispersal of
potentially tragic elements is most clearly apparent in the borrowing
from Pyramus and Thisbe because we see the story re-enacted on stage
in its original tragic form – in so far as any production by the mechani-
cals may be termed 'tragic'. There are additional obvious parallels
between the inset play and *A Midsummer Night's Dream* itself, for the
story of Hermia and Lysander might easily have ended as sadly as that
of Ovid's starcrossed lovers. But the debt to Pyramus and Thisbe in *A
Midsummer Night's Dream* is just one overheard fragment of Shake-
speare's dialogue with Ovid.

This tale is one facet of a discrete episode comprising numerous
stories and incidents which has for its framework the conflict between
the new god Bacchus and the recalcitrant daughters of Minyas who
refuse to obey Bacchus' command to join in the general merrymaking
and instead continue spinning. To pass away the time they tell various
stories until Bacchus punishes them for their temerity by transforming
them into bats. He also causes their looms to burst into a mass of fecund
vegetation:

> The web they had begun
> Immediatly waxt fresh and greene, the flaxe the which they spun
> Did flourish full of Ivie leaves. And part thereof did run
> Abrode in Vines. The threede it selfe in braunches forth did spring.
> (IV 488-91)

4. A Midsummer Night's Dream and The Tempest

An analogous invasion of an ordered world by riotous nature can be seen in *A Midsummer Night's Dream*; Theseus' controlled rule of the court is contrasted with the anarchic world of the fairies' wood. Yet in contrast with the *Metamorphoses* the barrier between the two worlds is only temporarily breached. The lovers' brush with fairyland seems a carnivalesque diversion compared with the violence which attends Bacchus' interference in the affairs of men. What is tragic or anarchic in the *Metamorphoses* is made subordinate to comic order in *A Midsummer Night's Dream*. The cruelty of the Ovidian universe is particularly apparent in Book IV of the *Metamorphoses* where Bacchus' treatment of the Minyades compounds the ruthlessness which he had already shown in his treatment of Pentheus in Book III. There are few parts of the *Metamorphoses* where Ovid seems so like Mann's Goethe.

Yet the Bacchanalian principle seems to be safely contained in *A Midsummer Night's Dream*. The irresponsible, mischief-making aspect of Bacchus is transferred to Puck, in whom these potentially anarchic traits are rendered harmless by the superior power and judgement of his master Oberon. The god's power is given to Theseus who exercises his authority more justly than Bacchus – he may have a Dionysiac side to his character but it is tempered by Apollonian control. It is Theseus who, like Bacchus, commands general revelry. The Duke's very forthright insistence upon the need for all the 'Athenian youth' to be merry, and his scorn for melancholy, is analogous to Bacchus' command for revelry at the beginning of *Metamorphoses* IV. Although both Bacchus and Theseus meet some resistance to their schemes for universal mirth their solutions are different. Bacchus deals with the daughters of Minyas savagely, whereas Theseus confronts the problem of Egeus and Hermia with justice and compassion.

The play that the mechanicals perform, like Ovid's own version of Pyramus and Thisbe, is designed to pass the time:

> whyle that others idelly doe serve the God of wine,
> Let us that serve a better Sainct Minerva, finde some talke
> To ease our labor while our handes about our profite walke.
> And for to make the time seeme shorte, let eche of us recite,
> (As every bodies turne shall come) some tale that may delight. (IV 46-50)

> Come now; what masques, what dances shall we have,
> To wear away this long age of three hours
> Between our after-supper and bed-time? (V.i.32-4)

Both the eldest daughter and Theseus consider a few unsatisfactory alternatives before deciding that the tale of Pyramus and Thisbe shall provide their entertainment. It is their stubborn refusal to join the joyous worship of Bacchus which forces the daughters to devise this

61

entertainment. Theseus and Hippolyta, on the other hand, epitomise the festive principle and are its chief celebrants.

The shade of Pyramus and Thisbe hovers over the entire play, not just the mechanicals' scenes. One example of its pervasive influence derives from an incident in the story which is not represented by the players – the metamorphosis effected by Pyramus' blood which turns the white-berried tree into the mulberry tree. This change of colour is transferred to the magic flower, 'Love in Idleness', which plays such a prominent part in the mechanics of the plot. The little legend which Oberon relates to account for its magic properties has plenty of Ovidian ingredients: an arrow from Cupid's bow, a lovely nymph and a metamorphosis connected with a flower. But these elements are put together by Shakespeare in a way more fitting to his play than a more typically Ovidian tale might have been. No peril overtakes the nymph for the power of Cupid's arrow is 'Quench'd in the chaste beams of the wat'ry moon' (II.i.162). Neither is she changed into a flower as the only alternative to death. Instead all the arrow does is change a flower from being 'milk-white' to 'purple with love's wound'. The mulberry tree in Ovid's tale of Pyramus and Thisbe is turned purple by a more concrete and literal 'love's wound', for it is dyed that colour by Pyramus' blood. The kind of wound Shakespeare talks about here is a benevolent one, as is appropriate to the flower's new use. The equivalent of the metamorphosis which signified the death of Pyramus and Thisbe's love allows the four lovers in *A Midsummer Night's Dream* to resolve their problems happily.

In the mechanicals' play banal verse and ludicrously inappropriate comparisons contrive to turn Thisbe's tragic discovery of Pyramus' corpse into a farce:

> Asleep, my love?
> What, dead, my dove?
> O Pyramus, arise,
>   Speak, speak. Quite dumb?
>   Dead, dead? A tomb
> Must cover thy sweet eyes.
>   These lily lips,
>   This cherry nose,
> These yellow cowslip cheeks,
>   Are gone, are gone;
>   Lovers, make moan;
> His eyes were green as leeks. (V.i.315-26)

Helena's discovery of Lysander asleep in the wood seems to echo the same incident:

> But who is here? Lysander! on the ground!
> Dead, or asleep? I see no blood, no wound.
> Lysander, if you live, good sir, awake. (II.ii.100-2)

Her irrational fear strengthens the parallel with Thisbe's discovery of Pyramus – there is no reason why Lysander should be dead. This little scene exemplifies Shakespeare's tendency to threaten the audience with tragedy and then change it into comedy. Lysander's awakening brings comic relief because he immediately begins to protest his love to Helena:

And run through fire I will for thy sweet sake.
Transparent Helena! Nature shows art,
That through thy bosom makes me see thy heart. (II.ii.103-5)

Even though we know what will happen because we have seen Puck put the juice on his eyes, the contrast between the possibility of Lysander's being dead and what actually happens is dramatically both suspenseful and satisfying.

The mechanicals' performance itself may be seen as a cathartic experience for the audience of lovers, and also for the wider audience in the theatre as a whole. The mixture of comedy and tragedy in their play is very different in effect from the mixture of similar elements that we find throughout the *Metamorphoses*. The farce of the one is matched by the ironic humour of Ovid, and there is little that can be called tragic in the *Metamorphoses*, although pathos and seriousness are present. Yet comparable procedures are deployed in both texts to dispel tragedy. By placing narratives inside one another, as when Ovid puts stories into the mouths of Orpheus and Venus, attention is drawn to the fictive nature of the *Metamorphoses* in a way which alienates our emotional involvement. Similarly a play within a play exaggerates our awareness that what we are seeing is only a fictional representation. We cannot possibly suspend our disbelief at two removes – especially when this second layer of fiction is presented with such egregious incompetence. Our awareness of the unreality of the mechanicals' play is heightened by the facetious interpolations of Theseus and the other courtiers. This function is performed by the voice of Ovid himself in the *Metamorphoses*; when, for example, he tells us that Perseus is so taken with Andromeda that he forgets to fly Ovid reminds us that he is able to manipulate the givens of myth in a playful way, thus checking our involvement in the story. When the players start to comment on the characters they are acting *in propria persona* during the performance itself we are jolted out of any belief in their play, just as we are prevented from feeling absolute empathy with the many Ovidian characters who are able to speak at length and with apparent composure when they are supposedly in the throes of anguish. Both the mechanicals and such characters in Ovid are simultaneously commentators and actors.

The self-reflexive wit inherent in Theseus' sceptical response to the lovers' experiences has often been noted – he is himself no more than an antique fable:

> More strange than true. I never may believe
> These antique fables, nor these fairy toys.
> Lovers and madmen have such seething brains,
> Such shaping fantasies, that apprehend
> More than cool reason ever comprehends. (V.i.2-6)[2]

In Book VIII of the *Metamorphoses* Ovid describes the similarly misplaced scepticism of Pirithoüs. (He is one of Theseus' companions, all of whom have been forced to shelter in the grotto of river-god Acheloüs who has just told his guests of Perimele's metamorphosis into an island.)

> 'ficta refers nimiumque putas, Acheloe, potentes
> esse deos,' dixit 'si dant adimuntque figuras.'

> 'These are but fairy-tales you tell, Acheloüs,' he said,
> 'and you concede too much power to the gods, if they give
> and take away the forms of things.' (VIII 614-15)

His scoffing words are rebuffed by Lelex, who relates the strange metamorphosis of Philemon and Baucis as a counter argument. It is interesting to note that although the whole company is impressed by this story, it is Theseus who responds with most enthusiasm to Lelex. Although Pirithoüs, like Shakespeare's Theseus, is the butt of his creator's irony, his sceptical vision is in tune with Ovid's own – the *Metamorphoses* is full of warnings that we should not believe all we read.

The other tales narrated by the daughters of Minyas in *Metamorphoses* IV are as full of violence and tragedy as Pyramus and Thisbe, but when Shakespeare incorporates them into *A Midsummer Night's Dream* they are purged of such elements in order to make them conform with the comic mode of the play. Immediately after the story of Pyramus and Thisbe, another sister tells how Apollo discovered that Venus had become the lover of Mars and betrayed her affair to Vulcan. In her fury Venus decides to punish the sun god by making him fall in love himself, with a nymph called Leucothoë. Shakespeare may well have been influenced by Golding's translation of this episode which emphasises the faultiness of Apollo's judgement due to the enchantment that has been put on his eyes: 'The fancie of thy faultie minde infects thy feeble sight' (244). This line has no direct equivalent in the original and seems to be entirely Golding's idea; the prominent alliteration makes it all the

---

[2] Shakespeare reran the joke in *Twelfth Night* when he made Fabian remark that 'if this were play'd upon a stage now, I could condemn it as an improbable fiction' (III.iv.121-2).

more emphatic. This connection between sight and judgement is very important in *A Midsummer Night's Dream*. Although every use of the magic flower contributes to Shakespeare's exploration of this theme, the episode which most resembles Venus' revenge, because of the power of those involved and the fact that the flower is used as a punishment, is Oberon's punishment of Titania. The effects of Venus' vengeance are described in an apostrophe to Apollo which has an incantatory force, as though we were listening to the words of a spell spoken by the goddess. Similarly portentous is the charm spoken by Oberon when he squeezes the juice on Titania's eyes:

> What now avayles (Hyperions son) thy forme and beautie bright?
> What now avayle thy glistring eyes with cleare and piercing sight?
> For thou that with thy gleames art wont all countries for to burne,
> Art burnt thy selfe with other gleames that serve not for thy turne.
> And thou that oughtst thy cherefull looke on all things for to show
> Alonly on Leucothoë doste now the same bestow. (233-8)

> What thou seest when thou dost wake,
> Do it for thy true-love take;
> Love and languish for his sake.
> Be it ounce, or cat, or bear,
> Pard, or boar with bristled hair,
> In thy eye that shall appear
> When thou wak'st, it is thy dear.
> Wake when some vile thing is near. (II.ii.27-34)

The ridiculous consequences of the enchantment laid on Titania have no counterpart in Ovid, for Apollo's passion has a tragic issue. However the tale's denouement may be linked with the tribulations of Shakespeare's lovers. Clytie, Apollo's former love, is enraged at being neglected and informs Leucothoë's father of his daughter's secret affair. His wrath is as severe as Egeus':

> He cruell and unmercifull would no excuse accept,
> But holding up hir hands to heaven when tenderly she wept,
> And said it was the Sunne that did the deede against hir will:
> Yet like a savage beast full bent his daughter for to spille ... (288-91)

In Ovid's tale of Pyramus and Thisbe parental opposition, although reported, is not vividly depicted as it is in both the story of Leucothoë and *A Midsummer Night's Dream*. The violence of Egeus' reaction to his daughter's disobedience and the fact that only the father and not the mother is mentioned suggest that the key Ovidian subtext here is not Pyramus and Thisbe, but the tale which immediately follows it.

Yet again Shakespeare modifies his source, making it subordinate to the spirit of comedy. In the *Metamorphoses* there is no dispassionate

Theseus to prevent Leucothoë's father from killing her as Egeus is prevented from doing. The betrayed Clytie stands in the same relation to Leucothoë as Helena does to Hermia. Ovid addresses Apollo directly when he tells us how the god is so enamoured of his new mistress that he neglects Clytie, encouraging the reader to infer that he wants to reprove Apollo for his fickleness:

> Thou lovest this Leucothoë so far above all other,
> That neyther now for Clymene, for Rhodos, nor the mother
> Of Circe, nor for Clytie (who at that present tyde
> Rejected from thy companie did for thy love abide
> Most grievous torments in hir heart) thou seemest for to care. (248-52)

This direct and reproachful response to Apollo's change of heart recalls Lysander's condemnation of Demetrius at the beginning of the play (I.i.106-10).

Ovid does not allow the tragic results of Clytie's talebearing to alienate our sympathy from this slighted nymph altogether. He cites her wounded feelings as an excuse for her behaviour:

> At Clytien, quamvis amor excusare dolorem
> indiciumque dolor poterat, non amplius auctor
> lucis adit Venerisque modum sibi fecit in illa
>
> But Clytie, though love could excuse her grief, and grief her
> tattling, was sought no more by the great light-giver, nor did
> he find aught to love in her. (256-8)

Golding picks up on the hint and carries Ovid's apologia one step further. Apollo's cessation of interest in Clytie is related as a simple fact by Ovid, but Golding makes it seem as if the god is actively spurning her in an unpleasantly malicious way, again making him more like the ungracious Demetrius:

> Yet would the Author of the light resort to hir no more
> But did witholde the pleasant sportes of Venus usde before. (313-14)

But the two girls' eventual fates are very different. The only remedy for Clytie's predicament is metamorphosis into a sunflower whereas the more fortunate Helena regains the love of her ungallant suitor – the fact that this is only possible because Demetrius remains under the magic flower's spell lends a little Ovidian equivocation to this 'happy ending'.

The final tale told by the daughters of Minyas is that of a vain and languid nymph, Salmacis, who refuses to go hunting with Diana and falls in love with a beautiful youth, Hermaphroditus, who is unmoved by her charms. She pretends to accept his decision, but secretly hides in a thicket until he undresses to bathe. She follows him into the pool and clings to him, praying to the gods that they might never be parted. Her prayer is answered and they are transformed into an androgyne. The feminised Hermaphroditus begs his parents to give the pool the power to emasculate anyone who bathes in it. In her amorous enthusiasm Salmacis may be linked both with Titania and with Helena.

It is the comparison with Titania that is most strongly suggested by the first movement of the tale. Interestingly Golding has anglicised Ovid's word *naiad* into 'Waterfairy' (IV 370). The nymph's lyrical declaration of love for Hermaphroditus resembles Titania's speeches to Bottom more than Helena's to Demetrius, for it expresses sudden passion rather than enduring affection. Both Titania and Salmacis are so smitten that they have difficulty deciding what kind of creatures the objects of their desire are. In both cases their first impulse is to think their lovers divine, and then concede that they might be mortal:

> Which done shee thus begon: O childe most worthie for to bee
> Estemde and taken for a God, if (as thou seemste to mee)
> Thou be a God, to Cupids name thy beautie doth agree.
> Or if thou be a mortall wight, right happie folke are they,
> By whome thou camste into this worlde ... (389-93)

> What angel wakes me from my flow'ry bed? ...
> I pray thee, gentle mortal, sing again: (III.i.118,125)

Salmacis is compared, and Titania compares herself, to ivy entwined around a tree, 'Or like as Ivie runnes on trees about the utter rinde;' (453), 'the female ivy so/ Enrings the barky fingers of the elm' (IV.i.40-1). The traditional emblem of feminine dependence is particularly well suited to these tenacious, clinging females.

But whereas Bottom's response to Titania's blandishments is one of bemused acquiescence, Hermaphroditus is determined not to be seduced by Salmacis. Clytie recalled the pathetic aspect of Helena's love for Demetrius; the ludicrous side of her devotion is analogous with Salmacis' unmaidenly determination to get her own way. Demetrius is as cruelly scornful of Helena as Hermaphroditus is of Salmacis. Both men react with exasperation to the advances of their lovers:

> I love thee not, therefore pursue me not ...
> Hence, get thee gone, and follow me no more ...
> Do I entice you? Do I speak you fair?
> Or rather, do I not in plainest truth
> Tell you I do not nor I cannot love you? (II.i.188, 194, 199-201)

> Leave of (quoth he) or I am gone, and leeve thee at a becke
> With all thy trickes. (413-14)

The girls are equally active in pursuit:

Run when you will; the story shall be chang'd
Apollo flies, and Daphne holds the chase;
The dove pursues the griffin; the mild hind
Makes speed to catch the tiger – bootless speed
When cowardice pursues and valor flies. (II.ii.230-4)

The price is won (cride Salmacis aloud) he is mine owne.
And therewithall in all post hast she having lightly throwne
Hir garments off, flew to the Poole and cast hir thereinto,
And caught him fast betweene hir armes for ought that he could doe
(440-3)

Both Salmacis and Helena have their wishes granted by superior powers. The gods cause Salmacis and Hermaphroditus to become one androgynous creature, and Demetrius' eyes, unlike Lysander's, remain enchanted with the magic Love-in-idleness and he continues to dote on Helena. But the two men's different reactions underline the fact that *A Midsummer Night's Dream* is a comedy whereas the *Metamorphoses* is not. Demetrius is happily oblivious to his bewitchment and to the irony of his conviction that he has returned to his 'natural' state:

The object and the pleasure of mine eye,
Is only Helena. To her, my lord,
Was I betroth'd ere I saw Hermia.
But, like a sickness, did I loathe this food;
But, as in health, come to my natural taste,
Now I do wish it, love it, long for it,
And will for evermore be true to it. (IV.i.167-73)

Hermaphroditus on the other hand is far from reconciled to his fate and curses Salmacis' pool.

Supernatural dealings in *A Midsummer Night's Dream* seem rather better organised than they do in the *Metamorphoses*. Whereas Ovid's metamorphoses are rarely better than a compromise, the rather muddled machinations of the fairies actually culminate in a solution which is pleasing to everyone – with the possible exception of Egeus. But Bacchic frenzy is not completely banished from the play. The apparently harmonious final tableau where we see the fairies give their blessing to all the newly weds contains an ominous warning:

To the best bride-bed will we,
Which by us shall blessed be;
And the issue there create
Ever shall be fortunate. (V.i.392-5)

The issue of Theseus and Hippolyta is far from fortunate. Theseus may be presented as a sceptic in *A Midsummer Night's Dream*, but later his credulity will bring about disaster. In the last book of the *Metamor-*

68

phoses Ovid relates how his second wife, Phaedra, wrongly accuses her stepson Hippolytus (Hippolyta's son) of seeking an incestuous relationship with her. Theseus curses him, and he is torn apart by horses – this is a typically 'Bacchic' punishment, such as that which the Athenian court might have witnessed had they chosen the play of 'The riot of the tipsy Bacchanals,/ Tearing the Thracian singer in their rage' (V.i.48-9) rather than the mechanicals' effort.

Also pertinent is the fate of Pentheus, torn apart by his maddened mother, because he, like Theseus, refused to believe a fantastic tale, remaining quite unmoved by Acoetes' account of how his fellow sailors (themselves scoffing sceptics) were transformed into dolphins by Bacchus while their ship, like the Minyades' loom, sprouted vine clusters: 'Praebuimus longis ... ambagibus aures', 'We have lent ear to this long rambling tale' (III 692) he sneers. Significantly the story of Pentheus immediately precedes the account of the daughters of Minyas, a link which is strengthened by the sisters' similarly sceptical response to their own narratives of metamorphosis:

> Some denide
> Hir saying to bee possible: and other some replide
> That such as are in deede true Gods may all things worke at will
> But Bacchus is not any such. (329-32)

Ovid's gods all have their fair share of *amour propre*, and Bacchus, perhaps because he is such a new god, is especially irked by any doubts about his power and divinity. In a play with such a strong Bacchic presence as *A Midsummer Night's Dream* Theseus' scepticism could be read as a danger signal; for the reader or spectator who knows the Ovidian subtext the reference to Hippolyta's progeny is a threat rather than a promise.

Perhaps it is fanciful to import a quite different phase of Theseus' eventful life into the end of *A Midsummer Night's Dream*. But we still have evidence that Shakespeare's metamorphosis of Book IV's tragedy into comedy was neither stable nor complete. The tale of Salmacis was an influence upon Shakespeare's disturbing if comical *Venus and Adonis* which ends in violent death, and although the lovers of *A Midsummer Night's Dream* are offered a reprieve, the full tragedy of Pyramus and Thisbe is replicated in *Romeo and Juliet*.

*

Although the principal Ovidian subtext in *The Tempest* – the story of Medea – is at least as disturbing as anything in *Metamorphoses* IV, Shakespeare seems in some ways more in step with his source in this later play than he does in *A Midsummer Night's Dream*, more truly

'Ovidian' perhaps. Francis Meres' suggestion that Ovid lives again in Shakespeare is almost justified by *The Tempest*, although this particular interface between the two writers finds neither at their most honeyed.

Towards the end of Shakespeare's career Ovidianism is less obviously apparent in his plays – we don't have clear signals such as the enactment of Pyramus and Thisbe provides. However the strong Ovidian presence in Shakespeare's late plays has been increasingly acknowledged. Overt allusions to stories in the *Metamorphoses* give way to a more oblique engagement with Ovid. David Armitage suggests in his own discussion of the subject that 'Myth has become more integral to the poetic fabric of the plays, developing from decorative spangling in the early work to concealed fertile allusion' (Armitage pp. 123-33). The aspects of Ovid's work which are most relevant in connection with *The Tempest* are his fondness for calling attention to the fictive nature of his writing, his manipulation of readers' expectations, the identifications he makes between himself and the creators in the *Metamorphoses*, whether gods or artists, and the blurring of boundaries between what is real and unreal, art or nature.

The most obvious starting point for any discussion of this play's Ovidianism is a speech by Prospero which has long been recognised as a very close imitation of Medea's incantation in Book VII of the *Metamorphoses*. Medea is the Colchian witch who helped Jason steal the Golden Fleece from her father. After they are married Jason begs Medea to prolong the life of his own father, Aeson. The invocation which is drawn on so heavily by Shakespeare comes just before she cuts up Aeson and places him in a cauldron full of magic potion from which he emerges as a youth. This feat later enables her to trick the daughters of Jason's enemy Pelias into cutting their own father's throat in the hope that the same miracle will be performed on him. This time the potion is neutral and Pelias remains dead.

> Ye elves of hills, brooks, standing lakes, and groves;
> And ye that on the sands with printless foot
> Do chase the ebbing Neptune, and do fly him
> When he comes back; you demi-puppets that
> By moonshine do the green sour ringlets make,
> Whereof the ewe not bites; and you whose pastime
> Is to make midnight mushrooms, that rejoice
> To hear the solemn curfew; by whose aid –
> Weak masters though ye be – I have bedimm'd
> The noontide sun, call'd forth the mutinous winds,
> And 'twixt the green sea and the azur'd vault
> Set roaring war. To the dread rattling thunder
> Have I given fire, and rifted Jove's stout oak
> With his own bolt; the strong-bas'd promontory

Have I made shake, and by the spurs pluck'd up
The pine and cedar Graves at my command
Have wak'd their sleepers, op'd, and let 'em forth,
By my so potent art. But this rough magic
I here abjure; and, when I have requir'd
Some heavenly music – which even now I do –
To work mine end upon their senses that
This airy charm is for, I'll break my staff,
Bury it certain fadoms in the earth,
And deeper than did ever plummet sound
I'll drown my book. (V.i.33-57)

auraeque et venti montesque amnesque lacusque,
dique omnes nemorum, dique omnes noctis adeste,
quorum ope, cum volui, ripis mirantibus amnes
in fontes rediere suos, concussaque sisto,
stantia concutio cantu freta, nubila pello
nubilaque induco, ventos abigoque vocoque,
vipereas rumpo verbis et carmine fauces,
vivaque saxa sua convulsaque robora terra
et silvas moveo iubeoque tremescere montis
et mugire solum manesque exire sepulcris!
te quoque, Luna, traho, quamvis Temesaea labores
aera tuos minuant; currus quoque carmine nostro
pallet avi, pallet nostris Aurora venenis! (VII 197-209)

Ye Ayres and windes: ye Elves of Hilles, of Brookes, of Woods alone,
Of standing Lakes, and of the Night approche ye everychone.
Through helpe of whom (the crooked bankes much wondring at the thing)
I have compelled streames to run cleane backward to their spring.
By charmes I make the calme Seas rough, and make ye rough Seas plaine
And cover all the Skie with Cloudes, and chase them thence againe.
By charmes I rayse and lay the windes, and burst the Vipers jaw,
And from the bowels of the Earth both stones and trees doe drawe.
Whole woods and Forestes I remove: I make the Mountaines shake,
And even the Earth it selfe to grone and fearfully to quake.
I call up dead men from their graves: and thee O lightsome Moone
I darken oft, though beaten brasse abate thy perill soone
Our Sorcerie dimmes the Morning faire, and darkes ye Sun at Noone.
(VII 265-77)

Critics have suggested different ways of responding to Shakespeare's decision to put the words of such a problematic character into the mouth of Prospero, and in particular the troubling retention of Medea's claim that she can raise the dead. Is there an ironic interplay between the very different characters, the bad witch who destroys and the benign enchanter who renews? Are we supposed to infer a darker side to Prospero's character? Or is Shakespeare simply responding to Ovid's poetry without really considering the context?

I would like to offer an explanation which is perhaps more truly

71

Ovidian (at least according to one reading of his work) than any of these – that Prospero *has* raised the dead – and has in fact done so in the play itself – but only by means of *illusion*. And, although his claim to have raised the tempest might at first seem uncontroversial, the reality even of this feat is possibly called into question. Although most readers would find *A Midsummer Night's Dream* a gayer play than *The Tempest* it is in the later work that Shakespeare seems most at ease with Ovid's ludic qualities.

Jonathan Bate correctly observes that 'the earlier part of the speech seems to be a lightening of the original' (p. 251), and this makes the retention of Medea's necromantic claim all the more striking and curious. This lightening may be seen in the activities with which the elves are associated, such as making magic rings and mushrooms. These are natural phenomena, not the violent alterations of nature which Medea claims to have the power to carry out. The beginning of this speech perhaps sounds more impressive than its content warrants, for the sonorous invocation is belied by the actual triviality of the phenomena described and the elves' lack of influence upon their surroundings. This victory of effect over content might be said to characterise *The Tempest* as a whole, and is consistent with the idea that both the storm and the necromancy are illusions. For within the context of *The Tempest* some of Medea's claims seem to have as much to do with the artistry of the playwright Shakespeare as with Prospero's magic powers. This suggestion of self-reference is in itself very Ovidian – the *Metamorphoses* is a supremely self-conscious work.

In the Medea speech Prospero evokes the storm he created in far more literary terms than either Golding or Ovid, ' 'twixt the green sea and the azur'd vault/ Set roaring war', and this seems to reflect its presentation at the opening of the play.

> If by your art, my dearest father, you have
> Put the wild waters in this roar, allay them. (I.ii.1-2)

Miranda's use of the word 'art' is perfectly appropriate simply as a synonym for magic and on one level this is clearly what it is. But if we follow the lead given by the hint of artifice attached to the storm in Prospero's Medea speech, then the implications of the word 'art' may be extended. Despite its vivid presentation in the first scene, the tempest takes on an air of unreality after it has died away. No one has been harmed and there are not even any stains of salt water on the sailors' clothes – the violent effects of the storm to which Prospero refers in the Medea speech are not at all in evidence. His reassurances to Miranda also serve to shift it beyond the realms of concrete reality into the province of illusion:

The direful spectacle of the wreck, which touch'd
The very virtue of compassion in thee,
I have with such provision in mine art
So safely ordered, that there is no soul –
No, not so much perdition as an hair
Betid to any creature in the vessel
Which thou heard'st cry, which thou saw'st sink. (I.ii.26-32)

The word 'spectacle' suggests that the storm was only a chimera, a pageant with no substance, and indeed has connotations of dramatic representation which become problematic in the context of a play and recall the connections that have been made between Prospero and Shakespeare himself – the parallels between the enchanter's eventual repudiation of magic and the playwright's farewell to the stage have proved irresistible to critics, although there is no evidence that Shakespeare himself intended such an identification to be made. Peter Greenaway's film *Prospero's Books* responds very strongly to this aspect of the play, and we see his Prospero playing with a toy boat as he writes the opening storm scene in a book, trying out different ways of reciting the first lines. The ease with which Prospero, and other characters in Shakespeare, invite us to align them with their creator is another sign of his Ovidianism, for Ovid too encourages his readers to detect affinities between himself and his artist characters such as Arachne and Mulciber. Prospero might be termed a stage manager as well as a playwright because when he describes his ability to summon music he seems to include a little cue directed at his tardy technicians: 'and, when I have requir'd/ Some heavenly music – which even now I do –/ To work mine end upon their senses' (V.i.51-3).

A spectator might initially be surprised by the suggestion that the storm was not a reality, only to reflect that the special effects which made it seem real were themselves an illusion which had never really deceived him. Artificial rolls of thunder, for example, could be perceived, not as the stage manager's attempt to convince an audience that the storm is real, but as Prospero using his magic to persuade Miranda of the same thing. By emphasising Miranda's cognizance of the storm through her faculties of sight and hearing, Prospero seems to be suggesting that this is the only sense in which the storm was a reality and that it had no existence outside Miranda's (and implicitly the audience's) perception.

Whereas Ovid is in the controlling position of narrator and can remind the reader that he is reading fiction, no single person or scene in *The Tempest* has this complete authority. Thus our perception of the storm in the very first scene of the play and the subsequent events which give an impression of its unreality undercut each other in a shifting interplay where no version of events is certain. Whereas in the *Metamorphoses* Ovid contrives to remind the reader wittily that there is no 'true' version of events because the poem is no more than a literary construct, Shakespeare makes his audience, whether it responds consciously or unconsciously, unclear what version of events to believe. The characters themselves seem undecided about the nature of their situation, disagreeing as to whether the island is bleak or fertile and, most significantly in the context of a storm whose reality is questioned, whether their clothes are wet or dry.

Deaths by drowning are usually the result of any storm. In *The Tempest* such deaths are not simply omitted; strong suggestions are given that people may have died which are then reassuringly contradicted. Death, like the storm, seems to have occurred at first but we become progressively less sure. Prospero's second claim was to have raised the dead to life and this detail, at first so impressively sinister, may, like his claim to have raised a storm, be reduced to a matter of audience manipulation.

Critics' preoccupation with the theme of rebirth and renewal in the Romances might incline the reader to interpret Prospero's words metaphorically and infer that spiritual rather than physical renewal is the miracle Prospero has carried out. The emphasis placed by commentators upon this theme makes it possible to regard Shakespeare's close imitation of Medea's speech as particularly significant, rather than being prompted by the local verbal and atmospheric felicities of this passage. Medea's invocation is a prelude to her rejuvenation of Aeson, a spectacular display of the very magic powers which Prospero vows to abjure at the end of his rendition of the speech. But the critic eager to emphasise the supposed reconciliation at the end of the play could argue that the element of miraculous physical resurrection in Medea's story is so happily consistent with the spiritual regeneration with which *The Tempest* concludes that Medea's speech is a far from incongruous source. Alonso and his companions, through their remorse, undergo the metaphorical equivalent of Aeson's rejuvenation. But if Shakespeare was thinking about the context of Medea's speech, and not merely appropriating a dramatic set piece, it is unlikely that he would have delighted in the apposite nature of the theme of rebirth and quite overlooked the trick Medea played on Pelias and the murder of Jason's new wife and children, only fleetingly mentioned by Ovid but notorious.

Prospero cites his 'so potent art' as having enabled him to perform the feat of raising the dead to life, and although 'magic' would seem to be the understood qualifier of 'art', certain elements in *The Tempest* suggest that the only way the dead are raised to life is by literary art. There is a subtle distinction between Prospero's claim and that of Ovid's (and Golding's) Medea which is significant although easily overlooked. Medea does not claim that she can raise the dead to life, but only 'manes … exire sepulcris!', 'call up dead men from their graves', zombie-fashion. By using the metaphor of waking those who are asleep Prospero suggests both that he is restoring the dead to their original state, i.e. life, and, even though the metaphor of sleep for death is well worn, hints that the dead were not really dead.

An evocation of a death which does not happen is contained in Ariel's song in which he seems to tell Ferdinand that his father has drowned. Although Prospero has already assured Miranda that the storm has harmed no one, Ferdinand does not know this and responds to the song by saying 'The ditty does remember my drown'd father' (I.ii.405). It is not simply death that Ariel suggests Alonso has undergone, but metamorphosis:

> Full fathom five thy father lies;
>   Of his bones are coral made;
> Those are pearls that were his eyes;
>   Nothing of him that doth fade
> But doth suffer a sea-change
> Into something rich and strange.
> Sea-nymphs hourly ring his knell ... (I.ii.396-402)

Any perceived contradiction in Prospero's ineffectual 'demi-puppets' helping him raise people from the dead is explained if we accept that this apparent necromancy consists of no more than the conjunction of a haunting song, an impressionable young man and an audience which is open to suggestion.

The song illustrates one common strand in Ovidian metamorphosis. Those who undergo transformation frequently retain many of their features after they have been metamorphosed, but these are modified to conform with their new identity. An obvious example is the metamorphosis of Daphne into a laurel:

> mollia cinguntur tenui praecordia libro,
> in frondem crines, in ramos bracchia crescunt,
> pes modo tam velox pigris radicibus haeret,
> ora cacumen habet: remanet nitor unus in illa. (I 549-52)

> And therwithall about hir breast did grow a tender barke.
> Hir haire was turned into leaves, hir armes in boughes did growe,
> Hir feete that were ere while so swift, now rooted were as slowe.
> Hir crowne became the toppe, and thus of that she earst had beene,
> Remayned nothing in the worlde, but beautie fresh and greene. (I 672-6)

But the two passages create quite different effects. Daphne's changes are presented as part of a consistent process, signalled in particular by the balanced symmetry of line 550. In Ariel's song this ordered clarity is replaced by dreamlike imprecision. Lines 397-8 illustrate the divergence of Shakespeare's methods from those of Ovid. The line 'Of his bones are coral made' is syntactically elusive; we are not sure whether

Ariel is describing a completed or an ongoing process. In the next line, in comparison to the symmetry of line 550 of the Daphne passage, the order of the transformed feature and the thing it has become is reversed, and whereas 397 suggests that the metamorphic process is ongoing, the transformation of the eyes into pearls is mysterious and absolute. The overall impression is one of disintegration rather than the strange logical integrity of Daphne's metamorphosis.

The song may be described as Ovidian for more than one reason. The most obvious is the use of metamorphic imagery. But the generation of uncertainty surrounding an assertion is also typical of Ovid, as two similar incidents in the *Metamorphoses* illustrate. Ovid suggests that the drowned king Ceyx may have lifted his head from the water to meet his wife Alcyone's kiss, 'Folk dowt if Ceyx feeling it too rayse his head did strayne/ Or whither that the waves did lift it up' (XI 851-2). He similarly implies that another apparently drowned man, Orpheus, may still be alive as his head floats along the Hebrus and 'his livelesse toong did make/ A certeine lamentable noyse as though it still yit spake' (XI 55-6). Although we know that Alonso is still alive, it is impossible to forget Ariel's strange evocation of his metamorphic decay just as, at the end of *The Winter's Tale* it is the arresting image of a statue apparently coming to life, rather than Paulina's rational explanation for this marvel, which has most impact upon a spectator's imagination.

Even though we know that Alonso is alive the song still represents a powerful evocation of the general strangeness of the isle and it is rendered more unsettling because we have only heard that Alonso is safe from Prospero and do not actually see him again until Act II. The association of Alonso with metamorphosis might be taken as a portent of the regenerative moral change he apparently undergoes. Yet it is eloquent of the haphazard nature of such regeneration in this play that Alonso's metamorphosis is presented as the result neither of Prospero's grace nor his own will but simply of the disinterested forces of a morally neutral environment.

*

As Jonathan Bate notes in *Shakespeare and Ovid*, one entire phase of the *Metamorphoses* seems to have particular affinities with *The Tempest*. This is the sequence which describes Aeneas' progress from Troy to Italy, and which comprises roughly the second half of Book XIII and the first half of Book XIV. Here too we can see how Ovid is a dynamic, informing presence in Shakespeare's plays – the source has been internalised, not simply imitated.

As with Medea, the importance of this debt to Ovid lies in more than the surface similarities of language or plot. The Medea speech helps to highlight the way Shakespeare undermines our expectations and plays with his audience's capacity to suspend its disbelief. The influence of Ovid's 'Little *Aeneid*' has a comparable effect because Shakespeare is looking at a section of the *Metamorphoses* which is very much concerned with defeated expectations and the subversion of literary authority.

A number of critics have detected traces of the *Aeneid* in *The Tempest* – and a full length study has been devoted to the relationship between the two (Hamilton 1990). The fact that the noblemen are travelling from North Africa to Italy, a reference to Dido in Act II, the affinity between Ferdinand's first sight of Miranda and Aeneas' meeting with Venus in disguise, the appearance of a harpy in both works, have all been adduced as evidence of Virgil's influence upon Shakespeare. But there are good reasons for privileging Ovid's *Aeneid* above Virgil's as a context for *The Tempest*. Interwoven with details of Aeneas' voyage are accounts of legends concerning minor ocean deities, and here, more than at any other time in Ovid's poem, we are aware of the sea and its denizens. Some of these stories have interesting points of contact with the action of *The Tempest*, and many of the different places mentioned by Ovid seem to have lent something to Shakespeare's conception of Prospero's island. In Golding's translation they seem very much to be 'sea pastorals', as it were, with a particular quality of their own, dreamily idyllic, but bucolic, almost rustic, and not in the least austere or 'classical'. It seems probable that Shakespeare was using these tales, if only subconsciously, as models for the magical seascape of *The Tempest*.

The most obvious link between these interludes and *The Tempest* is that between Polyphemus and Caliban. Polyphemus is an interesting mixture of contrarieties whose unrequited love for the nymph Galatea has a touching quality for all his grotesqueness and violent jealousy of his favoured rival, Acis. Similar contradictions, more problematically presented, focus around the character of Caliban. They both have a particular affinity with the natural world, an attribute which is treated ambiguously by both Shakespeare and Ovid and which determines both their positive and their negative aspects, emerging in their use of images taken from their surroundings and in the proprietorial pride they feel in relation to their environment. This latter quality is partly dictated by the fact that they both live on islands to which they feel they have a special claim.

Although he is dismissed by Galatea as an 'owgly Giant' (896) whose attempts to beautify himself, 'His sturre stiffe heare he kembeth nowe with strong and sturdy rakes,/ And with a sythe dooth marcussotte his bristled berd:' (XIII 903-4) only serve to accentuate his grotesqueness, his lengthy love complaint has its own plangent charm despite its lack of sophistication.

More whyght thou art than Primrose leaf my Lady Galatee,
More fresh than meade, more tall and streyght than lofty Aldertree,

More bright than glasse, more wanton than the tender kid forsooth,
Than Cockleshelles continually with water worne, more smoothe,
More cheerefull than the winters Sun, or Sommers shadowe cold,
More seemely and more comly than the Planetree too behold,
Of valew more than Apples bee although they were of gold ...
(XIII 929-35)

It is significant that Polyphemus is a musician of sorts, because the passage always cited to support Caliban's status as a complex and sensitive character is the following famous speech:

Be not afeard. The isle is full of noises,
Sounds, and sweet airs, that give delight, and hurt not.
Sometimes a thousand twangling instruments
Will hum about mine ears; and sometime voices,
That, if I then had wak'd after long sleep,
Will make me sleep again; and then, in dreaming,
The clouds methought would open and show riches
Ready to drop upon me, that, when I wak'd,
I cried to dream again. (III.ii.130-8)

The beauty of Caliban's speech is accentuated by Stephano's crass rejoinder, 'This will prove a brave kingdom to me, where I shall have my music for nothing' (III.ii.139-40). However one should not overemphasise Caliban's spirituality. Although he is able to respond to music, the one image which it summons up for him is one of boundless riches, even though he does express this vision of wealth in terms of a Danaën epiphany and thus prevents it from seeming too overtly materialistic.

Another point of contact is that between the Cercopes, who are changed into apes on account of perjury, and Caliban, who also abuses the language he has been taught by Miranda. Bate suggests that the Ovidian subtext problematises Prospero:

It is Jove who metamorphoses the Cercopes into apes, Prospero who has the power to do the same to Caliban. ... But might such actions also be indications that Prospero is usurping powers which should properly belong only to a god? (pp. 248-9)

Then follows Bate's analysis of the Medea speech which he finds similarly disturbing.

But for Prospero, imagined as a virtuous ruler, to bring a pagan image of raising the dead into the Christian era, in which that power should belong uniquely to Christ and his Father, is deeply disturbing. (pp. 251-2)

I would like to offer an alternative way of looking at Shakespeare's use of the 'Little *Aeneid*', as a counterpart to my reading of the Medea speech.

The evidence that Shakespeare was drawing on a substantial section of the *Metamorphoses*, rather as he used Book IV in *A Midsummer Night's Dream*, is interesting because it tells us something about the workings of the playwright's poetic imagination. But, as with the relationship between Ovid's Fama and *The House of Fame*, the surface similarities are but the visible tip of a veritable iceberg of Ovidianism. Shakespeare has imported the structure as well as the verbal detail and individual stories of these books of the *Metamorphoses*. Perceiving this relationship may help us to illuminate some of the stranger qualities of *The Tempest*. Throughout the play a curious impression that something is escaping us is created, an elusive sense that what we are seeing or reading is taking place somehow outside the main action. The same is true of the 'Little *Aeneid*'.

The reason for this destabilising effect is more easily accounted for in the case of Ovid. He is retelling a work which despite its relatively recent composition was already revered and definitive. The *Heroides* provide evidence that Ovid was interested in the ingenious literary possibilities of retelling aspects of canonical works from an unusual angle and in the *Metamorphoses*, as we saw in Chapter 2, the *Iliad* as well as the *Aeneid* is subjected to this treatment. While there was nothing new in writers of epic making up material – Virgil is credited with having originated the idea of a love affair between Dido and Aeneas – Ovid draws attention to and thematises the gap between two versions rather than attempt to make his own telling oust a previous rendering from its position of supremacy. Indeed, Ovid's version of Aeneas' voyage would lose much of its point and interest if it succeeded in dispelling all memory of the *Aeneid* from our minds. It differs principally from the *Aeneid* itself in being far less concerned with the historic nature of the hero's mission. Aeneas drifts along comparatively aimlessly in the *Metamorphoses* whereas in the *Aeneid* his objective is constantly impressed upon the reader. He is of course the protagonist of Virgil's poem whereas in the *Metamorphoses* not only is his story dispatched within the space of two books but even in these books Ovid constantly marginalises Aeneas and diverts his readers' attention to other stories and characters. Like Christ in *The Life of Brian*, Aeneas is consigned firmly to the sidelines.

The connections with *The Tempest*, which does not have a single source, are not immediately apparent. But it too raises expectations in its audience only to defeat them, not in relation to a particular work but to fiction and narrative in general. We have already seen that Prospero may be in some sense identified with a stage manager, and also with an author. One might say that he is not a very good author – losing track of the different strands of his narrative such as Caliban's plot and getting sidetracked on to less important matters such as the masque. In the section of the *Metamorphoses* under discussion, Ovid, on the surface, seems to be a similarly incompetent narrator who loses sight of his hero in order to deal with the affairs of less important characters, such as Polyphemus and Galatea, at length.

A similarly desultory quality may be detected in both *The Tempest* and the *Metamorphoses*. The action of *The Tempest* lacks the sense of purpose and motivation which we expect from a narrative and Ovid's version of the *Aeneid* lacks that specific *telos* which we expect after having read Virgil. We assume that Prospero has a clear aim because he is presented as a powerful magician with very specific grievances to avenge, whereas we assume Aeneas has a definite goal because we have read the *Aeneid*. But our expectations are similarly thwarted in both works.

In the very first lines of the *Aeneid* we are informed that the Trojan is no ordinary traveller – the gods themselves take a keen and active interest in his wanderings, 'multum ille et terris *iactatus* et alto/ vi superum, *saevae* memorem Iunonis ob iram', 'much buffeted on sea and land by violence from above, through cruel Juno's unforgiving wrath' (I 3-4). Ovid effects a contrast by using similar vocabulary to describe the far more mundane framework for the problems which beset his own Aeneas, '*saevit* hiems *iactatque* viros', 'the wintry seas raged and tossed the heroic band' (XIII 709). In fact Juno's anger is only mentioned once, very briefly, at the end of Aeneas' story when all his troubles are over. These departures from the *Aeneid*, in particular the trivialisation of his destiny, have to be read in the light of the tremendous importance placed upon the hero during the rule of his supposed descendant, Augustus.

Similarly, the action of *The Tempest* progresses in a way which leads us to assume that some great purpose lies behind all Prospero's actions. It would appear that he is about to give Miranda a more precise account of his plan when she falls asleep (I.i.75-186). By being given a hint of a strategy which is not then explained the audience might feel that something is lacking. Our expectation of Prospero's revenge is changed into an anticipation that the play will climax in a scene of forgiveness – but although we may *think* we have been shown this scene in the last act, at this crucial moment the play falls victim to inertia and loses its momentum. As soon as Prospero has everyone in his power he decides not to exact vengeance. His portentous machinations suddenly seem like the actions of a novice chess player who can devise an apparently subtle strategy which disintegrates after a few moves because he has failed to take into account either his opponent's response or long term developments. His actions, which have hitherto appeared so complicated, dissolve into nothing for Alonso resigns his right to tribute voluntarily and Sebastian and Antonio maintain a truculent silence, an absence of reaction rather than positive defiance, until the arrival of Stephano and Trinculo prompts them to make a few characteristically sarcastic quips. Edmund and Iachimo repent fulsomely, yet the chief villains in this play, so often characterised by its supposed engagement with ideas of reconciliation and forgiveness, remain defiant. The audience might justly feel cheated of a more fitting climax – easily imagined by a moderately seasoned theatre goer – involving a dramatic exposure of Antonio and Sebastian's designs against Alonso, followed by their suitably abject public recantation and Prospero's lofty forgiveness extended to all. But the plot formed by Antonio and Sebastian is prevented from reaching a climax because Alonso and Gonzalo never realise they were in danger and Prospero decides to keep quiet about it. (We have only to think of a play which *does* satisfy all our expectations, such as *Twelfth Night* or *As You Like It* to realise how curious *The Tempest* is in this respect.) Stephano and Trinculo seem extraneous to the main story – their much vaunted plot, too, is never attempted – and they are completely distracted by the tawdry costumes left as bait. Also unresolved, and underlying all these other problems, is the question of the nature and extent of Prospero's powers. At times he seems a beneficent, almost godlike figure, at others a cantankerous and forgetful old man, and, although more than natural forces seem to be at work in the play, it is not always clear whether they stem from Prospero, the island itself or from some mysterious external agency.

This aspect of *The Tempest* parallels the lack of almost any sense of destiny or significance in Ovid's account of Aeneas' journey. But although I wish to emphasise the presence of Ovid in this play, this does not necessarily mean that Virgil has to be absent. The two poets' influences are not mutually exclusive. Perhaps we might align the ending of the *Aeneid* with the closing scenes of *The Tempest*. Both seem destined to end on a note of reconciliation with the forgiveness of Antonio on the one hand and the union of Lavinia and Aeneas on the other. But Antonio, as we have seen, does not repent in a satisfactory manner, and the *Aeneid* ends, not with a marriage or scene of triumph, but with the murder of Turnus and the descent of his unforgiving soul to the underworld.

The general sense of a lack of purpose in the 'Little *Aeneid*' is accompanied by a more specific lack of narrative drive, whereby we are prevented from becoming really engaged with Aeneas' adventures because the story keeps breaking off, jumping from one plot strand to another. Similarly in *The Tempest* evidence may be found to suggest that we are missing all the action, almost as if we were continually being shown the wrong part of the island. Alonso and Gonzalo have only just woken up at the end of II.i, yet when we next see them at III.iii they want to go to sleep again. Gonzalo's words 'here's a maze trod, indeed,/ Through forth-rights and meanders!' (III.iii.2-3) seem an appropriate comment on the action of the play. Admittedly both occasions when they sleep serve as spurs to the murderous ambitions of Sebastian and

Antonio, yet even they seem infected by a kind of *vis inertiae*. In II.i we hear Antonio's very effective Iago-like persuasion of Sebastian to kill Alonso. Sebastian is convinced:

> Thy case, dear friend,
> Shall be my precedent; as thou got'st Milan,
> I'll come by Naples. Draw thy sword. One stroke
> Shall free thee from the tribute which thou payest;
> And I the king shall love thee. (281-5)

Antonio replies

> Draw together;
> And when I rear my hand, do you the like,
> To fall it on Gonzalo. (285-7)

They presumably draw their swords at this point and some tension will have been generated in the audience, who will be wondering whether or not they will succeed.

But at this exciting point the tension is suddenly deflated. Sebastian says 'O, but one word.' [they talk apart]. The action is halted and Ariel comes on and makes the following reassuring speech:

> My master through his art foresees the danger
> That you, his friend, are in; and sends me forth -
> For else his project dies – to keep them living. (288-90)

He then sings a little song – goodness knows what Antonio and Sebastian are talking about all this time – the words of which have an ironic aptness which is presumably unintentional on Shakespeare's part.

> While you here do snoring lie,
> Open-ey'd conspiracy
> His time doth take.
> If of life you keep a care,
> Shake off slumber and beware.
> Awake, Awake! (291-6)

'Open eyed conspiracy his time doth take' should be paraphrased 'now is the hour of conspiracy' but the modern sense of taking one's time would certainly fit the context. Finally Antonio returns to the situation with the words 'Then let us both be sudden' – (!) – (297) but Alonso and Gonzalo are wakened by the noise of bellowing. The whole interval between the decision to assassinate them and the attempt itself seems superfluous – killing the tension. We might expect a playwright to manipulate his material in order to allow the hero to thwart the plans of the villains, yet we don't expect the villains to create their own completely gratuitous delays if the hero – in this case Ariel – appears to be detained.

The development of the love interest presents parallel problems; the play raises expectations in its audience, based on their previous experience of fiction and narrative, only to defeat them. Despite Prospero's approval of the love which develops between Ferdinand and Miranda, he decides to test the prince's worth by affecting anger. The audience might expect to witness a touching scene where Prospero reveals his motives for making Ferdinand carry logs and gives the couple his blessing. In fact, not for the only time in this play, we seem to arrive just too late. Prospero's words at the beginning of Act IV, 'If I have too austerely punish'd you,/ Your compensation makes amends' (IV.i.1-2) would seem to be spoken immediately after this pleasant revelation. This sense of an inept camera operator at a football match showing us the hugging but not the goal is paralleled in the 'Little *Aeneid*', for just as we get to the point where the reader would expect the tale of Dido – the *Aeneid*'s erotic highlight – we are swept off into the long excursus of Polyphemus and Galatea, leaving Ovid time only for the most hasty summary of her involvement with the hero.

The play's most famous speech provides a fitting note on which to end:

Our revels now are ended. These our actors,
As I foretold you, were all spirits, and
Are melted into air, into thin air;
And, like the baseless fabric of this vision,
The cloud-capp'd towers, the gorgeous palaces,
The solemn temples, the great globe itself,
Yea, all which it inherit, shall dissolve,
And like this insubstantial pageant faded,
Leave not a rack behind. We are such stuff
As dreams are made on, and our little life
Is rounded with a sleep. (IV.i.148-58)

This follows the masque which celebrates the lovers' betrothal. On one level it seems to be wholly nugatory, indeed this is the impression given by Prospero himself:

                  Go bring the rabble,
O'er whom I give thee pow'r, here to this place.
Incite them to quick motion; for I must
Bestow upon the eyes of this young couple
Some vanity of mine art ... (IV.i.37-41)

On the other hand the apparent appearance of three goddesses and the convincing majesty of their speeches undercut Prospero's disclaimer to some extent. These conflicting impressions confuse the audience, unsure whether the masque is divinely inspired or merely a flimsy and delusive conjuring trick. This elusiveness is the hallmark of Shakespeare's Ovidianism throughout the late plays; the explanations for such strange events as Hermione's descent from the pedestal and Thaisa's return to life in *Pericles* are neither wholly rational nor decidedly magical. As with the storm, whose special effects can be attributed either to stage machinery or Prospero's magic, the masque becomes problematic in its theatrical context. The goddesses speak with regal grandeur and the actors who portrayed them would presumably be dressed in all the sumptuous finery that the theatre's budget would permit. An audience might therefore be surprised that Prospero refers to them as 'rabble'. Yet, fully aware of the nature of theatre, even though he may have temporarily suspended his disbelief, a spectator might recall that the boys (now women) who represent the goddesses are at least as far from being divine as Prospero's airy minions. Ovid undercuts his poem in a similar way in the middle of the 'Little *Aeneid*', when he introduces Scylla, and then says, 'et, si non omnia vates/ ficta reliquerunt, aliquo quoque tempore virgo', 'and, if all the tales of poets are not false, she was herself once a virgin' (XIII 733-4). We might also remember Ben Jonson's witty exploitation of an audience's acceptance of theatrical convention at the climax of *Epicoene*, when its 'heroine' is revealed to be a boy in disguise – a secret which in one sense its audience would have known all along. The masque's contradictory combination of impressive effects which turn out to have only flimsy substance also anticipates the Medea speech, whose claims appear to be awe-inspiring and supernatural but may be reduced to mere theatrical devices. The Revels speech shares this playful ambiguity, for 'globe' suggests the Globe as well as the world, just as *orbis* could be the world or a ball of wool for Ovid (I 35, V 19), and although the 'insubstantial pageant' is ostensibly the masque, it could equally well refer to *The Tempest* as a whole or indeed to life itself.

If we choose to associate Prospero with Shakespeare and the Mage's magic art with literary sleight of hand then we might also (fancifully) want to suggest that a copy of Ovid's *Metamorphoses* makes a second appearance on Shakespeare's stage (the first being in *Titus Andronicus* IV.i.42):

> I'll break my staff,
> Bury it certain fathoms in the earth,
> And deeper than did ever plummet sound
> I'll drown my book. (V.i.54-7)

The submerged *Metamorphoses* of *The Tempest* reveals Shakespeare's understanding of Ovid's art still more strikingly than the more obviously 'Ovidian' early works.

Untroubled Ovidianism: Andrew Marvell's Ovidian Wit

Unlike his near contemporary Milton, Marvell was completely at home in the world of the *Metamorphoses*. We cannot know whether Marvell was like Ovid, but 'Marvell' and 'Ovid' certainly have a great deal in common – both have been described as urbane, witty, sophisticated and dispassionate, and both have the power to alienate as well as attract. Marvell is perhaps the most unreservedly Ovidian writer discussed in this book. His engagement with the *Metamorphoses* seems almost entirely free of tensions or misgivings of any kind, yet his Ovidianism is strangely resistant, at least at first, to analysis. Marvell's poetic voice, ambivalent, disengaged, continually eluding the reader who wishes to pin him down to a moral or a meaning, and distinguished, as Eliot remarked, by an 'alliance of levity and seriousness' (*Selected Essays* p. 296), reflects a sensibility, a frame of mind, which might be styled 'Ovidian'. But beyond a vague sense of some general affinity it is not easy to define the relationship between the two poets with any degree of precision. It might seem that Marvell was not profoundly engaged by the *Metamorphoses* – allusions to Ovid seem scant and casual on a first reading of his poetry. But this very elusiveness is itself a symptom of Marvell's complete absorption in Ovid (or perhaps we should say in 'Ovidianism') whose presence is embedded into the very texture of his poems, influencing their style as much as their content. It is certainly possible to point to details and references in Marvell's poetry, and trace them back to Ovid, generally to his *Metamorphoses*.[1] But such stories as Apollo's pursuit of Daphne, Zeus' transformation into a shower of gold in order to woo Danaë, and the fall of Phaethon, all alluded to by Marvell, cannot really be used as evidence of a truly profound engagement with Ovid, any more than a casual reference to the *id* in a twentieth-century novel proves the author was a student of Freud. They

[1]However, Horace is perhaps the Roman poet whom we most instinctively associate with Marvell, if only because Marvell himself entitled one of his most famous poems 'A Horatian Ode'. Asserting Ovid's importance for Marvell need not involve depressing the influence of Horace, particularly as the two influences are far from incompatible. The description of the flood in 'Upon Appleton House', for example, is generally traced back to Ovid, yet similar topsy-turvy floods are described twice by Horace, in the *Ars Poetica* and in *Odes* (1.2).

represent part of the furniture of the Renaissance mind, and, although Ovid might be the principal source for these and many other legends, poets and painters had incorporated them into their works so frequently that by the time Marvell was writing they were very common coin. If we want to assert that Marvell was an Ovidian poet in any meaningful sense we must look for more than a few name-dropped gods and nymphs.

The relationship between the two poets may perhaps best be defined in terms of a shared disdain for boundaries. Both flout the parameters of genre, both fragment the idea of a stable selfhood, entire of itself, both problematise the relationship between the poet as artist and the poem as object, and, perhaps most strikingly, both refuse to maintain the distinctions between different orders of creation. Before discussing one of his best known poems, 'Upon Appleton House', I will attempt to offer a more general survey of Marvell's appropriation of Ovidian tropes.

In Marvell's 'Mourning' the tears of a bereaved woman are not really signs of grief:

> She courts her self in amorous rain;
> Herself both Danae and the shower. (19-20)

Marvell may or may not have learnt this tale from Ovid – it is alluded to three times in the *Metamorphoses* – we cannot tell, and in any case it is perhaps inappropriate to attempt to identify a definite source for any one person's knowledge of such a familiar myth – can any of us say for sure where we first learnt the story of Cinderella? The reason why this couplet contributes to our sense of Marvell as an Ovidian poet lies less in its subject matter than its style. The essence of the style is its epigrammatic wit – but although Ovid and Marvell are both obviously 'witty' poets, so are many others, and it is necessary to refine our sense of what we mean by wit in this particular context in order to make the connection between the two meaningful. A useful analysis of the lines is included in Christopher Ricks' essay 'Its Own Resemblance' where he carefully analyses Marvell's playful variation on the Danaë myth, and notes that 'the ancient ingenuity of Zeus' rape-seduction of Danae, ensconced by her father in her tower but not safe from a golden shower of amorous rain, is matched by the modern ingenuity of this turn' (p. 113). The same could be said of the final reference to Danaë in the *Metamorphoses*. Ovid, like Marvell, is exploiting the story in order to make a witty comparison with a quite different phenomenon, Midas' golden touch.

> And when he washed; that water, showered in rain,
> Might simple Danaë have deceived again. (Sandys, p. 371)

5. *Andrew Marvell's Ovidian wit*

But Ricks is more particularly interested in Marvell's reflexive wit:

> Marvell's lyrical succinctness compacts the reflexive verb and the reflex-
> ive image ... in an acknowledgement of one strange yet natural form
> which self infolded self division may take. (p. 113)

Ricks includes a great many instances of Marvell's use of this trope –
'The river in itself is drowned,/ And isles th'astonished cattle round'
('Upon Appleton House' 471-2) is just one further example. It would be
possible to write at similar length about Ovid's own fondness for the
self-reflexive mode. One example, analogous to Marvell's couplet, oc-
curs in his description of Envy:

> sed videt ingratos intabescitque videndo
> successus hominus carpitque et carpitur una
> supplicium suum est. (II 780-2)

> Who looks on good success with eyes that weep;
> Repining, pines: who, wounding others, bleeds:
> And on herself revengeth her misdeeds. (Sandys, p. 62)

As in the Danaë couplet a sense of circularity is achieved by the lack of
distinction between subject and object. But perhaps the most celebrated
and extended example of this reflexive quality in the *Metamorphoses* is
the tale of Narcissus, whose love for his own reflection is echoed in the
poetry itself (see pp. 9-10). Marvell, like Shakespeare and Milton, was
drawn to Ovid's Narcissus, and in one of his Latin poems, 'Ros', the
imitation is particularly striking. The subject of the poem is a drop of
dew who, like Narcissus, is scornful and self-absorbed:

> Inque *rosas roseo* transfluat orta sinu. (2)
> And, sprung from the rosy breast of Dawn, flows onto the roses.

> Tristis, et in liquidum mutata *dolore dolorem* (13)
> Sad, changed by sorrow into liquid sorrow.

The wish of the narrator of 'The Garden' for solitude might recall
Narcissus not only because of his self-absorption, but also because of the
imagery of reflection and doubleness which Marvell employs.

> Meanwhile the mind, from pleasure less,
> Withdraws into its happiness:
> The mind, that ocean where each kind
> Does straight its own resemblance find ...

> Two paradises 'twere in one
> To live in paradise alone. (41-4, 63-4)

Another Ovidian detail which seems to elude discussion by virtue of its very obviousness is that famous stanza from 'The Garden' which ends on a note of aetiological subversion:

> Apollo hunted Daphne so,
> Only that she might laurel grow.
> And Pan did after Syrinx speed,
> Not as a nymph, but for a reed. (29-32)

At first it might seem that only the bare bones of two tales have been taken from Ovid, a borrowing which the independent fame of the legends in any case makes less telling. But we can find the same kind of pithy paradox in the *Metamorphoses*, as for example in the following description of Atalanta racing:

> How often lagged she when she might o'regoe!
> And gazing on him, sighed t'out-strip him so! (Sandys, p. 352)

And in Ovid's account of Daphne's flight from Apollo itself we may discover a similarly gleeful invitation to protest at another ludicrous yet somehow superficially logical assertion – Apollo's promise that, if Daphne will only slow down, he will moderate his own pace to match hers (I.510-11).

One distinctive feature of the Ovidian universe is the lack of respect with which his deities are treated – the gods of Homer and Virgil certainly display many human qualities, but are never treated quite so cavalierly as they are in the *Metamorphoses*. Typical of Ovid's somewhat irreverent treatment of his immortals is the way he clearly enjoys reminding us of the physical realities of the minor gods' existence – a river god, for example, is the river itself, with all that that implies, not simply a numinous deity. After the death of Orpheus we are told that 'lacrimis quoque flumina dicunt/ increvisse suis', 'They say that the rivers also were swollen with their own tears' (XI 47-8). A similar emphasis on physicality infects Marvell's personifications. In 'The Character of Holland' we are told that 'the sea laughed itself into a foam' (122).

We might expect a wonderful city to be compared to heaven as a way of expressing its splendour, but Ovid strikes a curious note when he inverts the expected order and compares heaven to the Palatia in Rome – or, to use Sandys' translation, to Whitehall.

> This glorious roof I would not doubt to call,
> Had I but boldness lent me, Heaven's Whitehall. (p. 5)

A similar kind of bathos may be found in Marvell's description of an open space in 'Upon Appleton House':

The world when first created sure
Was such a table rase and pure.
Or rather such is the Toril
Ere the bulls enter at Madril. (445-8)

But the dominant note of the *Metamorphoses* is derived not from such
individual strokes of humour, although they contribute to the poem's
overall tone, but from the phenomenon of metamorphosis itself. As with
all facets of Ovid's possible influence upon Marvell, the fact that the
latter poet uses images of metamorphosis must be approached with
caution. Transformation may be the keynote of Ovid's greatest poem,
but not all metamorphoses are Ovidian.

One of the most noticeable features of Ovidian metamorphosis is the
care with which he delineates the degree of continuity between the two
states. A typical example is the transformation of Myrrha into a tree:

> nam crura loquentis
> terra supervenit, ruptosque obliqua per ungues
> porrigitur radix, longi firmamina trunci,
> ossaque robur agunt, mediaque manente medulla
> sanguis it in sucos, in magnos bracchia ramos,
> in parvos digiti, duratur cortice pellis. (X 489-4)

> Even then the ground
> Covered her legs; a downward-spreading root
> Burst from her toes; whose ever-fixed foot
> Sustained the lengthful bole. Bones turn to wood,
> To pith her marrow, into sap her blood:
> Her armes great branches grow, her fingers spine
> To little twigs, her skin converts to rine. (Sandys, p. 348)

A series of equivalents are found between Myrrha the woman and
Myrrha the tree, and one detail is identified as remaining unchanged –
the Latin word *medulla* means both bone marrow and pith. Ovid's love
of making ingenious connections might perhaps lie behind the unex-
pected wit of the soul's complaint in 'A Dialogue between the Soul and
Body':

> O who shall, from this dungeon, raise
> A soul enslaved so many ways?
> With bolts of bones, that fettered stands
> In feet; and manacled in hands. (1-4)

A closer analogue may be found in 'The Mower against Gardens' in
which the mower complains about the artificiality of man's attempts to
cultivate nature – 'The Pink grew then as double as his Mind' (9).

A passage from 'A Poem upon the Death of O.C.' owes an obvious debt to the whole tradition of metamorphic description, and thus might in a general way be styled 'Ovidian'.

> So have I seen a vine, whose lasting age
> Of many a winter hath survived the rage.
> Under whose shady tent men every year
> At its rich blood's expense their sorrows cheer,
> If some dear branch where it extends its life
> Chance to be pruned by an untimely knife,
> The parent-tree unto the grief succeeds,
> And through the wound its vital humour bleeds;
> Trickling in watery drops, whose flowing shape
> Weeps that it falls ere fixed into a grape. (89-98)

But the use of this epithet might be rash. The chief features of the metamorphosis, the violence done to the tree and the way it bleeds, perhaps find their most obvious counterpart in Virgil's account of the transformed Polydorus, an episode which was memorably reinvented by Dante (*Inferno* XIII) and Spenser (*Faerie Queene* I.ii):

> accessi, viridemque ab humo convellere silvam
> conatus, ramis tegerem ut frondentibus aras,
> horrendum et dictu video mirabile monstrum.
> nam quae prima solo ruptis radicibus arbos
> vellitur, huic atro liquuntur sanguine guttae
> et terram tabo maculant. mihi frigidus horror
> membra quatit, gelidusque coit formidine sanguis. (III 24-30)

> I drew near; and essaying to tear up the green growth from the soil, that I might deck the altar with leafy boughs, I see an awful portent, wondrous to tell. For from the first tree, which is torn from the ground with broken roots, drops of black blood trickle and stain the earth with gore. A cold shudder shakes my limbs, and my chilled blood freezes with terror. (III 24-30)

Yet although the *Aeneid* may be Marvell's principal source here, the passage is still more Ovidian than Virgilian. The last two lines of the description are particularly significant. The phrase 'weeps that it falls' eludes attempts to resolve its precise meaning. The watery drops are surely themselves the tears, yet the act of falling – in other words crying – is with curious illogic also the *cause* of their tears. They are particularly distressed that they must fall 'ere fixed into a Grape', and yet in some strange way this process is in fact achieved. The suggestion that the drops of blood, associated in our minds with drops of wine by the earlier reference to men cheering themselves 'at its rich blood's expense', might somehow *become* fixed into a grape, effects a kind of metamorphosis in the readers' minds as the 'flowing shapes' which have, after all, been at the same time tears, drops of blood and drops of wine, can also be visualised as grapes. The additional image of the watery drops joining together to form some larger shape – perhaps at least momentarily human in our mind's eye as it is described as weeping – is reminiscent of Ovid's account of the metamorphosis of Arethusa into a stream as she is being pursued by Alpheus.

> occupat obsessos sudor mihi frigidus artus,
> caeruleaeque cadunt toto de corpore guttae,
> quaque pedem movi, manat lacus, eque capillis
> ros cadit, et citius, quam nunc tibi facta renarro,
> in latices mutor. sed enim cognoscit amatas
> amnis aquas ... (V 632-7)

> Cold sweats my then-besieged limbs possessed:
> In thin thick-falling drops my strength decreased.
> Where-ere I step, streams run; my hair now fell
> In trickling dew; and, sooner then I tell
> My destiny, into a flood I grew.
> The river his beloved waters knew ... (Sandys, p. 185)

A detail from Sandys' translation may be aligned with the way Marvell's description of the grapes puts pressure on its own internal logic, and forces us to juggle with contradictory signals, as though we were trying to resolve a picture which might be viewed either as a duck or a rabbit. Sandys translates Ovid's 'capillis ros cadit' as 'My hair now fell/ In trickling dew'. We reach the end of the line perhaps unconsciously expecting the verb 'fell' to be resolved by a phrase such as 'in curls' – in other words the fact that hair is being described inclines us to gloss 'fell' as 'descended' rather than 'dropped'. But the significance of the word 'fell' shifts, and a further stage of the metamorphosis has been achieved.

As we saw in the last chapter the most profound Ovidianism is not always the most easily identifiable. In 'Upon Appleton House' as in *The Tempest*, the one immediately obvious borrowing does not tell the whole story of the work's Ovidianism.

> Let others tell the paradox,
> How eels now bellow in the ox;
> How horses at their tails do kick,
> Turned as they hang to leeches quick;
> How boats can over bridges sail;
> And fishes do the stables scale.
> How salmons trespassing are found;
> And pikes are taken in the pound. (473-80)

This description is clearly derived from Ovid's account of the flood, quoted in Chapter 1. Obvious similarities between the two topsy-turvy worlds are immediately apparent. Both poets offer an inversion of normality in which the normally discrete domains of sea, sky and air are seen to merge, another aspect of their shared attraction to the breaking of boundaries. But more specifically Ovidian motifs may be identified in Marvell's imitation of the passage. The inversions of Ovid's world are not so clear cut as they seem to be. The verb *aro* (1 294) is so often used of the action of a ship going across the water that the paradox of a man rowing where he had once ploughed is not so startling as one might expect. Similarly, Marvell uses the word 'pound' which has two meanings; that of an enclosure in which cattle are kept is signalled by the context, yet as a once common variant of 'pond' we are almost returned to normality. In each passage the vocabulary's ambiguous register destabilises the inversion. The pun on 'scale' is similarly Ovidian in spirit, for its reliance upon two meanings may be compared with the way the word *medulla* is used in the description of Myrrha's metamorphosis. In the *Metamorphoses* the flood may be read as a foretaste of the even stranger inversions effected by metamorphosis, and forms an important part of Ovid's vision of the fluidity of all boundaries between different orders of creation. As we shall see, Marvell's poem also goes on to explore the phenomenon of metamorphosis, and his sense of a similar relativism in the universe is hinted at just two stanzas before the description of the flood, when he describes the cattle in the gleaming meadow.

> They seem within the polished grass
> A landskape drawn in looking-glass.
> And shrunk in the huge pasture show
> As spots, so shaped, on faces do.
> Such fleas, ere they approach the eye,
> In multiplying glasses lie.
> They feed so wide, so slowly move,
> As constellations do above. (457-64)

The narrator seeks a refuge from the upheaval:

> But I, retiring from the flood,
> Take sanctuary in the wood;
> And, while it lasts, myself imbark
> In this yet green, yet growing ark ... (481-4)

The double meaning of 'imbark' allows the reader to imagine the narrator either setting off in a boat or being contained within one of the trees. This ambiguity is itself Ovidian in spirit, as the pun serves to connect two stages of something's existence, and suggests a kind of continuity between the tree and the boat into which it is made. This Ovidian trait has already been mentioned, but a particularly pertinent example occurs towards the end of the *Metamorphoses*, when Ovid describes the metamorphosis of Aeneas' ships back into the nymphs of the trees from which the vessels were made. He lists all the ways in which the ships have been changed – for example the oars become toes – but also emphasises the one thing which remains the same – 'quodque prius fuerat, latus est', 'what had been body before remained as body' (XIV 552) – we might translate *latus* as 'waist', part of a ship as well as a body, to retain the pun. Of course, as in Marvell's play on the word 'imbark' or Ovid's own use of *medulla*, the stability is more linguistic than actual; the primary meaning of *latus* is the flank of the body, but it may also be used in a more technical sense in the context of shipbuilding. In that 'imbark' forces us to hold two pictures in our mind at once – the trees are simultaneously themselves and potential vessels – its use can be seen as analogous with Ovid's love of indeterminacy, and his alertness to the idea of an alternative state existing as something potential within an object or person. Additionally, the idea of the narrator turning into a tree is of course an Ovidian image in its own right, most obviously recalling Daphne's metamorphosis.

It is this latter, metamorphic, picture of the poet turning into a tree which resonates most strongly during the remainder of the poem. A few stanzas later the opposite phenomenon is hinted at when the music of the Orphic nightingale seems to animate the trees into consciousness:

> The nightingale does here make choice
> To sing the trials of her voice.
> Low shrubs she sits in, and adorns
> With music high the squatted thorns.
> But highest oaks stoop down to hear,
> And listening elders prick the ear.
> The thorn, lest it should hurt her, draws
> Within the skin its shrunken claws. (513-20)

A little later the poet expresses his willingness to fly like a bird, and again refers to his possible affinity with trees:

> Thus I, easy philosopher,
> Among the birds and trees confer:
> And little now to make me, wants
> Or of the fowls, or of the plants.
> Give me but wings as they, and I
> Straight floating on the air shall fly:
> Or turn me but, and you shall see
> I was but an inverted tree. (561-8)

The sentiments and the buoyant tone recall stanza 7 of 'The Garden', in which the poet's soul is described as ascending to the trees like a bird. The next two stanzas, in which he explains how his language is already beginning to resemble that of the natural world, are more complex. He associates writing and nature together with a wit which is Ovidian in its reliance on connections which are the creations of language rather than reality:

> Already I begin to call
> In their most learned original:
> And where I language want, my signs
> The bird upon the bough divines;
> And more attentive there doth sit
> Than if she were with lime-twigs knit.
> No leaf does tremble in the wind
> Which I returning cannot find.
> Out of these scattered sibyls' leaves
> Strange prophecies my fancy weaves:
> And in one history consumes,
> Like Mexique-paintings, all the plumes.
> What Rome, Greece, Palestine, ere said
> I in this light Mosaic read.
> Thrice happy he who, not mistook,
> Hath read in Nature's mystic book. (569-84)

The leaves on the tree are transformed into leaves in a book as we move from one stanza to the next, for the reference to the Sybil immediately makes us think of something written down. The plumes are ostensibly those used in South American designs, but in the context might as easily recall the bird's feathers or quill pens. The adjective 'Mosaick' seems to refer to the chequered patterns of light in the leafy trees but, particularly because of the reference to Palestine, we also think of Moses. As in the description of the flood, two apparently opposite frames of reference are more similar than they at first appear.

Two stanzas later we find another curious association between the poet and the natural world:

> Thanks for my rest ye mossy banks,
> And unto you cool zephyrs thanks,
> Who, as my hair, my thoughts too shed,
> And winnow from the chaff my head. (597-600)

However, the end result of the poet's hinted-at metamorphosis is continually shifting, and in the light of the previous reference to his 'embarkation' the stanza which follows might almost evoke the poet as a kind of Daphne figure, an image which is reinforced by the invitation he then gives to various plants to surround him entirely:

> How safe, methinks, and strong, behind
> These trees have I encamped my mind;
> Where beauty, aiming at the heart,
> Bends in some tree its useless dart;
> And where the world no certain shot

Can make, or me it toucheth not.
But I on it securely play,
And gall its Horsemen all the Day.

Bind me ye woodbines in your 'twines,
Curl me about ye gadding vines,
And oh so close your circles lace,
That I may never leave this place:
But, lest your fetters prove too weak,
Ere I your silken bondage break,
Do you, O brambles, chain me too,
And courteous briars nail me through. (601-16)

As in 'The Garden' we receive a sense, less of the poet foregoing sexual pleasure, than of him simply replacing one kind of eroticism with another, and a pretty recherché one at that. Here too, we may trace an affinity with the *Metamorphoses*, as the following description of the poem suggests:

> Is the world to be populated by people produced from the rapes of the gods? From Iphis-like lesbianism? From Pygmalian union with stones? The poem is an extraordinarily tense mixture of the generative and the perverse. And Ovid is not interested in reconciling them. (Burrow 1988, p. 100)

(Here, as so often, an account of one of these kindred spirits serves equally well to invoke the other.) Later the narrator seems to identify himself more generally with the whole landscape.

O what a pleasure 'tis to hedge
My temples here with heavy sedge;
Abandoning my lazy side,
Stretched as a bank unto the tide;
Or to suspend my sliding foot
On the osier's undermined root,
And in its branches tough to hang,
While at my lines the fishes twang! (641-8)

The fact that in 'The Garden' it is the fountain which has a 'sliding foot' (49) makes the hint at metamorphosis even stronger. We can trace a movement in both the *Metamorphoses* itself and in 'Upon Appleton House' whereby the phenomenon of metamorphosis is adumbrated in the flood, and then realised in the main body of the poem, even if this realisation is not explicit in Marvell. Both poems also contain a kind of coda in which metamorphosis, although present, is demystified. Much of the final book of the *Metamorphoses* is concerned with the philosopher Pythagoras who describes transformations which may be

miraculous but which are also entirely natural. His description of the
effects of time's passing seems intended to recall the flood in Book I.

> Where once was solid land, seas have I seen;
> And solid land, where once deep seas have been.
> Shells, far from seas, like quarries in the ground;
> And anchors have on mountain tops been found. (Sandys, p. 497)

Pythagoras also gives examples of metamorphoses from natural history
which, if familiarity had not bred contempt, might seem just as startling
as Daphne's transformation:

> The caterpillars, who their cobwebs weave
> On tender leaves (as hinds from proof receive)
> Convert to poisonous butterflies in time.
>
> And birds of every kind; did we not know
> Them hatched of eggs, who would conjecture so? (p. 499)

The very last stanza of 'Upon Appleton House' presents us with a picture
of what might at first glance seem to be some new kind of monster, but
which turns out to be no more than a fisherman.

> But now the salmon fishers moist
> Their leathern boats begin to hoist;
> And, like Antipodes in shoes,
> Have shod their heads in their canoes.
> How tortoise-like, but not so slow,
> These rational amphibii go?
> Lets in: for the dark hemisphere
> Does now like one of them appear. (769-76)

Yet metamorphosis itself is only part of this poem's Ovidianism. As we
have already seen, another hallmark of the *Metamorphoses* is its preoc-
cupation with various kinds of artists, and the nature of the art they
produce. This topic exercised a similar fascination upon Marvell. In the
arresting opening of 'Upon Appleton House' the creating mind and the
created object merge together.

> Within this sober frame expect
> Work of no foreign architect;
> That unto caves the quarries drew,
> And forests did to pastures hew;
> Who of his great design in pain
> Did for a model vault his brain,
> Whose columns should so high be raised
> To arch the brows that on them gazed. (1-8)

Although Marvell appears to be writing about the poem's subject, Appleton House, other possibilities also emerge. The phrase 'sober frame', when read in isolation, might most easily be taken to refer to the poet himself, and even when the unfolding of the stanza reveals the house to be the subject, there still remains the possibility that the poem, if not the poet, might also be the construct whose simplicity Marvell is describing. (An analogous use of the word can be found in 'The Coronet' when Marvell refers to the possibility of shattering 'my curious frame', a phrase which, in the context of that poem, may be said to invoke both the poet's body and his poetry.) Lying behind all these possibilities is the idea of a creating artist still greater than any architect or poet – God himself. The portentous phrase 'great design' hints at this, as does the sweeping, expansive, nature of the architect's actions, 'That unto caves the quarries drew,/ And forests did to pastures hew' (4-5). Although such feats may certainly in time be carried out by mortal hands, the impression given is one of mysterious, immediate movement. We might compare Sandys' translation of the creation of the world, 'Bids trees increase to woods, the plains extend,/ The rocky Mountains rise, and vales descend' (p. 2).

Another hint that God is being invoked is provided by the rhyme which is effected between 'drew' and 'hew'. Taken together their alternative meanings 'sketched; and 'colour' are revealed, and we are perhaps reminded that what are huge tasks for men, were to God no more demanding than touching up a picture. Later in the poem God's handiwork is associated with that of a more specialised kind of artist – a scene painter.

No scene that turns with engines strange
Does oftner than these meadows change. (385-6)

A similar comparison is used by Ovid to describe the emergence of armed men from serpents' teeth.

So in our theatre's solemnities,
When they the arras raise, the figures rise ... (Sandys, p. 83)

The close correspondence between the brain of the architect and the building he creates is strengthened by an apparent shift in subject between the two in the stanza's final lines. The phrase 'whose columns' seems at first to refer back to 'brain', and the curious picture of these columns arching the brows is consistent with this, yet the last four words 'that on them gaz'd' effects a strange split between the brows and the columns – if the brows – eyes – can gaze at the columns then surely they must be the columns on the house rather than part of the structure of the architect's head?

97

These confusions, the analogies we are encouraged to draw between God, Marvell, and the creating artists he writes about, find their counterpart in the *Metamorphoses*. The closest analogues are perhaps the doors of the Palace of the Sun and Arachne's web, both of which were discussed in Chapter 3. Just as the brain of Marvell's architect becomes almost inextricably involved with the building he creates, so Arachne seems to become part of the tapestry she weaves. Similarly, Marvell writes of Appleton House in a way which makes him appear to be paying a compliment to his own poetry at the same time.

> Humility alone designs
> Those short but admirable lines,
> By which, ungirt and unconstrained,
> Things greater are in less contained. (41-4)

An analysis of individual points of contact between the *Metamorphoses* and 'Upon Appleton House' perhaps fails to do justice to the latter poem's Ovidianism. Something must be said of the poem as a whole. It eludes discussion in its entirety, inviting the reader to focus on one section at a time. It is generically uncertain, drawing on traditions of pastoral, panegyric, lyric, history and even epic, or perhaps mock epic. It is witty and delightful, yet it touches on important theological and philosophical questions. It ends with a paean of praise which not all critics have found entirely straightforward, the description of Maria Fairfax (681-752). All these qualities are of course shared by the *Metamorphoses*.

In 'Marvell's Metaphysical Wit' A.J. Smith sketches some of the principal characteristics of the poet's style, noting his 'sense of the relativeness of things' and his 'impulse to entertain issues wittily in conceited arguments, emblems, images, nice nuances of tone, which themselves have a distinctive metaphysical life in the way they hold unlike orders of being together in the one apprehension.' Smith concludes:

> Marvell's metaphysical wit amounts to something more than his speculative interests or bizarre trappings. I think of the way his poetry wittily embodies tensions which we can only call metaphysical, gets its special power and quality from a distinctive apprehension, a kind of double or multiple vision realized in the wit. It is a manner of metaphysical wit which has little to do with the clever game Johnson so brilliantly characterized in his essay on Cowley. (p. 86)

Smith's analysis of Marvell's wit is equally applicable to Ovid's. If the epithet 'Metaphysical' is not generally applied to Ovid, and if we do not think of his work as containing 'conceits', this may be partly put down to the chances of periodisation. Perhaps the very completeness of

5. Andrew Marvell's Ovidian wit

Marvell's Ovidianism somehow detracts from his importance within this study. Whereas tensions and disjunctures between Ovid and his imitators drive the tradition forwards, uncovering new layers of meaning in the *Metamorphoses*, the perfect equilibrium between Ovid and Marvell only produces inertia. In just one important respect is Marvell unovidian; he fails to metamorphose his source.

6

The anxious Ovidian: Milton's metamorphosis of Ovid

Despite their many points of contact, Milton and Marvell are very different practitioners of Ovidianism. Marvell's easy appropriation of Ovid gives way to a taut and complexly allusive engagement with the *Metamorphoses* in *Paradise Lost*. Milton at first seems to have successfully reconfigured the ingredients of Ovid's amoral universe within the Christian framework of his poem, invoking the beauty of pagan writings only to put them firmly in their place. But a more searching examination of Milton's use of Ovid reveals troubling fissures in the text which might lend some support to those who agree with Blake that Milton was 'of the Devils party without knowing it' (Blake, p. 107). Ovid is a snake in the grass in Eden as well as in Spenser's Bower.

Of all the poets considered in this study, Milton is perhaps the least obviously Ovidian. Whereas the works of his near contemporary, Marvell, possess almost all the hallmarks we have come to expect from a writer steeped in the *Metamorphoses*, Milton's poetry might seem to show a greater temperamental affinity with Virgil. Yet his comparatively little known early Latin poetry is greatly indebted to Ovid's love elegies, and his daughter Deborah reported that the *Metamorphoses* – along with Isaiah and Homer – was one of the books which the blind Milton most often wished to have read to him. This apparent predilection is borne out by his extensive use of the poem in *Paradise Lost*. He was particularly indebted to Book 1, drawing freely on Ovid's description of the beginning of the world in his own account of the creation. This is one of Milton's less problematic uses of Ovid because, as many previous commentators had noted, the similarities between the opening of the *Metamorphoses* and the first chapters of Genesis are so numerous and evident.[1] Ovid was not perhaps the most orthodox source he could have turned to, but neither would Milton's contemporaries have considered such an innovation heretical. In fact Golding, in the Prefatory

---

[1] The anonymous early fourteenth-century author of the *Ovide Moralisé*, for example, finds numerous points of contact between the first book of the *Metamorphoses* and Scripture. The two versions of Creation are obviously similar, but he also associates Ovid's silver age with Adam and Eve's expulsion from Paradise, and the tower of Babel with the revolt of the giants.

Epistle to his translation of the *Metamorphoses*, says that he is sure Ovid must have had access to Old Testament writings:

What man is he but would suppose the author of this booke
The first foundation of his worke from Moyses wryghtings tooke?
Not only in effect he dooth with Genesis agree
But also in the order of creation, save that hee
Makes no distinction of the dayes. For what is else at all
That shapelesse rude and pestred heape which Chaos he dooth call,
Than even that universall masse of things which God did make
In one whole lump before that ech their proper place did take.

(Golding, Prefatory Epistle 342-9)

A different basis for the validity of mythical writings was the belief that ancient knowledge after the flood was disseminated not simply through Biblical writings, but through the myths of other peoples. Therefore *Metamorphoses* I could be seen as a variant, although one far more distant and less authoritative, of Genesis.

The inevitable slippage in both language and culture makes an account of the opening of Ovid's poem tend to drift inevitably towards some Christianisation of vocabulary. It might be summarised, 'God creates the world, and then mankind; they descend into sin and a flood is sent to punish them; two righteous people, Pyrrha and Deucalion, survive and then miraculously create a new race of men out of stones; an ominous snake, the Python, threatens mankind but is killed by a god.' However, even when we have firmly sifted out any Christian accretions from our reading of the *Metamorphoses* – in so far as it is possible to evade the pressures of such a powerful tradition – we might tentatively suggest that there is a greater 'seriousness' in the very opening section of Ovid's poem than in the rest of the *Metamorphoses*. Of course, we still have to accept that a characterisation of certain incidents or topics as 'serious' is perhaps a function of their congruence with that inescapable Judaeo-Christian tradition – itself firmly labelled as 'serious' in our minds. The description of the creation as told by Ovid is strikingly close, in some ways, to the account in Genesis. (We may be inclined to overestimate the similarity thanks to our memories of Milton who was of course influenced by Ovid.) Perhaps it is the *topic* of creation, rather than its particular, local characteristics, which strikes the modern reader as 'serious'. The fact that the creating god is unidentified helps make Ovid's account susceptible to Christianisation. He is deliberately vague, disclaiming all exact knowledge of his identity:

Sic ubi dispositam quisquis fuit ille deorum
congeriem secuit sectamque in membra coegit,

6. Milton's metamorphosis of Ovid

> When he, whoever of the gods it was, had thus arranged in order and
> resolved that chaotic mass, and reduced it, thus resolved, to cosmic
> parts...(I 32-3)

Although the notion of such an indeterminacy surrounding man's begin-
nings is most unchristian, this vagueness makes it particularly easy for
him to be identified with the Christian God, far more so than if Ovid
had identified him unequivocally with Jove himself (whom we see so
frequently in less dignified capacities) or with his father Saturn. (In
Book I of *Paradise Lost* Milton includes Jove as one of the fallen angels
who became gods among the heathen peoples). The destructive flood is
an obviously potent story within the Christian tradition, and Ovid's
Golden Age, again partly thanks to Milton's mediating Ovidianism, will
irresistibly align itself with Eden in the mind of the Christian or
post-Christian reader.

But however felicitous Ovid's description of the Creation may be, he
is still a pagan talking about pagan gods, and in this respect Milton
must negotiate his source carefully. Often in *Paradise Lost* the *Meta-
morphoses* is a more antagonistic presence, and in order to fulfil the
promise of his poem's opening lines Milton must invoke Ovid as a
challenger rather than a disciple. By contrast with Christianity's sharp
divide between good and evil, God and Satan, the divinities in the
Metamorphoses – and within the Classical tradition more generally –
have a thoroughly human capacity for both vice and virtue. Their
treatment of mankind is prompted by spite or whimsy more often than
justice. Such equivocal deities belong neither in Milton's Hell nor in his
Heaven, but lend something to each nonetheless. Reading Milton
through Ovid alerts us both to the similarities and to the crucial
differences between the two locations, the one offering a skewed mirror
image of the other. The separation of loyal and rebel angels may only be
recent, but the schism's effects are far more absolute and decisive than
Satan and his crew yet realise.

This multi-layering effect is consistent with Milton's use of the
Metamorphoses elsewhere. In *Milton and Ovid* DuRocher notes that the
wicked Comus and his virtuous opponent Sabrina both owe something
to the metamorphosed Scylla (p. 57), and Jonathan Collett observes
that in *Paradise Lost* itself Echo, an absent presence when Eve gazes
on her reflection Narcissus-like, is invoked in the description of Sin
(herself a descendent of Scylla) suggesting a disquieting link between
the poem's only female characters (pp. 87-9).

At the beginning of the *Metamorphoses* Jove calls a meeting to inform
the gods of the wickedness of man, and particularly Lycaon who doubted
Jove's divinity and served him human flesh to test his powers of
observation. This episode is somewhat unusual for we don't often see
Jove preoccupied with such serious matters; Ovid normally portrays

him within an amorous context. Whereas elsewhere he is fiercely opposed by other gods, for example Juno, whom he cannot prevent from further punishing the victims of his lust, here Jove is in full control; the entire pantheon is united behind their ruler, answering his summons with alacrity. Perhaps more important than his enhanced power and authority is the sense that his anger is appropriate:

> Quae pater ut summa vidit Saturnius arce,
> ingemit et facto nondum vulgata recenti
> foeda Lycaoniae referens convivia mensae
> ingentes animo et dignas Iove concipit iras
> concilium vocat: tenuit mora nulla vocatos.

> When Saturn's son from his high throne saw this he groaned, and, recalling the infamous revels of Lycaon's table – a story still unknown because the deed was new – he conceived a mighty wrath worthy of the soul of Jove, and summoned a council of the gods. Naught delayed their answer to the summons. (I 163-7)

By depicting him throned in state and using an appellation which reminds us of his ancestry, Ovid emphasises Jove's function as an awesome god rather than a philanderer.

The presentation of Jove is not the only element in this episode which is uncharacteristic of the *Metamorphoses* as a whole. The character of Lycaon's metamorphosis differentiates it from most of the transformations in Ovid, for as well as being both appropriate and deserved, it seems to be the result of a tacit divine decree. The use of a flood to punish mankind is also unusual. Such metamorphoses as Actaeon's into a stag or the Lycian peasants' into frogs are the result of a god's spontaneous and spiteful anger, whereas Jove has clearly deliberated the matter for at least at long as it takes to assemble all of Heaven. The submissive response to Jove's decision to send the deluge may be contrasted with the gods' reaction to Diana's treatment of Actaeon. That more unruly and self-willed picture of the gods' behaviour is far more typical of the *Metamorphoses* as a whole than is the council scene in Book I, but it is this very untypicality which makes it an appropriate source for Milton to exploit when he retells the scriptural account of creation.

Jove's convocation of the gods has a number of points of contact with Milton's presentation of God in Book III. In both poems a victory had just been achieved over an impious and overreaching foe who is sceptical of God's power and omniscience, and both rebels receive appropriately severe punishments – Lycaon is turned into a wolf and Satan is sent to Hell. Usually Ovid's focus is on a few named deities, but in this description of Olympus he evokes vast numbers of anonymous gods, comparable with the countless unindividuated angels in Milton's

Heaven. Other epic accounts of Olympus do not suggest hundreds of obedient underlings under one supreme deity as both Milton and Ovid do.

In Book VII of *Paradise Lost* God proclaims his decision to create a new race of men who are destined to replace the fallen angels, although they will not immediately be permitted to enter Heaven:

> ... and in a moment will create
> Another world, out of one man a race
> Of men innumerable, there to dwell,
> Not here, till by degrees of merit raised
> They open to themselves at length the way
> Up hither, under long obedience tried ... (VII 154-9)

This promise of eventual admission into Heaven recalls Jove's reference to the minor deities who live on Earth and who must neither be contaminated by the sins of men nor injured by the flood. It could be argued that God's words reflect Christian doctrine, and need owe nothing to the *Metamorphoses*. But the timing of the statement at a meeting of Heaven when God is aware that men are under threat from a vicious foe, the fact that the nymphs are, like men, eventually going to earn a place in Heaven, and particularly Lycaon's importance as a source for the portrait of Satan, are all factors which heighten the resemblance to Jove's declaration in similar circumstances:

> sunt mihi semidei, sunt, rustica numina, nymphae
> faunique satyrique et monticolae silvani
> quos quoniam caeli nondum dignamur honore,
> quas dedimus, certe terras habitare sinamus.

> I have demigods, rustic divinities, nymphs, fauns and satyrs, and sylvan deities upon the mountain-slopes. Since we do not yet esteem them worthy the honour of a place in heaven, let us at least allow them to dwell in safety in the lands allotted them. (I 192-5)

Like the descendants of Adam, these nymphs will thus be 'by degrees of merit raised' (VII 157).

But although the beginning of the *Metamorphoses* lends itself well to Christian adaptation, Ovid is not a sacred text. This means that Milton is able to use Book I as a model for the meeting called by Satan as well as that which is summoned by God. When Satan addresses the devils he refers to them as 'Synod of gods' (II 391). By describing the fallen angels in this way he not only shows his temerity, but also makes the reader think of pagan contexts, such as *Metamorphoses* I, where the concept of a plurality of gods would be acceptable. It is interesting that Sandys, with whose translation of the *Metamorphoses* Milton was

105

familiar, also uses the word 'Synod' when he describes Jove's convocation (p. 4).

Pandaemonium is described in much the same way as Olympus, and Satan proclaims his summons in a similar fashion to Jove. Sandys renders the scene as follows:

> A synod called, the summoned appear.
> There is a way, well seen when skies be clear,
> Them milky named; by this the gods resort
> Unto th'almighty thunderer's high court.
> With ever-open doors on either hand,
> Of nobler deities the houses stand:
> The vulgar dwell dispersed; the chief and great
> In front of all, their shining mansion's seat.
> This glorious roof I would not doubt to call,
> Had I but boldness lent me, Heaven's Whitehall.
> All set on marble seats ... (pp. 4-5)

Satan's heralds:

> with awful ceremony
> And trumpet's sound throughout the host proclaim
> A solemn council forthwith to be held
> At Pandaemonium, the high capital
> Of Satan and his peers: their summons called
> From every band and squared regiment
> By place or choice the worthiest; they anon
> With hundreds and with thousands trooping came
> Attended. (753-61)

In its grandeur Pandaemonium resembles Jove's mansion, and Milton, like Ovid, follows this description with a modern analogy:

> the gates
> And porches wide, but chief the spacious hall
> (Though like a covered field, where champions bold
> Wont ride in armed, and at the soldan's chair
> Defied the best of paynim chivalry
> To mortal combat or career with lance)
> Thick swarmed ... (I 761-7)

Neither of these anachronistic comparisons is arbitrary. In likening Heaven to the Palatia, Ovid appears to pay a compliment to Rome and hence, indirectly, to Augustus. However, the reversal of the usual pattern of such comparisons, the way that Ovid compares Heaven to the Palatia rather than vice versa, undermines the value of the compliment to Rome, subverting the emperor's pretensions with a deference too exaggerated to be taken at face value. Milton's use of chivalric imagery is peculiar to his descriptions of Hell. Like Ovid, he uses an ostensibly positive comparison to encourage a questioning response. Ovid's sly undercutting of divinity would be quite inappropriate in Milton's Heaven, but consorts well with the persistent undermining and belittling of the fallen angels.

Further details from *Metamorphoses* I are similarly better adapted to an infernal context. When the gods first hear of Lycaon's wickedness their response is very violent and not particularly angelic. Sandys' translation of the passage seems to have influenced Milton's description of the devils' reaction to Mammon's speech:

> All bluster, and in rage the wretch demand.
> So, when bold treason sought, with impious hand,
> By Caesar's blood t'out-race the Roman name;
> Mankind, and all the world's affrighted frame,
> Astonished at so great a ruin, shooke.
> Nor thine, for thee, less thought, Augustus, took,
> Than they for Jove. He, when he had suppressed
> Their murmur, thus proceeded to the rest. (p. 5)

Milton also uses the words 'murmur' and 'bluster', and describes the reaction in terms of a comparison:

> He scarce had finished, when such murmur filled
> The assembly, as when hollow rocks retain
> The sound of blustering winds, which all night long
> Had roused the sea ... (II 284-7)

The Ovidian passage quoted above might have had an extra significance for Milton. The account of the world's horrified reaction to the assassination of Caesar is reminiscent of Eve's fall:

> Earth felt the wound, and nature from her seat
> Sighing through all her works gave signs of woe,
> That all was lost. (IX 782-4)

Thus far it seems that Milton has successfully negotiated his way around the potential hazards of his Ovidian source, allowing the positive aspects of the *Metamorphoses* into heaven and banishing the less reputable elements down to hell where they belong.

Sometimes Milton doubles rather than splits an Ovidian episode. Not surprisingly the flood which Ovid describes so graphically is used as source material for Michael's revelation of the future. Ovid is Milton's main source, and although the depiction of Noah's flood is less flamboyant and surreal than Ovid's the two are obviously connected. Particularly striking is Milton's imitation of Ovid's 'omnia pontus erat, derant quoque litora ponto' (I 292), 'Sea covered sea,/ Sea without shore'

107

(XI 749-50). We might also note the lines which immediately follow, 'and in their palaces/ Where luxury late reigned, sea monsters whelped/ And stabled' (XI 750-2). As in the *Metamorphoses* – and 'Upon Appleton House' – the topsy-turvy flood allows Milton to play with the way our use of metaphors transposes sea, land and sky almost without our realising it:

> the floating vessel swum
> Uplifted; and secure with beaked prow
> Rode tilting o'er the waves (XI 745-7)

Whereas the epithet 'beaked' might suggest a bird, the phrase 'rode tilting', like Ovid's own *arabat* (ploughed), reflects an activity associated with the earth rather than the sea, but through a metaphor which is so commonplace that we hardly notice it.

Ovid's flood is also used to help Milton evoke the less spectacular but comparable climatic disturbances which accompany the Fall. After Adam has eaten the apple, the eternal spring – which reigns in Eden just as it reigns during Ovid's Golden Age – is taken away and replaced by the usual flux of seasons and weather. Milton says: 'the sun, as from Thyestean banquet, turned/ His course intended' (X 688-9). In Seneca's play *Thyestes* a human being, Thyestes' son, is served up at a banquet. Milton describes the change in the weather as if it stemmed from just such a horrible act. In the *Metamorphoses* it does. Lycaon's cannibal feast is the direct cause of the flood which only Pyrrha and Deucalion survive. Thus a tacit connection is made between the flood in the *Metamorphoses* and the upheaval which takes place in Paradise. The disruption is not only external, for the minds of Adam and Eve are also troubled as if by storm:

> Nor only tears
> Rained at their eyes, but high winds worse within
> Began to rise, high passions, anger, hate,
> Mistrust, suspicion, discord, and shook sore
> Their inward state of mind, calm region once
> And full of peace, now tossed and turbulent … (IX 1121-6)

Milton creates further links between the Flood and the Fall. In the middle of Michael's account of Mankind's future fate he pauses 'betwixt the world destroyed and world restored' (XII 3). The meaning of this statement is ambiguous. It could refer to the present time – to Adam and Eve's exile from Paradise and the distant hope of salvation – but it could also allude to Michael's prophecies, for Adam has just witnessed the aftermath of the deluge and the advent of the rainbow which signifies God's covenant with humanity. Michael's words to Adam are similarly two-edged:

Thus thou hast seen one world begin and end;
And man as from a second stock proceed. (XII 6-7)

These words might be equally well applied to Adam's witnessing of the creation of Eden, his expulsion, and his own sons or to the flood, its destruction of the world, and the new beginning made by Noah and his descendants. Such recurring patterns are not of course the prerogative of Christianity; Ovid's Iron Age is on one level an historical epoch which was brought to an end by the flood. However, its faults are indistinguishable from those of the poet's own era and we are slyly reminded that Augustus has not quite succeeded in bringing in a second Golden Age.

Pyrrha and Deucalion lie behind one of Milton's most significant doublings. As the only righteous humans to survive a flood sent to punish mankind they are most obviously equivalent to Noah and his wife – indeed, their intrinsic worthiness, and thus their fitness to survive, is given a prominence in the *Metamorphoses* which is perhaps unexpected in the light of the poem's often arbitrary treatment of humanity. Yet Milton's use of them as analogues to Adam and Eve is the logical conclusion of his association of the world's first sinful men, including Lycaon, with Satan and his followers. As commentators have noted, their individuality and mutual devotion make them the obvious originals for Adam and Eve. Deucalion would have been willing to drown rather than live without Pyrrha, 'namque ego (crede mihi), si te quoque pontus haberet,/ te sequerer, coniunx, et me quoque pontus haberet', 'For be assured that if the sea held you also, I would follow you, my wife, and the sea should hold me also' (I 361-2). Adam is similarly devoted: 'for with thee/ Certain my resolution is to die;/ How can I live without thee', 'Bone of my bone thou art, and from thy state/ Mine never shall be parted, bliss or woe' (IX 906-8, 915-16). Here Milton is doing rather more than divide up the Ovidian sheep and goats; the echo of Deucalion in Adam's rash promise to Eve dramatises the difference between the two poets' perspectives in the most telling manner. What is virtuous in the pagan world is culpable (though appealing to most fallen readers) in Paradise.

In that they have transgressed knowingly against God's law Adam and Eve perhaps have more in common with Lycaon than Pyrrha and Deucalion. However, their sin is not totally unforgivable. They are permitted to live, with the hope of giving birth to a new race of men. At this point Milton complicates his use of Ovid by comparing them not just to Pyrrha and Deucalion but also, implicitly, to the new men whom they create by throwing stones behind them:[2]

---

[2]Pyrrha and Deucalion are told by an oracle to throw behind them the bones of their great mother. They correctly infer that their 'mother' is the earth, and that they must throw stones behind them. These stones metamorphose into men and women (I 381-415).

Prevenient grace descending had removed
The stony from their hearts, and made new flesh
Regenerate grow instead ... (XI 3-5)

The seeming contradiction of their being aligned with both Pyrrha and
Deucalion *and* the race they create is echoed in Milton's apparently
contradictory (yet transcendently lucid) description of Adam and Eve:

Adam the goodliest man of men since born
His sons, the fairest of her daughters Eve. (IV 323-4)

The metamorphosis of stones into men is reinvented as the hardness of
Adam and Eve's fallen hearts which become softened by repentance and
'prevenient grace'. The metaphor invests the quality of stoniness with
a moral weighting and reminds us of the couple's previous sin which has
brought on their punishment. (For Ovid the stone in this case connotes
nothing more sinister than hardiness and endurance, although the
Metamorphoses includes more than one story about hard hearted people
who are turned into stone.) To sum up, the image created in these lines
reminds us of the similarities between Adam and Eve and three quite
separate elements from *Metamorphoses* I: Lycaon, Pyrrha and Deu-
calion, and the new race of men. This palindromic pattern of Adam and
Eve becoming stony through sin and then softened through grace
recalls a similar sequence in the *Metamorphoses*. In Book X Orpheus
relates how the Propoetides turned to stone because they became
prostitutes and lost all shame. The process is then reversed, not within
the same characters as in *Paradise Lost*, but by the miracle worked by
Venus in causing Pygmalion's statue to come to life. The fact that Adam
and Eve can represent three distinct aspects of Ovid's narrative re-
minds us that the possibilities for development are in some ways even
greater in Milton's world than in Ovid's, for grace can allow those who
succumb to evil to escape divine wrath and destruction and even aspire
to eventual reward in Heaven. In *A Map of Misreading* Harold Bloom
describes Milton 'troping upon his forerunners' tropes' (p. 132), and the
metamorphosis of Ovid in *Paradise Lost* is consistent with this account
of the poet's method. Ovid may blur the boundaries between different
orders of creation, but Milton overgoes him by merging together three
quite separate parts of the flood narrative, combining them in the
figures of Adam and Eve.

One important distinction can be drawn between the different ways
the metaphor of stoniness is used in the two poems. Deucalion begs to
be told how the wrath of the gods may be averted, ' "si precibus"
dixerunt "numina iustis/ victa remollescunt, si flectitur ira deorum ..." ',
'If deities are appeased by the prayers of the righteous, if the wrath of
the gods is thus turned aside ...' (I 377-8). The verb *remollesco* is an

110

example of the connection that both poets make between literal and metaphorical stoniness. But whereas it is the gods' hearts which must be softened in Ovid, for Milton the crucial mollification takes place within Adam and Eve. This perhaps suggests the greater power which they have over their own destiny. Yet again the *Metamorphoses* is simultaneously invoked and rejected by Milton.

Finally I want to turn to a further example of Milton's 'splitting' of Ovidian material, more complex and more problematic than his use of Jove's meeting, to demonstrate that Milton didn't always get the better of Ovid. Eve is explicitly aligned with Pomona on two occasions in *Paradise Lost*, and at least once implicitly. (Pomona was a Latin nymph who shunned all suitors until successfully wooed by shape-shifting Vertumnus who came to her in the guise of an old woman and warned her against frigid self-sufficiency.) Both are gardeners. Milton compares Eve to Diana in Book IX with the following qualification: 'Though not as she with bow and quiver armed,/ But with such gardening tools as art yet rude,/ Guiltless of fire had formed, or angels brought' (IX 390-2). Ovid describes Pomona in almost identical terms. Like Eve she is defined by reference to what she is not, and the gardening tools she carries are contrasted with the weapons of Diana and her nymphs:

> non silvas illa nec amnes,
> rus amat et ramos felicia poma ferentes;
> nec iaculo gravis est, sed adunca dextera falce,

> She cared nothing for wood and rivers, but only for the fields and branches laden with delicious fruits. She carried no javelin in her hand, but the curved pruning-hook. (XIV 626-8)

There are also striking resemblances between the meticulous attention shown to their gardens by Pomona and Adam and Eve. In Book IX Eve makes her fatal suggestion to Adam that they should carry out their tasks separately so as to be more efficient:

> Let us divide our labours, thou where choice
> Leads thee, or where most needs, whether to wind
> The woodbine round this arbour, or direct
> The clasping ivy where to climb, while I
> In yonder spring of roses intermixed
> With myrtle, find what to redress till noon: (IX 214-19)

Pomona's activities are described in similar detail:

> qua modo luxuriem premit et spatiantia passim
> bracchia conpescit, fisso modo cortice virgam
> inserit et sucos alieno praestat alumno;

111

nec sentire sitim patitur bibulaeque recurvas
radicis fibras labentibus inrigat undis.

With which now she repressed the too luxuriant growth and cut back the branches spreading out on every side, and now, making an incision in the bark, would engraft a twig and give juices to an adopted bough. Nor would she permit them to suffer thirst, but watered the twisted fibres of the thirsty roots with her trickling streams. (XIV 629-33)

Sandys' translation of the beginning of this passage, 'Now prunes luxurious twigs, and boughs that dare/ Transcend their bounds' (469), seems to be echoed in Eve's statement that 'the work under our labour grows,/ Luxurious by restraint; what we by day/ Lop overgrown, or prune, or prop, or bind' (IX 208-10) and also in another account of gardening in Paradise, where Milton describes Adam and Eve seeing where 'any row/ Of fruit-trees over-woody reached too far/ Their pampered boughs, and needed hands to check/ Fruitless embraces' (V 212-15). The impression given in these passages is that both Eve and Pomona, despite the former's protestations that she is overtasked, have to look hard to find any real work to do in their gardens, and have plenty of time to attend to the intricate niceties of their craft.

Like Eve, Pomona is at first wary of lovers, although her fear lasts far longer, and she carefully guards herself from all unwelcome attentions. But Vertumnus is a particularly determined wooer, and he uses many disguises in order to catch a glimpse of her. Eventually, while disguised as an old woman, he makes a long speech to Pomona on the desirability of marriage, not forgetting to recommend himself as a husband in warm terms:

sed tu si sapies, si te bene iungere anumque
hanc audire voles, quae te plus omnibus illis,
plus, quam credis, amo: vulgares reice taedas
Vertumnumque tori socium tibi selige! pro quo
me quoque pignus habe: neque enim sibi notior ille est,
quam mihi; nec passim toto vagus errat in orbe,
haec loca sola colit; nec, uti pars magna procorum,
quam modo vidit, amat:

But if you will be wise, and consent to a good match and will listen to an old woman like me, who love you more than all the rest, yes, more than you would believe, reject all common offers and choose Vertumnus as the consort of your couch. You may also have my guaranty for him; for he is not better known to himself than he is to me. He does not wander idly throughout the world, but he dwells in the neighbourhood here alone; nor, as most of your suitors do, does he fall in love at sight with every girl he meets. (XIV 675-82)

At this point he throws off his disguise and Pomona, unswayed by his arguments until she sees his beauty, falls in love with him straight away. The impudence with which he prosecutes his suit and the deliberate and gleeful mendacity he uses seem innocuous within the context of the *Metamorphoses* because Ovid is more tolerant of deceit and imposture than Milton. In the *Metamorphoses* such doubtful methods are employed by more or less the whole pantheon to effect their designs on mankind, which may be malevolent, as with Juno and Semele, or beneficent, as when Jove and Mercury visit Philemon and Baucis. When disguises are assumed for such different reasons, and in a world where involuntary metamorphosis seems to be an integral part of life, what might seem morally dubious in a different context, such as Vertumnus' trickery, becomes more acceptable. But in *Paradise Lost*, although Milton assures us that all heavenly spirits can change their shape at will (I 423-31), such disguises are associated almost exclusively with Satan and are assumed in order to harm Mankind.

Eve's relationship with Pomona is straightforward enough, invoked by Milton to suggest one aspect of her role and character, just as he uses Narcissus and Proserpina for the same purpose at different stages of the poem. The presence of Vertumnus in *Paradise Lost* is more complex, for although his most obvious analogue is Adam, his dealings with Pomona also suggest links with both Satan and Milton himself.

We only hear retrospective accounts of Eve's early tentativeness, and it is not in these reports that she is overtly compared to Pomona, although her account of her acquiescence to Adam might suggest Pomona's capitulation. Adam, like Vertumnus, conquers Eve by physical assertion, 'with that thy gentle hand/ Seized mine, I yielded' (IV 488-9). Vertumnus discards his disguise, 'vimque parat: sed vi non est opus, inque figura/ capta dei nympha est et mutua vulnera sensit', 'He was all ready to force her will, but no force was necessary; and the nymph, smitten by the beauty of the god, felt an answering passion' (XIV 770-1).

Considering the very short-lived nature of Eve's 'sweet reluctant amorous delay' it might seem strange that she is compared to Pomona at that point in Ovid's narrative when the nymph is still holding herself aloof from men. Eve is first compared to Pomona when Raphael comes down to visit Eden.

> So to the silvan lodge
> They came, that like Pomona's arbour smiled
> With flowerets decked and fragrant smells; but Eve
> Undecked, save with her self more lovely fair
> Than wood nymph, (V 377-81)

We might assume that the comparison was only superficial, simply noting that Eve's arbour is like Pomona's, and not intended to suggest any further similarity between them. But the idea of needing a defence against some danger is mentioned immediately after the comparison has been made, recalling Pomona's own careful defences of her garden.

>   No veil
> She needed, virtue-proof, no thought infirm
> altered her cheek. (V 383-5)

The nymph's precautions were against wooers. This is clearly not applicable to Eve. The defence must be against some other kind of maleficent influence.

The same impression is given by another comparison between Eve and Pomona in Book IV. The nymph's name is not mentioned, but the conjunction of a bower with a strong verbal echo of Book XIV of the *Metamorphoses*, suggests that Milton was thinking of Pomona:

>   In shady bower
> More sacred and sequestered, though but feigned,
> Pan or Silvanus never slept, nor nymph,
> Nor Faunus hunted. Here in close recess
> With flowers garlands, and sweet-smelling herbs
> Espoused Eve decked first her nuptial bed. (IV 705-10)

> quid non et Satyri, saltatibus apta iuventus
> fecere et pinu praecincti cornua Panes
> Silvanusque, suis semper iuvenilior annis,

> What did not the Satyrs, a young dancing band, do to win her, and the Pans, their horns encircled with wreaths of pine, and Silvanus, always more youthful than his years, (XIV 637-9)

Pomona's precautions against rustic deities presumably become irrelevant once she has accepted Vertumnus as her lover. But the need to be careful of outside influences is evoked in *Paradise Lost* even though Eve is married to Adam, even, in fact, when her nuptial bed is being described. The intimation of danger suggested by allusions to these demigods seems to be a real, proleptic one, as is borne out by the reference to the Fall which follows. Five lines later Milton says that Eve is:

> More lovely than Pandora, whom the gods
> Endowed with all their gifts, and O too like
> In sad event. (IV 714-16)

These darker associations which crop up when Eve is compared to Pomona suggest that Milton is using the Ovidian story to do more than make a parallel with Eve's bashfulness when she first encounters Adam.

114

6. Milton's metamorphosis of Ovid

The final explicit mention of Pomona is ambiguous. It occurs when Eve has left Adam on the fatal day of her fall:

> To Pales, or Pomona thus adorned,
> Likeliest she seemed, Pomona when she fled
> Vertumnus, or to Ceres in her prime,
> Yet virgin of Proserpina from Jove. (IX 393-6)

The fact that she is compared to Pomona at a very specific moment in that nymph's history – 'when she fled Vertumnus' – fits in with the idea of Pomona being used to evoke Eve's shy reception of Adam. But this episode is long over in the chronology of *Paradise Lost*. Still retaining the connection between Vertumnus and Adam, we might see this as a reference to Eve's unwise departure from him at this dangerous time, with Satan at large in Eden. But taken in conjunction with the next comparison, which is with Ceres, the whole passage takes on a wistful tone, a sense of action suspended in mid flight, an image arrested before some final and portentous event. Remembering that Vertumnus did indeed catch Pomona eventually, and that Jove did catch Ceres, and knowing that the snake is about to catch Eve, we are prepared for Vertumnus ceasing to be a type of Adam and starting to be analogous with Satan. DuRocher in *Milton and Ovid* states correctly that 'Milton nowhere compares Adam to Vertumnus, perhaps because the god's shiftiness is inappropriate to Adam's stable character' (p. 98), but does not entertain the possibility that Vertumnus might have been used as a model for Satan.

Vertumnus' instability of reference within *Paradise Lost* is unsettling, drawing attention to potential faultlines in the text's ideological coherence. If Vertumnus may suggest either Adam or Satan, does that mean that the two apparently opposed figures have something in common? The idea of Satan's temptation of Eve as an essentially sexual one has perhaps coloured Milton's writing here, despite the fact that he is very anxious to demonstrate that sexuality was part of prelapsarian life, and even part of heavenly life as Raphael somewhat coyly informs us (VIII 618-29). Pomona's imminent loss of virginity is implied by the phrase 'Pomona when she fled Vertumnus'; the same idea is made explicit in the description of Ceres 'or to Ceres in her prime/ Yet virgin of Proserpine from Jove'. Earlier in the poem Milton refers to Eve's 'virgin majesty' (IX 2670) as though he associated prelapsarian and sexual innocence together.[3] Eve's blushing capitulation to her new husband (VIII 511) and her yielding to the serpent's temptation are thus curiously cognate moments.

Like Vertumnus when he is spying on Pomona Satan changes from

---

[3]'Virgin' may signify no more than 'pristine' but the choice of word is still significant.

one form to another to watch Adam and Eve. Ovid describes in some detail Vertumnus's various disguises:

> o quotiens habitu duri messoris aristas
> corbe tulit verique fuit messoris imago!
> tempora saepe gerens faeno religata recenti
> desectum poterat gramen versasse videri;
> saepe manu stimulos rigida portabat, ut illum
> iurares fessos modo disiunxisse iuvencos.
> falce data frondator erat vitisque putator;
> induerat scalas: lecturum poma putares;
> miles erat gladio, piscator harundine sumpta;

> Oh, how often in the garb of a rough reaper did he bring her a basket of barley-ears! And he was the perfect image of a reaper, too. Often he would come with his temples wreathed with fresh hay, and could easily seem to have been turning the new-mown grass. Again he would appear carrying an ox-goad in his clumsy hand, so that you would swear that he had but now unyoked his weary cattle. He would be a leaf-gatherer and vine-pruner with hook in hand; he would come along with a ladder on his shoulder and you would think him about to gather apples. He would be a soldier with a sword, or a fisherman with rod. (XIV 643-51)

This long account of all the different disguises which Vertumnus assumes reveals Ovid's admiration for his ingenuity. Their convincing accuracy is particularly emphasised. Satan is equally clever and adaptable; however, Milton, unlike Ovid, but like Spenser, disapproves of metamorphosis in general, and especially when it is being used to deceive:

> Down he alights among the sportful herd
> Of those-four footed kinds, himself now one,
> Now other, as their shape served best his end
> Nearer to view his prey, and unespied
> To mark what of their state he more might learn
> By word or action marked: about them round
> A lion now he stalks with fiery glare,
> Then as a tiger, who by chance hath spied
> In some purlieu two gentle fawns at play,
> Straight couches close, then rising changes oft
> His couchant watch, as one who chose his ground
> Whence rushing he might surest seize them both
> Griped in each paw: (IV 396-408)

For Satan and Vertumnus this succession of disguises is only the beginning; so far neither has been allowed to speak to their prey. The culminating metamorphoses are the ones that permit Vertumnus to speak to Pomona, and Satan to speak to Eve. Vertumnus adopts the appearance of an old woman, Satan that of a serpent. Vertumnus enjoys looking at Pomona, 'denique per multas aditum sibi saepe figuras/ repperit, ut caperet spectatae gaudia formae', 'in fact, by means of his many disguises, he obtained frequent admission to her presence and had much joy in looking on her beauty' (XIV 652-3). Satan feels the same pleasure in spite of his evil designs, when he looks at Eve:

> Such pleasure took the serpent to behold
> This flowery plat, the sweet recess of Eve
> Thus early, thus alone; her heavenly form
> Angelic, but more soft, and feminine,
> Her graceful innocence, her every air
> Of gesture or least action overawed
> His malice, and with rapine sweet bereaved
> His fierceness of the fierce intent it brought: (IX 455-62)

Both Vertumnus and Satan go about gaining their very different ends by means of persuasive eloquence. Both use flattery, and suggest that the two women are throwing themselves away – Eve by monogamy, Pomona by virginity. Vertumnus says:

> Helene non pluribus esset
> sollicitata procis nec quae Lapitheia movit
> proelia nec coniunx nimium tardantis Ulixis.
> nunc quoque, cum fugias averserisque petentes,
> mille viri cupiunt et semideique deique
> et quaecumque tenent Albanos numina montes.

> Then would you have more suitors than ever Helen had, or she for whom the Lapithae took arms, or the wife of the all too slow-returning Ulysses. And even as it is, though you shun them and turn in contempt from their wooing, a thousand men desire you, and half-gods and gods and all the divinities that haunt the Alban hills. (XIV 669-74)

Satan uses similar arguments:

> Thee all things living gaze on, all things thine
> By gift, and thy celestial beauty adore
> With ravishment beheld, there best beheld
> Where universally admired; but here
> In this enclosure wild, these beasts among,
> Beholders rude, and shallow to discern
> Half what in thee is fair, one man except,
> Who sees thee? (And what is one?) Who shouldst be seen
> A goddess among gods, adored and served
> By angels numberless, thy daily train. (IX 539-48)

Both temptations take place near trees. The snake leads Eve to the tree of knowledge, Vertumnus gains admittance to Pomona's orchard, 'cultosque intravit in hortos/ pomaque mirata est "tanto" que "potentior!"

inquit/ paucaque laudatae dedit oscula', '[he] entered the well-kept garden and, after admiring the fruit, said: 'but you are far more beautiful,' and he kissed her several times' (XIV 656-8). Both temptations are successful. Although eloquence is a key to the success of each, the actual objects of temptation – the apple and Vertumnus' appearance – are also important in swaying Eve and Pomona:

> Haec ubi nequiquam formae deus aptus anili
> edidit, in iuvenem rediit et anilia demit
> instrumenta sibi talisque apparuit illi,
> qualis ubi oppositas nitidissima solis imago
> evicit nubes nullaque obstante reluxit,
> vimque parat: sed vi non est opus, inque figura
> capta dei nympha est et mutua vulnera sensit.

> When the god in the form of age had thus pleaded his cause in vain, he returned to his youthful form, put off the old woman's trappings, and stood revealed to the maiden as when the sun's most beaming face has conquered the opposing clouds and shines out with nothing to dim his radiance. He was all ready to force her will, but no force was necessary; and the nymph, smitten by the beauty of the god, felt an answering passion. (XIV 765-71)

> He ended, and his words replete with guile
> Into her heart too easy entrance won:
> Fixed on the fruit she gazed, which to behold
> Might tempt alone, and in her ears the sound
> Yet rung of his persuasive words, impregned
> With reason, to her seeming, and with truth. (IX 733-8)

Eve delivers a final self-deceiving speech before plucking the apple. The earth's response offers an ironic echo of Pomona's amorous wounding by Vertumnus – 'vulnera sensit' (771).

> So saying, her rash hand in evil hour
> Forth reaching to the fruit, she plucked, she ate:
> Earth felt the wound (780-2)

Although the appearance of the apple is allowed to be important, Milton does not let us forget that without Satan she would not have looked at the fruit. But Ovid's description shows us that Vertumnus might have saved both his breath and his ingenuity in disguising himself, for he could have conquered Pomona simply by appearing before her in his true form. Thus the tempter's metamorphosis and rhetoric, which seem so sinister in *Paradise Lost*, are comically undercut by Ovid's hint that they are extraneous to Vertumnus' purpose and delay his eventual triumph.

In *Paradise Lost* two aspects of Vertumnus' temptation – his persuasive rhetoric and his physical beauty – have been divided between the snake and the apple. Despite his beauty the snake poses no temptation through his physical form, but only through his arguments, and the apple tempts by its appearance alone. If the word 'fruit' were replaced by the word 'man' in the passage from *Paradise Lost* quoted above we would conflate the two halves of the temptation, just as Ovid did, and would end up, to all intents and purposes, with a paraphrase of the story of Vertumnus and Pomona.

Pomona, like Eve, has a special affinity with the plants and flowers she tends. Her name links her with the fruits of her orchard, and one of Vertumnus' disguises thus reflects his lustful intent; when he dresses as a vine-pruner 'lecturum poma putares', 'you would think him about to gather apples' (650). Satan's metamorphosis into a tiger, quoted above, similarly hints at his destructive purpose. But Vertumnus, unlike Satan, wishes Pomona no harm, even though his own gratification is uppermost in his mind. He warns as well as tempts the nymph, and these two strands of his discourse take on very different resonances within the context of *Paradise Lost*. He uses the comparison between a vine and an elm as a potent emblem of heterosexual love, arguing that Pomona, like the vine, requires a support. This image is imitated by Milton, and he is in full agreement with Vertumnus as to the desirability of such a relationship. And Eve, like Pomona, is saved from fruitless self-sufficiency when God leads her away from her own reflection and into the arms of Adam. It seems as though Vertumnus might not be of the devil's party after all. And for readers who are alienated by Milton's presentation of Eve, the congruity of his voice with that of tricksy Vertumnus may not come as so much of a surprise. Neither the god nor the poet appears to have much respect for women as autonomous beings; both cast them in subordinate roles; both tell stories (the metamorphosis of hard-hearted Anaxarete into stone, the narrative of the Fall) to inspire women with anxiety about their possible wish for self-sufficiency.

The last words Vertumnus speaks to Pomona, his final plea, are also suggestive:

sic tibi nec vernum nascentia frigus adurat
poma, nec excutiant rapidi florentia venti!

So may no late spring frost ever nip your budding fruit, and may no rude winds scatter them in their flower. (763-4)

Eve's vulnerability is strikingly aligned with the frailty of flowers. When Satan first glimpses her in Book IX she is propping up roses, 'mindless the while,/ Herself, though fairest unsupported flower,/ from her best prop so far, and storm so nigh' (431-3). When Adam realises Eve

119

has eaten the forbidden fruit he lets fall the garland he has woven for her, 'and all the faded roses shed' (893). Vertumnus is a straightforward – not to say single-minded – character, and his wooing of Pomona has a perfectly coherent internal logic. Yet he acquires a strange complexity if his story is read in the shadow of *Paradise Lost* for his rhetoric is an unsettling compound of Miltonic pathos and Satanic threat.

Some of Ovid's earlier translators also treat Pomona as if her story reminded them of Eve being tempted by Satan. Golding seems to have connected the nymph's vulnerability in her orchard with that of Eve in Paradise for he refers to Priapus as a 'feend', which is a word he uses very rarely and which might suggest Satan:

> and eeke the feend that scares away
> The theeves and robbers with his hooke, or with his privy part,
> To winne her love ... (XIV 728-30)

Perhaps more interesting in the light of Milton's own apparent reaction to the story of Pomona is the retelling of this tale in Abraham Fraunce's *Third Part of the Countess of Pembroke's Yuychurch*, published in 1592. That Pomona had become identified with Eve on some level for Fraunce seems indicated by Vertumnus' outburst when he comes to her disguised as a 'beldame':

> O brave sweete apples, and o most bewtiful orchyard,
> O paradise-garden, fit for so lovely a gardner ... (p. 52)

Fraunce's rendition of Ovid is very free and the following description of Vertumnus' shapeshifting is his own interpolation and not a direct translation from the *Metamorphoses*:

> So, and so did this Vertumnus, slippery turnecoate
> Turne, and winde, transforme, and change himself to a thousand
> Shapes; and all, to behold Pomona the Lady of apples.

This description differs from Ovid in that Vertumnus is alleged to change shape, whereas in the *Metamorphoses* it is conceivable that he disguises himself by natural means as all his semblances are human. True metamorphosis is not ruled out by Ovid, but the account of Vertumnus' disguises is too sketchy for the question to be resolved. Fraunce's assertion that Vertumnus actually changed shape connects him with Satan who moved from one animal to another to watch Eve and, more strikingly, the way in which his manoeuvres are described is very serpentine. Milton characterises Vertumnus in the same way in *Tetrachordon*. He evokes the slippery logic of some debaters by comparing them with Vertumnus, 'let him try which way he can wind in his Vertumnian distinctions and evasions' (Milton 1645, p. 67). His emphasis on the god's sophistical tergiversations in this context strengthens the case for an alignment between Vertumnus and Satan in Milton's mind.

If Milton had read Fraunce and been struck by his treatment of the story then this might have provided a basis for his own identification of Satan with Vertumnus. If, as is likely, the two poets made the connection independently, this suggests that the elements which comprise the outline of the Pomona story, a woman in a garden being tempted by a disguised supernatural trickster in close proximity with a fruit tree, are likely to trigger off associations in the Christian reader's mind with the story of Adam and Eve. A felicitous reminder of the persistence of such archetypes can be found in a poem by A.S. Byatt, attributed to the Victorian poet hero of her novel *Possession*. The status of 'tricksy Herakles' is similar to that of Vertumnus. Transposed to a Christian context it would be equally difficult to put him firmly in the category of either hero or villain.

> These things are there. The garden and the tree
> The serpent at its root, the fruit of gold
> The woman in the shadow of the boughs
> The running water and the grassy space.
> They are and were there. At the old world's rim,
> In the Hesperidean grove, the fruit
> Glowed golden on eternal boughs, and there
> The dragon Ladon crisped his jewelled crest
> Scraped a gold claw and sharped a silver tooth
> And dozed and waited through eternity
> Until the tricksy hero Herakles
> Came to his dispossession and the theft. (p. 1)

The poem surprises the reader by appearing to offer a description of Eden which is gradually revealed to be the Garden of the Hesperides. The two locations are different and yet strangely similar, creating an effect similar to that produced by Ovidian metamorphoses, with their blend of continuity and change. Milton's transformations of Ovid are similarly arresting. Ovid's stories undergo transmutations whereby part of the original is left intact, rather as Io for example retains her whiteness when she changes from a heifer back to a woman (I 743), but the retention highlights the startling degree of metamorphosis. The rough congruence between Eve and Pomona underlines the impossibility of finding a single precise counterpart to Vertumnus, which in turn draws attention to the gulf between Milton and Ovid. Barkan's definition of metamorphosis as 'an image of simultaneous but divisible multiplicity' (p. 32) is suggestive of Milton's own metamorphosis of Ovid. Whether or not Milton was conscious of the complex cluster of analogues for Vertumnus, the effect – drawing attention to the difference between Christian and Pagan ideologies – mirrors his much discussed use of more obvious undercutting strategies, such as when he caps his memorable description of the fall of Mulciber by sternly reminding us that 'thus they relate/ Erring' (I 746-7), or when he describes the burnished apples of Eden as 'Hesperian fables true,/ If true, here only' (IV 250-1). Particularly striking – and Ovidian – is the following famous passage:

> Not that fair field
> Of Enna, where Proserpine gathering flowers
> Her self a fairer flower by gloomy Dis
> Was gathered, which cost Ceres all that pain
> To seek her through the world; nor that sweet grove
> Of Daphne by Orontes, and the inspired
> Castalian spring, might with this Paradise
> Of Eden strive (IV 268-75)

It is eloquent of Milton's relationship with Ovid that, although Eden's pre-eminent loveliness is asserted here, the passage's poignant beauty is dependent on the *loca amoena* of the *Metamorphoses*, ostensibly invoked as mere shadows of Paradise.

Milton's metamorphoses of Ovid may be aligned with the dramatic transformations within the poem's narrative. The most obvious metamorphoses in *Paradise Lost* are perhaps those undergone by Satan, culminating in the mass transformation of all the fallen angels into snakes, or else the promised incarnation of Christ. But the central metamorphosis in the poem involves no obvious physical alteration at all – the fall itself. We have seen how Ovid enjoyed using puns to suggest that something remains the same after even the most dramatic transformation – Myrrha's *medulla*, for example, or the *vena* (veins) in the rocks which Pyrrha and Deucalion throw behind them which remain (linguistically) the same even after the metamorphosis (I 410). Milton uses similar wordplay to link fallen and unfallen men. The lovely brooks in Eden roll 'With mazy error under pendant shades' (IV 239). The vocabulary contains ominous hints at what is to come; no taint has yet marred paradise, but we as fallen readers cannot help being aware of the negative potential of a word like 'error'. Similarly Eve's hair 'in wanton ringlets waved' (306). Although the word 'wanton' here certainly does not imply that Eve is in any sense sexually abandoned, we are encouraged to anticipate her fallen lasciviousness, transposing it onto her present sinless state. The *Metamorphoses* has managed to insinuate its way within the pale even of this most Christian poem, donning an uncharacteristically serious guise in order to tempt Milton into indulging his taste for Ovidian play.

7

Ovid translated: Sir Samuel Garth's *Metamorphoses*

It is fitting that this stage in the development of English Ovidianism is represented here by translators rather than imitators. This was the great age of English translation, as evidenced by Dryden's versions of Lucretius and Virgil and Pope's Homer. These are justly celebrated, but it is less widely known that the eighteenth century produced perhaps the most accomplished translation of the *Metamorphoses* – Garth's 1717 edition by several hands.

> This poem has been ever since the magazine, which has furnished the greatest poets of the following ages with fancy, and allusions; and the most celebrated painters with subjects and designs. (Garth's Preface to the *Metamorphoses*, p. xviii)

This brief quotation suggests the self-awareness of English Ovidianism in the Augustan age, the ability to reflect on the *Metamorphoses*' contribution to Western culture, and situate oneself within a well established Ovidian tradition. When examining a translation of Ovid, such as that edited by Garth, it is possible to assert with greater confidence that any departures from the text, whether in the spirit of the *Metamorphoses* or against the grain of the original, are likely to have been intentional. Whereas we cannot know to what degree Shakespeare and Spenser were aware of their engagement with Ovid at any particular moment, we may be sure that the *Metamorphoses*' Augustan translators were, if not fully in control of all the effects they created, at least conscious that every line they wrote took Ovid as its starting point. An examination of Garth's Ovid reveals a nuanced responsiveness to the *Metamorphoses*, and a confident facility for reproducing the chief features of its style.

Yet Garth's *Metamorphoses*' came into being just as Ovid's star was beginning, at least ostensibly, to wane. A little exchange in Fielding's *Amelia* demonstrates the poet's 'downgrading' very tellingly:

> 'Nay, Madam,' said the Doctor ... 'Are there no unreasonable Opinions in very learned Authors, even among the Critics themselves? For Instance, What can be a more strange, and indeed unreasonable Opinion, than to prefer the *Metamorphoses* of *Ovid* to the *Aeneid* of *Virgil*?

'It would be indeed so strange,' cries the Lady, 'that you shall not persuade me it was ever the Opinion of any Man.' (pp. 408-9)

It would be a long time before dissent from the confidently expressed views of the lady and the doctor became probable or even possible. The decline of Ovid's reputation meant that Garth's *Metamorphoses* was doomed to comparative obscurity even though the two greatest Augustan poets, Pope and Dryden, contributed to the volume, along with other leading figures such as Gay and Addison. No major poet would be profoundly influenced by Garth in the way Milton, Marvell and Shakespeare were by Sandys and Golding.

Although there is no need to dig for 'embedded' Ovidianism in a translation of the *Metamorphoses*, it is possible to identify a particular fluency in the response to Ovid in Garth which suggests the degree to which Ovidianism was now engrained in English poetry's subconscious, as it were. That Ovid's reputation suffered a falling off during the following two centuries is undeniable, but Ovidianism was too profoundly embedded in the poetry of the previous three hundred years for his influence to be completely destroyed, and the *Metamorphoses* continued to be a submerged but vital presence in English poetry.

In the next chapter I shall examine an extended example of Ovid's 'absent presence' in Keats' 'Ode on a Grecian Urn' but an earlier and particularly telling illustration of the same phenomenon can be found in the poetry of Pope. Ovidianism owes as much to his imitators as to Ovid himself, and it is perhaps significant that Pope turned to *The House of Fame* early in his career, producing an imitation of Book III of Chaucer's poem, *The Temple of Fame*, in 1711. We are reminded of the pervasiveness of English Ovidianism by Pope's account of his ascent into the air:

I stood, methought, betwixt earth, seas, and skies;
The whole creation open to my eyes:
In air self-balanced hung the globe below ... (11-13)

The first line comes via Chaucer (714-15) from *Metamorphoses* XII 39-40, 'orbe locus medio est inter terrasque fretumque/ caelestesque plagas, triplicis confinia mundi', but line 13 echoes Ovid's description of the world's creation, 'nec circumfuso pendebat in aere tellus/ ponderibus librata suis', 'nor yet did the earth hang poised by her own weight in the circumambient air' (I 12-13) and has no equivalent in *The House of Fame*. Although this is the first quotation from the *Metamorphoses* that Garth picks out for special praise in his preface, it is probable that for most of Pope's readers the presence of *Paradise Lost* is more strongly felt, 'And earth self balanced on her centre hung' (VII 242). By the eighteenth century Ovidianism was so deeply engrained in English

124

poetry that there is little to be gained in trying to pin down the provenance of such a borrowing too precisely. But whether he was responding to Ovid, Milton or indeed to both, Pope has clearly incurred debts to the *Metamorphoses* which cannot simply be traced back to Chaucer.

In Chapter 2 we saw how the differences between Ovid and Chaucer themselves reflected the operations of Fama. The process is extended by Pope, who offers a quite different selection of luminaries from Chaucer, reflecting the changes wrought by four hundred years of altering taste. His poem thus exemplifies the processes it describes:

> Inscriptions here of various names I viewed,
> The greater part by hostile time subdued;
> Yet wide was spread their fame in ages past,
> And poets once had promised they should last.
> Some fresh engraved appeared of wits renowned;
> I looked again, nor could their trace be found. (31-6)

There is perhaps a (rather Ovidian) pun on engrave here; for some writers' fame is so transient that inscription and erasure (here burial) are almost simultaneous. Marvell makes the same play on words in 'The Nymph Complaining for the Death of her Faun':

> For I so truly thee bemoan,
> That I shall weep though I be stone:
> Until my tears, still dropping, wear
> My breast, themselves engraving there. (114-17)

The line 'And poets once had promised they should last' (34) has no equivalent in Chaucer but is an allusion to *The House of Fame* nonetheless; Chaucer is himself one of these 'poets' and Pope here proclaims both his indebtedness to and his independence from his predecessor. This is not the only poem by Pope in which the very act of translation illustrates its central thesis. His 'The First Epistle of the Second Book of Horace Imitated', where the poet bemoans the way modern poets are overlooked in favour of their Renaissance predecessors, gains an extra edge if the reader recalls that Horace composed the original some 1500 years before these 'ancients' were born.

Whether influenced by Ovid himself or by earlier English Ovidian voices, Pope's *Temple of Fame* draws on the *Metamorphoses* independently as well as via *The House of Fame*. It is therefore ironic that one of the poets given prominence in Chaucer's poem but banished from Pope's is Ovid himself. However the omission is not entirely inappropriate. Although hardly less influenced by the *Metamorphoses* than their Renaissance predecessors, Augustan poets were cautious in their assessment of Ovid, criticising his extravagant wit. Pope's own love for

125

Ovid was seen as bad taste by Warton and Spence (Bush 1937, p. 32). But the major poets of the age still found the charm of the *Metamorphoses* hard to resist. Dryden may subject Ovid to some cutting criticisms in his preface to the *Fables Ancient and Modern*, but the translations themselves tell a different story, betraying his great affinity with Ovid, and his readiness to equal, or even cap, the witty 'boyisms' he condemns.

Garth's attitude towards Ovid is similarly compounded of admiration and disapproval. His preface to the translation acknowledges that Ovid's standing had already somewhat diminished, and he appears to wish to correct this tendency, observing that the poet 'is too much run down at present by the critical spirit of this nation' (37). Yet he finds fault with Ovid's 'boyisms' – the same word used by Dryden in his preface to *Fables Ancient and Modern* – even though he is full of praise for Ovid's wit, elegance and delicacy, and writes with particular enthusiasm about the *Metamorphoses'* clever use of transitions between stories, choosing a simile which anticipates modern critics' fondness for detecting an affinity between Arachne's art and her creator's:

> The texture is so artful, that it may be compared to the work of his own Arachne, where the shade dies so gradually, and the light revives so imperceptibly, that it is hard to tell where the one ceases, and the other begins. (p. viii)

Garth's praise might almost equally well be applied to his own edition. Although one perhaps ought to be able to tell the difference between, say, Dryden and Maynwaring at first glance, such discriminations are in practice not always so easy to make. Whereas Hofmann and Lasdun's anthology *After Ovid* is decidedly eclectic, embracing numerous verse forms and ranging from precise translation to distant imitation of the Latin original, all Garth's contributors have chosen the same verse form and (with very minor variations) the same principles of translation. Although Ovid has been translated into many verse forms, few have served his wit so well as the rhyming couplet. Its aptness can most clearly be seen in the translations of Pope and Dryden, but even Stonestreet, one of the weaker contributors, is capable of nicely Ovidian touches. The hyperbole and antithesis in the following lines, describing the plague of Aegina, have no precise equivalent in the *Metamorphoses* but are completely idiomatic:

> Here one, with fainting steps, does slowly creep
> O'er heaps of dead, and straight augments the heap.
> Another, while his strength and tongue prevailed,
> Bewails his friend, and falls himself bewailed. (pp. 240-1)

Each couplet opens with a line which uses caesuras to suggest the sufferers' exhaustion, slowing down the pace. The second lines both employ repetition – 'heaps ... heap', 'Bewails ... bewailed' – to point the transition from life to death, the contrast between being a spectator and a participant.

Another related characteristic of the volume is the receptivity of its contributors to Ovid's particular brand of wit, their alertness to his linguistic play. There is a daring in Garth's Ovid which we do not find in earlier translations; Sandys was confident enough to update Ovid by substituting 'Whitehall' for 'Palatia', and his successors still more boldly added entirely new turns and fancies of their own.

The description of a man who 'ducit remos illic, ubi nuper arabat', 'plying his oars where lately he has plowed' (I 294) has been discussed above in Chapter 5. Dryden makes explicit a joke which is only hinted at in Ovid when he translates the line, 'And ploughs above, where late he sowed his corn' (p. 14), and even sets up his joke by using the word 'ploughed' to describe the first sea voyages of the brazen age when 'ships in triumph ploughed the watery plain' (p. 6). Ovid encouraged us to recall that *aro* is commonly used to describe the motion of a ship; Dryden twice employs the verb in this figurative sense.

Dryden is also happy to invent his own Ovidian turns. When Clymene instructs Phaethon how he may find his father's house she explains:

> If still you doubt your mother's innocence
> His eastern mansion is not far from hence,
> With little pains you to his levée go.
> And from himself your parentage may know. (p. 36)

The pun – levée means both an audience held in the morning and a rising – demonstrates Dryden's immersion in the spirit of his author. The double meaning simultaneously invokes Apollo as a powerful ruler presiding at court – such as Louis XIV, the Sun King – and the sun itself. As a voguish word – the first listing in the OED is from Dryden's own *Marriage à-la-Mode* of 1672 – levée would have created the same frisson as the comparison between Heaven and the Palatia did for Ovid's first readers.

In a slightly different way, Addison also apparently aspires to make his translation more Ovidian than Ovid. He renders the petrifaction of Atlas more pointed than it is in the original: Perseus uses the gorgon's head because it is to hand; Addison refines the punishment by making the hero assert that he will grant the giant endless rest in return for refusing rest to his visitor (p. 132). A similar motivation appears to lie behind his embellishment of Medusa's own metamorphosis:

> The hissing snakes her foes more sure ensnare
> Than they did lovers once, when shining hair. (p. 139)

Again and again we see this confident willingness to improvise, to offer new variations in the Ovidian manner. We might adduce Ovid's praise of Arachne's art once more, for these little innovations are generally executed with such tact that the reader fails to notice where translation shades into imitation. More than two centuries later Paul Muldoon feels the same urge as Addison to make a punishment more pointed. When Latona turns the Lycian peasants into frogs she explains that 'Since you've shown ... no soft spot/ for me, in this soft spot you'll always stay' (Hofmann and Lasdun, p. 152).

The contributions of the editor himself sometimes read like the work of someone desperately finishing off the bits no one else wanted to do – he is always very happy to truncate. But there is one pleasing touch in his description of the transformation of Turnus' ships into nymphs. In the list of various before and after features he inserts a detail of his own, 'the prow a female face' (p. 497). It is possible that Garth is attempting to replicate a pun discussed in Chapter 6 – 'quodque prius fuerat, latus est' (XIV 552) – for the association between a prow and a female face might suggest a figurehead, something which, like 'latus', could remain the same after the metamorphosis.

Garth's enthusiasm for Ovid also manifests itself in his original compositions; a more extended example of a new turn in the Ovidian style can be found in his 'place' poem 'Claremont', which contains the story of a beautiful youth, Montano, 'Not lovelier than Narcissus to the eye' (p. 11). Like Narcissus, he is indifferent to the charms of nymphs, but unexpectedly it is Narcissus' slighted admirer Echo who finally inflames Montano; in a neat reversal of Ovid's story she is unresponsive to his ardour, and continues to sigh for Narcissus:

With pity he beholds her wounding woes;
But wants himself the pity he bestows. (p. 13)

Montano calls down a curse on Echo, just as Narcissus was himself cursed by a rejected suitor:

sic amet ipse licet, sic non potiatur amato!

So may he himself love, and not gain the thing he loves! (III 405)

Retake the life you gave, but let the maid
Fall a just victim to an injured shade. (p. 14)

It seems apt that Ovid's tale of mirror images should be subjected to a complete reversal in 'Claremont'. Ovid's reflexive word order remains a local stylistic effect when imitated by Milton, Marvell and Shakespeare, but the whole structure of Garth's poem operates together with its Ovidian source to form a larger chiastic pattern. Garth's ability to reproduce this pattern on a much larger scale is entirely characteristic of the ease with which Augustan writers, even those of the second rank, seemed to appropriate and internalise the procedures of the *Metamorphoses*.

One of the surprise stars of Garth's Ovid is the little known Arthur Maynwaring. Like his editor, Maynwaring imitates Ovid's fondness for puns (*medulla*, *latus*) which draw together two different phases of a character's existence. In the fight which ensues after Andromeda's rescue, Perseus uses the gorgon's head to petrify his enemies. Astyages rushes at an enemy, not realising he has already turned to stone:

> Astyages the living likeness knew,
> On the dead stone with vengeful fury flew;
> But impotent his rage, the jarring blade
> No print upon the solid marble made:
> Again, as with redoubled might he struck,
> Himself astonished in the quarry stuck. (p. 151)

Two meanings of quarry – prey pursued and stone – are suggested by the last line.

Another of Maynwaring's additions, a coda to the account of Cyane's transformation into a fountain, is still more clearly suggestive of his understanding of 'Ovidianism'. The entire description repays quotation as it demonstrates that the beauties of Garth's Ovid are not the prerogative of its more celebrated contributors:

> Her varied members to a fluid melt,
> A pliant softness in her bones is felt.
> Her wavy locks first drop away in dew,
> And liquid next her slender fingers grew.
> The body's change soon seizes its extreme,
> Her legs dissolve, and feet flow off in stream.
> Her arms, her back, her shoulders, and her side,
> Her swelling breasts in little currents glide,
> A silver liquor only now remains
> Within the channel of her purple veins;
> Nothing to fill love's grasp; *her husband chaste*
> *Bathes in that bosom he before embraced.* (p. 162)

This weird evocation of the nymph's admirably adaptable mate might recall Apollo's similarly stoical response to Daphne's metamorphosis; he is content to adopt her as his tree since she cannot be his mistress. Yet again we see how well Ovid is served by rhyming couplets. The process of metamorphosis seems to gather pace even as we read; at first each line describes just one aspect of the nymph's transformation, but then two and even four are fitted into the same little space. By framing the final line with two verbs – one invoking her present state, one her

129

former shape – the poet emphasises the poignant strangeness of the metamorphosis.

Maynwaring's insertion is a convincing touch, reflecting the inhumanity – or perhaps *non*-humanity – of Ovid's immortals. He combines with this responsiveness to the spirit of the *Metamorphoses* an alertness to local verbal nuance – describing Proserpina, for example, as a 'blooming maid' (p. 160), following Ovid's own implied comparison between the goddess and the flowers she plucks.[1] Maynwaring's intensification of the link between Proserpina and her flowers may have been suggested by Milton's evocation of Eve's affinity with the natural world. The similarities between Proserpina's fatal taste of the pomegranate and Eve's fall had been noted by Sandys (p. 195) and further details of Maynwaring's translation might indicate that his reading of Milton had coloured his response to Ovid's narrative. Ceres tells Jove that 'en quaesita diu tandem mihi nata reperta est', 'See, my daughter, sought so long, has at last been found' (V 517). In Maynwaring this becomes 'In vain I sought her the wide world around' – hardly a dramatic alteration, yet perhaps recalling the famous 'which cost Ceres all that pain/ To seek her through the world' (*Paradise Lost* IV 272-3). Similarly when he describes how Proserpina ate the pomegranate he places the act within a context of temptation, absent in Ovid, 'and tempting her to taste/ She plucked the fruit, and took a short repast' (p. 167).

Addison, too, may be said to read Ovid through Milton. The famous description of Mulciber's fall in Book I of *Paradise Lost* is clearly derived from the first book of the *Iliad* but also owes something to Phaethon. Ovid's comparison between this youth and a falling star gains a further detail in Addison's translation:

> like a falling star
> That *in a summer's evening* from the top
> Of Heaven drops down, or seems to drop ... (p. 49)

It seems likely that the addition derives from Milton:

> from morn
> To noon he fell, from noon to dewy eve,
> *A summer's day*; and with the *setting sun*
> Dropt from the zenith like a falling star (I 742-5)

---

[1] He thus shows a greater sensitivity to the pathos of that tale than the intolerant Prior, who remarks in his *Observations on Ovid's Metamorphoses*: 'Proserpine was indeed very young or very silly that when she was in the hands of Pluto, had her clothes torn and squalled out to her mother was grieved that she dropped the flowers out of her lap. This was a great while since, wenches that are big enough to be ravished are not so infinitely concerned for their nosegays' (Prior, vol. 1, p. 671). Prior's expression may be obscure, but his scorn is apparent.

7. Sir Samuel Garth's Metamorphoses

Yet again, English Ovidianism can be seen as a multi-layered phenomenon, dependent on much more than Ovid himself. Milton's great poem is enriched by the *Metamorphoses*, but the favour is returned when Addison draws on *Paradise Lost* to refresh a new *Metamorphoses* which is (like *After Ovid*) a tribute to Ovidianism and not just to Ovid.

Satire is a mode which we tend to associate – perhaps too readily – with the Augustan age. Where a Renaissance commentator would have offered a moral or theological interpretation of Ovid's fantastic tales, or perhaps adduced an analogue from natural history, Garth draws a parallel with contemporary politics:

> From Proteus we have this lesson, that a statesman can put on any shape; can be a spaniel to the lion, and a lion to the spaniel; and that he knows not to be an enemy, who knows not how to seem a friend; that if all the crowns should change their ministry, as often as they please, though they may be called other ministers, they are still the same men. (p. xviii)

In the same spirit Eusden embellishes Ovid's account of the underworld, making the most of an opportunity to have a dig at two favourite eighteenth-century targets:

> pars aliquas artes, antiquae imitamina vitae.

> others ply some craft in imitation of their former life. (IV 445)

> Th'unbodied spectres freely rove, and show
> Whate'er they loved on Earth, they love below.
> The lawyers still, or right, or wrong, support,
> The courtiers smoothly glide to Pluto's court. (p. 122)

The most celebrated satirist of the age, Jonathan Swift, did not contribute to Garth, but he too translated Ovid, reinventing the tale of Baucis and Philemon within a Christian setting; Jove and Mercury are replaced by a pair of hermits 'taking their tour in masquerade' (8) and the couple's house is transformed into a church rather than a temple. Although the metamorphosis is far more elaborate in Swift's version than in the original, it is strikingly Ovidian in spirit, with various items undergoing dramatic alterations, yet still retaining something of their old function:

> A wooden jack, which had almost
> Lost, by disuse, the art to roast,
> A sudden alteration feels,
> Increased by new intestine wheels:
> And what exalts the wonder more,
> The number made the motion slower ... (65-70)

131

The jack's apparent sentience makes him like one of Ovid's metamorphosed human characters, and like them it does not quite forget its previous incarnation, although transformed into the clock on the church steeple:

> And still its love to houshold cares
> By a shrill voice at noon declares,
> Warning the cook-maid, not to burn
> That roast meat which it cannot turn. (81-4)

A similarly ingenious link is discovered between the old couple's bedstead and its new form:

> A bedstead of the antique mode,
> Compact of timber many a load,
> Such as our ancestors did use,
> Was metamorphosed into pews;
> Which still their ancient nature keep;
> By lodging folks disposed to sleep. (101-6)

Ovid's Baucis and Philemon ask to be allowed to serve as the priests of their new temple. Their humble reverence is not matched by Swift's couple; his Philemon asks to be made Parson because he 'fain would live at ease' (115), and fulfills his ambition by revamping old sermons and assiduously gathering in his tithes. Although the parson and his wife are eventually metamorphosed into trees the poem ends on a decidedly sour note:

> Till once, a parson of the town,
> To mend his barn, cut Baucis down;
> At which, 'tis hard to be believed,
> How much the other tree was grieved,
> Grew scrubby, died a-top, was stunted:
> So, the next parson stubbed and burnt it. (173-8)

Although technically a 'Christianised' Ovid, Swift's mischievous satire reflects rather than contradicts the almost complete absence among Augustan writers of any urge to relate Ovid's stories to Christian teaching – Sandys represents the last gasp of this tradition. The very explicitness of Swift's Christianisation robs it of any of that anxiety we found in the works of earlier Christian Ovidians. Just occasionally we find a moralising note in Garth, such as when Stonestreet expresses a disapproval of suicide which would have been alien in Ovid's day:

> Strange madness, that, when death pursued so fast,
> T'anticipate the blow with impious haste. (p. 242)

Rather more interesting is Dryden's subtle alteration of the scene where

7. Sir Samuel Garth's Metamorphoses

Jove vents his wrath at Lycaon's impiety. Whereas in Ovid Jove informs the gods that he 'in domino dignos everti tecta penates', 'brought the house down upon its household gods, gods worthy of such a master' (I 231), Dryden's Jove says 'the tables I o'erturned' (p. 11), an apparent allusion to Christ's similarly righteous fury at the moneylenders' desecration of the temple. A few self-imposed bowdlerisations can also be detected if Garth is read side by side with the Latin text. Addison omits the unpleasantly suggestive comparison between the voracious Salmacis and a polyp, and makes the rejected suitor who curses Narcissus a nymph rather than a youth. Similarly Dryden omits the lines describing Orpheus' own love for beautiful youths. However, this prudishness is far from characteristic. Walter Scott censoriously remarked that 'Where there was a latitude given for coarseness of description and expression, Dryden has always too readily laid hold of it' (Kinsley, p. 375). Scott perhaps had Dryden's version of Lucretius in mind, but the translator's boldness is equally apparent in the *Fables*, most interestingly in his translation of Pygmalion which was later included in Garth.

Dryden's version of the legend is the first of many responses to Pygmalion which I have included in the second half of this book. I have not chosen the most obvious text, *The Winter's Tale*, as my starting point, partly because this aspect of the play has been extensively discussed elsewhere (Barkan 1981 and Bate, pp. 234-8), partly because I wish to focus on the 'darkening' of Pygmalion – although it could be argued that *The Winter's Tale* becomes darkened retrospectively by texts such as H.D.'s *Her*. Although Dryden's translation of the tale is ostensibly faithful to Ovid, alterations and additions, slight in themselves, combine to shift the tone and emphasis of the original, modifying our response to both sculptor and miracle.

This process is begun in the very first lines:

Quas quia Pymalion aevum per crimen agentis
viderat, offensus vitiis, quae plurima menti
femineae natura dedit, sine coniuge caelebs
vivebat thalamique diu consorte carebat.

Pygmalion had seen these women spending their lives in shame, and, disgusted with the faults which in such full measure nature had given the female mind, he lived unmarried and long was without a partner of his couch. (X 243-6)

Pygmalion loathing their lascivious life,
Abhorred all womankind, but most a wife:
So single chose to live, and shunned to wed,
Well pleased to want a consort of his bed. (1-4)[2]

---

[2]For ease of reference Kinsley's modern edition of Dryden is used here as lines are not numbered in Garth.

In the *Metamorphoses* the sculptor's decision to eschew wedlock seems judicious, or at least carefully deliberated. But Dryden has infected the lines with a touch of the ludicrous. Somehow the second line suggests a more instinctive repulsion from union with a female, such as that felt by Gulliver who recoils from his own unfortunate wife after his sojourn among the Houyhnhnms. And there is no hint of any special complacency in Ovid as there is in line four where the use of 'want', signifying lack but shading into desire, points to the perversity of his stance in rejecting normal human urges. But although Dryden significantly alters the Latin, it is still possible to trace the seeds of his own Pygmalion back to Ovid. The judgment on women is harsh even in the original, and not explicitly presented as Pygmalion's subjective opinion – he merely sees what is already there. Ovid more usually projects himself as a writer sensitive to the feelings and experiences of women, even those such as Myrrha and Iphis whose sexual urges are misdirected. But we might explain the misogynism here if we remember that Orpheus, not Ovid, is the narrator, and that he has reacted to the second loss of Eurydice by rejecting all women.

The couplet which follows hints that Pygmalion turns to sculpture to deflect sexual tension – the 'yet' is particularly pointed. There is no overt suggestion of such a motive in the Latin:

Yet fearing idleness, the nurse of ill,
In sculpture exercised his happy skill ... (5-6)

Ovid's simple account of his love for the statue, 'operisque sui concepit amorem', 'and with his own work he falls in love' (X 249) becomes

Pleased with his idol, he commends, admires,
Adores; and last, the thing adored, desires. (11-12)

'Idol' had the same connotations it does today, with the additional meaning of 'counterfeit'. The word is always used more or less pejoratively by Dryden. By calling the statue 'idol' and 'thing' rather than, say, ivory maid, Dryden brings out the ludicrousness of his infatuation, an effect compounded by the hyberbolical, almost hysterical, build-up of verbs. This hint at possible mental instability is reinforced with a couplet which has no precise equivalent in Ovid:

He knows 'tis madness, yet he must adore,
And still the more he knows it, loves the more. (19-20)

This recalls the hopeless passion of Narcissus, aware of the nature of his predicament, yet unable to fall out of love with his reflection. It may be that this is more than a chance similarity for, as J. Hillis Miller remarks, the statue can be seen as a mirror image of Pygmalion's desire.

When she awakes, he writes, 'it is as if Narcissus' reflection in the pool had come alive and could return his love' (p. 5).

When Dryden's Pygmalion caresses his creation the effect is both more and less passionate than in Ovid:

oscula dat reddique putat

He kisses it and thinks his kisses are returned (256)

Fired with this thought, at once he strained the breast,
And on the lips a burning kiss impressed.
'Tis true, the hardened breast resists the gripe,
And the cold lips return a kiss unripe:
But when, retiring back, he looked again,
To think it ivory, was a thought too mean. (23-8)

His ardour is more pronounced – 'fired', 'burning' – but his readiness to be deceived is less wholehearted than in Ovid. His awareness of her lack of response, coupled with his lingering suspicion that she is real, combine to make it seem almost that he is forcing himself on an unwilling victim. Lines 25-6 are entirely Dryden's own invention, and could as easily refer to a real woman as to a statue – if anything the adjective 'hardened' would make more sense in such a context as it seems to indicate that her hardness is the result of a gradual process rather than being her permanent state, and, like 'cold' and 'resists', is suggestive of a state of mind. When he fears he may have bruised her, Pygmalion 'explored her, limb by limb' (33) to check for blemishes. It is difficult to believe that this scrutiny is actuated purely by concern for her health.

Fired with hope by Venus' auspicious omens Pygmalion becomes still more eager:

And impudent in hope, with ardent eyes,
And beating breast, by the dear statue lies. (73-4)

When she appears to yield under his touch, 'the pleasing task he fails not to renew' (83). Once again this unattractively prurient quality is implicit in Ovid's story – Dryden emphasises but does not invent the sculptor's weird fetishisation of his creation. 'Pygmalion and the Statue' functions in the same way as a somewhat jaundiced piece of criticism and, although every translation is in some sense a new reading of the original, is perhaps unusual in the consistency of effect (if not purpose) achieved by each identifiable modification of the source.

It is not only Pygmalion whom Dryden subtly undermines. The statue herself is less artless, as it were, than the original, recalling the 'real' women depicted in the *Ars Amatoria* and the *Amores*. Yet again

135

this is a slanted but not a skewed reading of Ovid's story. In 'Womanu-facture' Alison Sharrock traces the relationship between Pygmalion and the masculine tradition of elegiac love poetry which objectifies the woman, making her as much an art object as the ivory statue. Feminist critics in particular have undermined the apparent 'realism' of elegiac woman; Maria Wyke, for example, compares the gait of Propertius' Cynthia to metrical movement: 'The Elegiac Woman's walk may also delineate metrical motion precisely because her body may be read as the anatomy of an elegiac text' (p. 56). The poem is about a woman, but it also in a sense *is* the woman. Cynthia and Corinna are as much – and as little – works of art as Galatea.

Dryden appears to draw on memories of Ovid's own elegiac poetry to create a female who is somehow more equivocally inanimate than the original. The humanly stony response to her lover's kisses has already been noted; another hint is given earlier in the poem when the account of the statue's creation gains a very Ovidian embellishment:

And carved in ivory such a maid, so fair,
As nature could not with his art compare,
Were she to work; but in her own defence
Must take her pattern here and copy hence. (7-10)

This suggestion of an *agon* between art and nature is missing from Ovid, although it might recall the description of Diana's grotto, dis-cussed in Chapter 3, or indeed Spenser's Bower of Bliss. Dryden interposes a similar elaboration when he describes Diana's temple in 'Palamon and Arcite', also included in *Fables Ancient and Modern*:

All these the painter drew with such command
That Nature snatched the pencil from his hand
Ashamed and angry that his art could feign
And mend the tortures of a mother's pain. (655-8)

Within the context of Pygmalion, Nature's need to emulate and even exceed Pygmalion's artistry might suggest the use of artifice by 'real', 'natural' women to captivate men. Dryden's elaboration of the original thus foregrounds an implicit link in the narrative between the sculptor and an elegiac poet such as Ovid himself. Women begin the work of turning themselves into works of art by resorting to various cosmetics and affectations, and the process is completed by any poet who makes them the subject of his poetry.

The following couplet, again an addition to the original, casts Pygma-lion in the role of victim; the vocabulary, if not the literal meaning, seems to involve the statue with the wiles traditionally associated with femininity:

Art hid with art, so well performed the cheat
It caught the carver with his own deceit. (17-18)

In the *Ars Amatoria* Ovid had advised women to affect a graceful negligence in their appearance, 'ars casum simulat', 'art counterfeits chance' (III 155) before going on to recommend the benefits of hair dye and wigs. And Dryden's own translation of the fourth book of Lucretius suggests that love is quite deceptive enough even when only normal men and women are involved:

So love with phantoms cheats our longing eyes
Which hourly seeing never satisfies;
Our hands pull nothing from the parts they strain,
But wander o're the lovely limbs in vain. (67-70)

Pygmalion follows the advice of the *Ars* in giving his beloved inexpensive rustic gifts and deploying flattery. Dryden calls these gifts 'the powerful bribes of love' (36), a note of cynicism which might seem more at home within the context of a more conventional liaison. The statue is further humanised in the following couplet:

He furnishes her closet first; and fills
The crowded shelves with rarities of shells (37-8)

'Closet' may mean either a bedroom or a cabinet; in either case the impression is given of a woman who already has a living space and some possessions rather than a work of art in a studio.

Still more telling is a veiled allusion to Ovid's Corinna in this section of the translation. In the *Metamorphoses* we are simply told that Pygmalion brings the statue 'parvas volucres', 'little birds' (X 261), but Dryden is more explicit, informing us that she is given 'parrots imitating human tongue' (41). Corinna's vocal parrot (deceased) is the subject of *Amores* II v. As well as invoking Corinna, a love-object who is (apparently) more 'real' than the ivory maid, the parrot's capacity to imitate speech makes him a suggestive addition to a tale about an artist's ability to infuse humanity into a senseless object. A parrot, like Echo, can only repeat what it is told – another hint that Pygmalion's love for the statue is somehow Narcissistic.

In keeping with the statue's greater reality is Pygmalion's treatment of her. In Ovid he simply calls her his consort and places her on downy pillows, but Dryden appends a further detail, 'With blandishments invites her to his side' (54). A nice ambiguity in the couplet which follows just hints at the possibility that she may already be animate:

And as she were with vital sense possessed
Her head did on a plumy pillow rest. (55-6)

Pygmalion may be the subject of 'rest' and her head merely the passive object. But it is equally possible that she rests her own head on the pillow, and line 55 is consistent with either reading. Another suggestion that she is rather more than a statue can be found in Venus' response to Pygmalion's prayers; she 'Well knew he meant th'inanimated fair' (69). The phrase 'Th'inanimated fair' is a clumsy, coy and curiously unattractive periphrasis. Furthermore, scansion aside, it is significant that Dryden calls her inanimated rather than inanimate. Whereas the latter signifies without life, inanimated only implies that she is lacking in animal spirits. Dryden creates an unappealing yet essentially human impression, comparable to the effect achieved by Tennyson when he describes Maud as 'icily regular, splendidly null' (*Maud*, line 82).

Dryden allows Pygmalion to insinuate himself even into non-Ovidian fables; in 'The Wife of Bath Her Tale', another narrative of fantasy fulfilled, he draws on a similar slippage between art and nature. When the crone is miraculously transformed into a beautiful woman a commonplace poeticism – 'ivory arm' – acquires an additional retrospective significance when Dryden compares the knight to Pygmalion:

> With joy he turned, and seized her ivory arm;
> And, like Pygmalion, found the statue warm. (533-4)

In a manner similar to Spenser's play in the Bower of Bliss the poet lulls us into reading ivory figuratively, and then forces us to think again. Barkan's remark that 'often the business of metamorphosis ... is to make flesh of metaphors' (23) is particularly pertinent in this context. The lady is transformed from elegiac woman to Galatea as well as from hag to maiden. Poets are, by their nature, adept at metamorphosis. (The possibility of an Ovidian miracle, another addition to Chaucer, had been invoked earlier in the poem when the knight wistfully wonders whether 'Medea's magic [could] mend thy face' (367).) It is perhaps significant, in the light of Dryden's subtle alterations to Ovid's story, that the invocation of Pygmalion at the point of metamorphosis allows a hint of unease to mar the triumphant conclusion of the Wife's narrative. Dryden follows Chaucer and informs us that their union was unclouded. However, the reader might recall the very different conclusion to Pygmalion's story, for his grandson is the unfortunate Cinyras, whose incestuous liaison with his daughter casts retrospective doubt on his grandfather's passion for his own creation. In his prefatory note to the two tales Dryden remarks that they are 'admirably well connected.'

Dryden's translation, which Judith Sloman inexplicably describes as having an effect 'distinctly more cheerful than in the *Metamorphoses*' (191) anticipates other negative responses to the legend which will be discussed in later chapters. But a more light hearted variation on the theme can be found in *The Rape of the Lock* where a reincarnation of

Pygmalion's statue, the lovely Belinda, breaks free from male control. Like the sculptor she sues to a goddess in her quest for beautification – her own reflection:

> Now awful beauty puts on all its arms;
> The fair each moment rises in her charms,
> Repairs her smiles, awakens every grace,
> And calls forth all the wonders of her face;
> Sees by degrees a purer blush arise,
> And keener lightnings quicken in her eyes. (139-44)

As both artist and goddess as well as statue Belinda nicely re-empowers her sex, even if she is ultimately as much a textual construct as Corinna and the heroine of the Wife of Bath's tale.

Our next Ovidian, Keats, turned to Sandys rather than Garth when he wanted an English Ovid. This is typical of the cool response Augustan poetry has too often met with from Romantic (and post-Romantic) readers. Although the age sought to distance itself from Ovid, it has been tarred with the same brushes used to denigrate his own works – elegance, wit, refinement and dispassion.

8

Absent presence: Keats' 'Ode on a Grecian Urn'

In the last chapter we saw how the ease with which the Augustan poets appropriated Ovidian tropes was a sign of Ovidianism's increasing 'embeddedness' in English literature. Another aspect of this 'embeddedness' is displayed in Keats' 'Ode on a Grecian Urn', a striking example of the way the *Metamorphoses* can function as a potent intertext within a poem even though it is not explicitly invoked. The Ode's undisputed canonicity reminds us that the Ovidian tradition remained central even when Ovid's reputation was supposedly in the doldrums. We can see in Keats' work the same anxieties and tensions that we found in the poetry of Spenser, Shakespeare and Milton, no longer perhaps inspired directly by that 'destructive tolerance' which characterises the Ovidian universe, but traceable to the *Metamorphoses* nonetheless by virtue of Keats' immersion in the works of all those poets who 'gild the lapses of time'.

Keats differs in one important respect from those poets discussed in the earlier part of this book. His education did not equip him to read Ovid in the original with ease, and he knew the *Metamorphoses* principally from Sandys' translation. With the examples of Coleridge and Wordsworth before him, he might easily have chosen to expunge classicism from his work. Yet although he affirms his desire to change the direction of English poetry, Keats may be seen to follow in the footsteps of his poetic predecessors, and continue the Ovidian 'line'.

Lamia is perhaps Keats' most obviously metamorphic poem; it opens with an account of Hermes' unrequited passion for a nymph which might equally easily be indebted to the *Metamorphoses* or to a similar tale in Marlowe's highly Ovidian *Hero and Leander* (I 386-464). Lamia herself is a notoriously ambiguous figure, a compound of beauty and grotesqueness. She is a serpent with the face of a woman at the opening of the poem, and Keats does not disclose whether this is her original state or whether she is the victim of some earlier metamorphosis:

She seemed, at once, some penanced lady elf,
Some demon's mistress, or the demon's self. (55-6)

Hermes gives her a woman's body so that she may fulfil her passion for Lycius, a youth of Corinth.

Lamia is aligned with two goddesses who feature in the *Metamorphoses*, but rather than providing us with a frame of reference within which to place her these allusions only serve to confuse our sense of her still further:

> And for her eyes: what could such eyes do there
> But weep, and weep, that they were born so fair?
> As Proserpine still weeps for her Sicilian air. (61-3)

This reference to the hapless, exiled goddess might appear to work in Lamia's favour. However, our reading of the passage may be complicated by memories of Eve, twice memorably compared with Proserpina by Milton (IV 268-75, IX 393-6). Eve in her turn might trigger associations with Satan, himself often depicted as a serpent with a woman's face by Renaissance painters. Equally problematic is a later reference to Lamia's 'Circean head'. Miriam Allott glosses Circean as 'beautiful and fatally enchanting like Circe' (p. 621). Yet the epithet immediately precedes Lamia's claim that she used to have a woman's shape – perhaps she resembles one of Circe's transformed victims more closely than the enchantress herself. This moral dubiety surrounding Lamia is almost more Ovidian than the central metamorphosis, for our distrust of her continues to be tempered by sympathy up until – and perhaps including – the moment she is unmasked as a serpent by the sage Apollonius, a crisis which may inspire the reader with similar feelings to those generated by Guyon's destruction of the Bower of Bliss.

But perhaps Keats' most interesting Ovidian poem is his 'Ode on a Grecian Urn'. At first glance it might not seem to owe any special debt to Ovid at all – vague references to gods and nymphs do not, after all, make a poem Ovidian. But I would suggest that the *Metamorphoses* is an informing presence within the poem, and that to place the Ode within an Ovidian context helps us to arrive at new answers to questions which have puzzled its readers.

Although 'Ode on a Grecian Urn' is perhaps Keats' best known and most discussed poem it has not met with universal critical approval. The final stanza is the main focus for contention; the puns contained in the first two lines have struck many readers as being out of place, but it is the final couplet which has proved most problematic:

> 'Beauty is truth, truth beauty,' – that is all
> Ye know on earth, and all ye need to know.

In her edition of the complete poems, Miriam Allott provides a summary of the range of critical positions on these lines, indicating the difficulties involved in gauging their significance.

8. Keats' 'Ode on a Grecian Urn'

Opinions about the meaning of the beauty-truth equivalent and its relevance to the rest of the poem can be roughly divided as follows: (1) philosophically defensible but of doubtful relevance (Murry); (2) a 'pseudo-statement', but emotionally relevant (I.A. Richards); (3) expressing the paradoxes in the poem and therefore dramatically appropriate (C. Brooks); (4) meaningless and therefore a blemish (T.S. Eliot); (5) an over-simplification, but attempting a positive synthesis of the oppositions expressed in the poem (F.W. Bateson); (6) emotionally and intellectually relevant when properly understood, but 'the effort to see the thing as Keats did is too great to be undertaken with pleasure' (Empson, p. 374).

It is possible to go some way towards resolving these problems – the apparent indecorum of register and the opacity of the final lines – by invoking a god whose importance for Keats is undisputed, Phoebus Apollo. ('Hyperion' and the two Odes to Apollo are only the most obvious examples of Apollo's presence in the poetry of Keats. References to the god are common in his work.) Apollo has many attributes. He is the god of healing, of the sun and, perhaps most importantly, of music. Many legends concern his exploits, one of the most famous being his unrequited passion for the nymph Daphne.

The only direct reference to Daphne in Keats' poetry comes towards the end of *Endymion* where an account of the constellations culminates in the line:

By Daphne's fright, behold Apollo! (IV 611)

This almost total neglect of Daphne is a little surprising as her tale is recounted elegantly and at length in Sandys' translation of Ovid's *Metamorphoses*.[1] Its companion piece, the story of Pan's frustrated passion for Syrinx, is referred to by Keats far more frequently yet, as we have already seen, the tale of Daphne's metamorphosis into a laurel is both more memorable and more celebrated. Keats' fascination with Apollo, a god whose presence is so strongly felt in his poetry, makes the omission still more unaccountable. Ian Jack's study *Keats and The Mirror of Art* devotes a whole chapter to Apollo, but Daphne is not even listed in the index.

Despite his apparent lack of interest in this tale it seems possible that it may have coloured and informed the 'Ode on a Grecian Urn'. The legend might usefully be thought of as embellishing at least a portion of the imaginary urn's elusive surface. The idea of permanence is explored and questioned through the unchanging but limited beauty of the urn. The tale of Apollo and Daphne shares this preoccupation with permanence, but here it is the result, not of art, but of metamorphosis and immortality. Another method of combating human transience is

---

[1] Keats is known to have used the Oxford Folio edition of Sandys' translation of Ovid (Colvin, p. 171).

tacitly suggested by both Ovid and Keats, the undying fame conferred by poetry.

If Keats did indeed have Apollo and Daphne in his mind then he might have owed a debt to a visual as well as a literary source. Many existing sculpted figures have been associated with this poem, including the Portland Vase and the Elgin Marbles (for a survey of the possible visual sources for the ode see Jack, pp. 214-24). The importance of these sources need not be dismissed in order to admit another memorable work of art into the group, Bernini's statue of Apollo and Daphne whose extravagant virtuosity Keats would surely have found congenial. In capturing the nymph mid-metamorphosis, Bernini has triumphantly fulfilled the requirements for successful composition described by Haydon in his diary:

> The great principle of composition in painting is to represent the event, doing and not done ... The moment a thing is done in painting half the interest is gone; our power of exciting attention depends ... upon the suspense we keep the mind in, regarding the past and the future. (W.B. Pope, ii, pp. 215-16)

Haydon's remark might also be a commentary on Keats' own urn. We cannot know if Keats ever came across a print of the statue, though his keen interest in art suggests that he would have known the work of such a celebrated sculptor – his contemporary Hazlitt was certainly familiar with Bernini (xi, p. 207, x, p. 162, xii, p. 89, xvi, pp. 300, 305, 306). A passage from 'I Stood Tip-Toe Upon a Little Hill' adds fuel to such speculation. Here we have a description of Apollo in conjunction with some metamorphic sweet peas, tremulously poised for flight:

> Dry up the moisture from your golden lids,
> For great Apollo bids
> That in these days your praises should be sung
> On many harps, which he has lately strung;
> And when again your dewiness he kisses,
> Tell him, I have you in my world of blisses:
> So haply when I rove in some far vale,
> His mighty voice may come upon the gale.
>
> Here are sweet peas, on tip-toe for a flight:
> With wings of gentle flush o'er delicate white,
> And taper fingers catching at all things,
> To bind them all about with tiny rings. (49-60)

Like Bernini's Daphne the sweet peas seem to be at some intermediate stage between plant and woman, and Keats, like Bernini, has evoked them with a beauty which is tinged with an element of the grotesque – a combination which he achieved most triumphantly when describing

Lamia's repulsive allure. The idea of the fingers catching at all things and then being bound implies their vulnerability and helplessness. But even if this is only a chance affinity, perhaps explained by a shared immersion in the strange atmosphere of the *Metamorphoses*, Keats' familiarity with Ovid's version of the story is incontrovertible.

It is easy to see how the story of Apollo and Daphne, in which a god pursues a reluctant nymph, might be said to have a loose generic connection with the figures which adorn Keats' urn. But a closer examination allows us to extend this general similarity, suggesting that the notion of metamorphosis, and particularly the kind of transformation which Daphne undergoes, is a significant undercurrent in the poem. The absent presence of this well known tale can be seen as an intertext in the fullest sense of the word; it fills in gaps in our understanding of the ode lending it a greater coherence. The problematic features of the ode identified above, the endlessly debated last lines and the uneasy mixture of registers, seem less puzzling once the poem is placed in its Ovidian context.

Through wordplay Keats invokes the idea of immortality so as to remind the reader that there are different ways of achieving this state. The first lines of the poem address the urn yet also look forward to the details of its subject matter. The description 'still unravished' is of course ambiguous. Although at first reading the word 'still' is most likely to be read as meaning 'motionless' the context of the whole poem allows the alternative 'yet' to emerge, through association with the fleeing maidens. The ode goes on to tell us slightly more about what might be depicted on the urn and, at the same time, alerts us to one of the conventional preoccupations of ecphrasis – the difference between written and artistic descriptions – by suggesting the speaker finds visual narratives more effective:

> Sylvan historian, who canst thus express
>   A flowery tale more sweetly than our rhyme:
> What leaf-fringed legend haunts about thy shape
>   Of deities or mortals, or of both ...

These lines contain two analogous collocations, 'flowery tale' and 'leaf-fringed legend'. The close proximity of two such similar phrases within the context of an expression of the differences between artistic and literary narratives is suggestive. Does a 'flowery tale' emphasise the language in which it is written and refer to high-flown vocabulary? Or does it, as seems more likely, instead emphasise the way the story is depicted through an illustration and refer perhaps to a decorative border of flowers? Or might it allude to the actual subject matter of the tale and imply that it is actually about flowers? The first possibility does not work with the phrase 'leaf-fringed legend' but there is still an

145

ambiguity as to whether the story, or only its depiction, is leaf-fringed. If we are being encouraged to imagine that the urn depicts a story where a leafy tree plays an important role, the legend of Apollo and Daphne would clearly be a strong contender in an uncompetitive field. The word 'legend' may of course refer to a written inscription as well as to a myth. The use of phrases which refer equally well to the urn's surface or to the actual content of the stories it depicts, 'still unravished', 'leaf fringed legend' and 'flowery tale', supports the notion that Keats might have been thinking about a tale which, because it deals with ways of evading death, may be linked with the imperishable urn. We may also be reminded of similar ambiguities in both Busirane's and Arachne's tapestries; both Ovid and Spenser fuse the web's fabric with its subject.

The poignancy of the poem's central image, the lover who can never kiss, but also never fade, is appropriate to the stasis of metamorphosis as well as art. If the tale of Apollo and Daphne is a subtext in this poem then the youth beneath the trees who cannot leave his song and the lover who can never reach his goal might both be the same figure:

> Ah, happy, happy boughs! that cannot shed
>   Your leaves, nor ever bid the spring adieu;
> And, happy melodist, unwearied,
>   For ever piping songs for ever new;
> More happy love! more happy, happy love!
>   For ever warm and still to be enjoy'd,
> For ever panting, and for ever young ...

The three apparently discrete exclamations may all be linked to this one tale. Although 'panting' is the kind of word which Keats would have used without being prompted, its use here might recall Sandys' description of Daphne; Apollo 'feels her heart within the bark to pant' (p. 13). Jack (p. 184) notes that Keats unusually associates Apollo with a pipe instead of his more traditional attribute, the lyre, in *Endymion*:

> A crowd of shepherds with as sunburnt looks
> As may be read of in Arcadian books;
> Such as sat listening round Apollo's pipe ... (I, 139-41)

But the possibility that the similar story of Syrinx, who was changed into reeds which in turn became Pan pipes, may share a place on the urn with Daphne should not be overlooked.

The fact that the tree is carved rather than real would account for its never being bare. But as a laurel Daphne too will never lose her leaves and Apollo, being a god, is no more susceptible to change than a carving. An evergreen tree and an immortal god are among the few things that share the permanence of art. In fact, the metamorphosis of Daphne gives her a double immortality. The laurel retains its leaves all year and, as is the case even with metamorphoses into more fragile plants, every laurel will henceforth be in some sense identical with Daphne. This idea of perpetual youth is articulated by Ovid's Apollo:

> And, as our uncut hair no change receives;
> So ever flourish with unfading leaves. (Sandys, p. 13).

Another significant reminder of Apollo's perpetual youth occurs in a poem which has been associated with Keats' own work but not with the 'Ode on a Grecian Urn'. This poem is Henry Hart Milman's 'The Belvidere Apollo' which, like the 'Ode on a Grecian Urn', was published in the *Annals of Fine Arts*. Although the Ode was published in a slightly earlier volume Milman's poem may have been known to Keats before its publication in the Annals as it was written earlier, and won an Oxford prize in 1812. Apollo's immortality is emphasised in the lines:

> The heavenly archer stands – no human birth,
> No perishable denizen of earth;
> Youth blooms immortal in his beardless face,
> A god in strength, with more than godlike grace ... (Milman, pp. 218-19)

We saw earlier how the phrases 'leaf fringed legend' and 'flowery tale' could refer equally well to the story itself or to the manner of its representation. Keats' use of these ambiguous phrases is consistent with the presence of this particular metamorphic subtext which allows the poem to offer two variations on the idea of an object being unchanging, perpetually on the brink of the climactic action – the transformation of Daphne which enables her to elude Apollo or the fixed representation of this or any other tale as a work of art. Keats would seem to have shared Ovid's playful enjoyment of exploiting the problems of writing a poem about a work of art, a representation of something which is itself a representation. Hazlitt shows his sense of the legend's 'just missed' quality when he uses it to illustrate his rather barbed description of Coleridge in *The Spirit of the Age*:

> He pursues knowledge as a mistress, with outstretched hands and winged speed; but as he is about to embrace her, his Daphne turns – alas! not to a laurel! (Howe, xi, p. 29)

It is worth noting that both Sandys and Keats rhyme 'kiss' with 'bliss'.

> Bold lover, never, never canst thou kiss,
> Though winning near the goal – yet, do not grieve;
> She cannot fade, though thou hast not thy bliss ...
>
> He sees her eyes, two stars! her lips which kiss
> Their happy selves, and longs to taste their bliss ... (Sandys, p. 11).

Sandys' own annotations also have a possible significance for Keats' reception of the tale:

> The laurel, by reason of her native heat, is ever young and flourishing: here fained such by the gift of Apollo, in imitation of his eternal youth, and unshorn tresses: attributed to the sun, in the rising and setting he is ever the same, his fair hair no other then his long and beautiful beams. (Sandys, p. 36).

Sandys emphasises and explicitly connects the different types of immortality achieved by the god and the nymph. The poetic instinct of Ovid's translator perhaps explains the hint of a symmetry between the expressions of each one's permanence: 'ever young', 'ever the same'. The same kind of repetition, in an intensified form, is used by Keats in the first four lines of Stanza III. Tooke's analysis of the legend in his *Pantheon*, a book Keats knew, is also significant as it emphasises the laurel's cool neutrality – another feature which serves to connect her metamorphic immortality with the urn's artistic immortality.

> She was changed into a laurel, the most chaste of trees; which is never corrupted with the violence of heat or cold, but remains always flourishing, always pure. (Tooke, p. 39)

The charm of Keats' evocation of an image perpetually arrested is ambivalent. His wistful admiration is partly tempered in the final stanza which suggests the possible sterility of such an unchanging image. Again, Milman's poem provides an interesting comparison:

> All, all divine – no struggling muscle glows,
> Through heaving vein no mantling life-blood flows,
> But animate with deity alone,
> In deathless glory lives the breathing stone.

We may find a similar evocation of Apollo's coldness if we jump forward to Alice Fulton's contribution to *After Ovid*, 'Daphne and Apollo':

> the classical glance of him
> visible for an instant as he
> ripples between stills, trying to settle
> into his perfection like a nest,
> trying to light,
> to don his marble artifice, flare into
> his precise foreverness. (p. 40)

Fulton perhaps recalls the way so many sculptors (including Bernini) have captured the dispassionate god in cool marble.

Keats' – and our – ambivalent response to the static urn is shared by the reader of Ovid; his metamorphoses are often the best available solution yet are rarely ideally satisfactory. A comparison between Hazlitt's account of Greek statuary in *On Poetry in General* and his reflections on metamorphosis reveals interesting parallels which perhaps reflect a similar association on the part of Keats.

> Greek statues are little else than specious forms. They are marble to the touch and to the heart. They have not an informing principle within them. In their faultless excellence they appear sufficient to themselves. By their beauty they are raised above the frailties of passion or suffering. By their beauty they are deified. But they are not objects of religious faith to us, and their forms are a reproach to common humanity. They seem to have no sympathy with us, and not to want our admiration. (Howe, v, p. 11)

The following extract from *On Personal Identity* reveals his similarly ambivalent attitude towards metamorphosis, and, although it is a pairing which never seems to be absent for long from the productions of this circle of writers, the reference to truth and beauty is interesting:

> It is an instance of the truth and beauty of ancient mythology, that the various transmutations it recounts are never voluntary, or of favourable omen, but are interposed as a timely release to those who, driven on by fate, and urged to the last extremity of fear or anguish, are turned into a flower, a plant, an animal, a star, a precious stone, or into some object that may inspire pity or mitigate our regret for their misfortunes. Narcissus was transformed into a flower; Daphne into a laurel; Arethusa into a fountain (by the favour of the gods) – but not till no other remedy was left for their despair. It is a sort of smiling cheat upon death, and graceful compromise with annihilation. It is better to exist by proxy, in some softened type and soothing allegory, than not at all – to breathe in a flower or shine in a constellation, than to be utterly forgot; but no one would change his natural condition (if he could help it) for that of a bird, an insect, a beast, or a fish, however delightful their mode of existence, or however enviable he might deem their lot compared to his own. Their thoughts are not our thoughts – their happiness is not our happiness; nor can we enter into it except with a passing smile of approbation, or as a refinement of fancy. (Howe, xvii, pp. 265-6)[2]

An allusion to Syrinx in 'I stood tip toe upon a little hill' echoes Hazlitt's sense of metamorphosis as a sweet but melancholy fate:

> Telling us how fair trembling Syrinx fled
> Arcadian Pan, with such a fearful dread.
> Poor nymph, – poor Pan, – how he did weep to find

---

[2]This essay was not published until 1828. However it is possible that similar ideas had formed part of his conversations with Keats. There is an interesting affinity between this passage and the opening stanza of 'Ode to a Nightingale', ' 'Tis not through envy of thy happy lot,/ But being too happy in thine happiness' (5-6).

Naught but a lovely sighing of the wind
Along the weedy stream; a half-heard strain
Full of sweet desolation, – balmy pain. (157-62)

The oxymoronic pairings of line 162 anticipate the poet's conflicting feelings about the urn. And in the elusive 'half-heard strain' we might recall the unheard melodies of the urn's piper. It is perhaps significant that Milman's poem ends with an account of a maiden who fell in love with the statue of Apollo and is beguiled by imagined music:

Oft breathless listening heard, or seemed to hear,
A voice of music melt upon her ear.

The teasing indeterminacy of 'or seemed to hear' is typically Ovidian – compare for example the comparison between Phaethon and a falling star (II 322).[3] The maid's eventual decline and death 'herself benumbed to stone' suggests that Milman and Keats share the same doubts about the efficacy of art as a source of solace.

In the first line of the Ode's final stanza we have a more prominent example of Keats' predilection for wordplay, just hinted at in the poem's opening line:

O Attic shape! Fair attitude! with brede
  Of marble men and maidens overwrought,
With forest branches and the trodden weed ...

The chiming effect of the pairing 'Attic/attitude' has been viewed with disfavour by, among others, William Empson who says that the line is 'very bad ... the half pun suggesting a false Greek derivation and jammed up against an arty bit of Old English seems .. affected and ugly' (Empson, p. 374) and the possibility of reading both 'brede' and 'over-wrought' as puns is intensified by their contiguity. This playfulness might be seen as jarring when contrasted with the apparently 'serious' content of the poem. But the incongruity, even indecorum, is itself very Ovidian. As we have seen, the *Metamorphoses* seems calculated to overturn generic expectancy; tales of erotic dalliance are freely mixed in with retellings of some the most revered ancient epics and even a discourse on Pythagorean philosophy. These qualities are apparent even within the account of Apollo and Daphne. The god's heroic con-quest over the terrible Python is swiftly followed by a fatal dart from one of Cupid's arrows and epic is transformed into elegy as he becomes smitten with passion for the virginal nymph. Even within the brief narrative of Apollo's pursuit the tone is not consistent, and the gulf

---

[3] But also compare Virgil's memorable description of Aeneas' glimpse of Dido's ghost: 'Doubtful as he who sees through dusky night,/ Or thinks he sees the moon's uncertain light' (Dryden, VI 614-15).

between the two participants' experience of the chase, discussed in Chapter 1, seems to have translated itself into a similarly troubling mixture of registers in both Bernini's and Keats' reinventions of the myth. The criticisms of Bernini voiced by John Moore (see above, pp. 15-16) could be made of Ovid himself, and in spirit they resemble unfavourable criticisms of the ode such as the remarks of Empson. The sculptor whom Hazlitt called a coxcomb (Howe, xvi, p. 300) and the poem whose final stanza incurs disapproval because of its puns would seem to have something in common. Ovid, too, has been accused of affectation, even by his contemporaries who, like Garth and Dryden, condemned his witty turns. The following translation of an anecdote told by the elder Seneca in his *Controversiae* exemplifies this quality in his poetry:

> Once, when he was asked by his friends to suppress three of his lines, he asked in return to be allowed to make an exception of three over which they should have no rights. This seemed a fair condition. They wrote in private the lines they wanted removed, while he wrote the ones he wanted saved. The sheets of both contained the same verses. Albinovanus Pedo, who was among those present, tells that the first of them was:
>
> 'Half-bull man and half-man bull,'
>
> the second
>
> 'Freezing north wind and de-freezing south.'
>
> It is clear from this that the great man lacked not the judgement but the will to restrain the licence of his poetry. He used sometimes to say that a face is the more beautiful for some mole. (Seneca, *Controversiae*, i, p. 265)

One feels that John Moore and William Empson might not have been on Ovid's side of this debate.

This sense of an affinity between the two poets is heightened by yet another possible echo of Daphne. In the manuscript of this poem the lines are punctuated quite differently from in standard modern texts. As the manuscript, although not in Keats' hand but his brother George's, represents the closest approximation to Keats' original intentions that we possess, the fact that a comma is placed after 'maidens' but not after 'overwrought' is significant:

> O Attic shape! Fair attitude! with brede
>   Of marble men and maidens, overwrought
> With forest branches and the trodden weed (Gittings, p. 49)

The more familiar punctuation of modern editions suggests that the brede contains two separate things, marble men and maidens and forest branches and weeds. Although this interpretation is not ruled out by the

MS version there is a much stronger possibility of reading the words 'overwrought/ With forest branches and the trodden weed' as standing in apposition to the men and maidens. Thus a hint at metamorphosis is allowed to emerge and the pun on 'overwrought' becomes particularly effective; it is perhaps fanciful to suppose that Keats had Daphne consciously in mind when penning these lines, but the double-edged adjective would certainly convey the simultaneity of Daphne's fear and her metamorphosis very successfully.

A discussion of this poem which omitted any mention of the final couplet might be considered incomplete. Keats' reproachful conclusion, beginning 'Cold pastoral', is clearly a continuation of his direct address to the urn. Yet the emphasis on immortality perhaps invokes those other ways of cheating death which have already been identified, metamorphosis and godhead. The latter is the most relevant to these lines:

> When old age shall this generation waste,
>   Thou shalt remain, in midst of other woe
> Than ours, a friend to man, to whom thou say'st,
>   'Beauty is truth, truth beauty' – that is all
>   Ye know on earth, and all ye need to know.

Keats is clearly drawing on the classical tradition of ecphrastic poems in which the object described speaks, yet perhaps the urn's is not the only voice heard in these last lines.

Gods, like urns, survive generations of men; they are also more obviously the friends of man than works of art. Assuming that the last two lines are spoken by a single voice, with the quotation marks simply indicating an aphorism, the idea of a shadowy divine figure, perhaps Apollo, not displacing the urn so much as speaking in unison with it, seems perfectly appropriate. Of course the friendship of any classical god for Mankind is rarely straightforward. The sense of superiority and inflexibility suggested by the last two lines seems fitting when we remember Apollo's ruthless flaying of Marsyas and his unpitying slaughter of all Niobe's children. Neither victim was guilty of anything worse than presumption. This idea of divine detachment makes the words 'on earth', which could be seen as redundant for any but metrical purposes, suddenly acquire a more specific meaning, reminding us of the gods' dispassionate elevation in the heavens as they look down on Mankind. Milman's description of Apollo as 'no perishable denizen of earth' helps to suggest why these final lines of the ode might be spoken by a god as easily as an urn.

Yeats' poem, 'Leda and the Swan' provides another analogue for Keats' apparent sense of the gulf between men and gods; the distance between Leda and her ravisher is rendered more terrifyingly absolute by the fact that, as a god who is also a swan, he is doubly alien. Ovid's account of the metamorphosis of Daphne contains nothing quite so chilling as the final lines of Yeats' poem:

> Did she put on his knowledge with his power
> Before the indifferent beak could let her drop? (p. 215)

Yet there is something essentially disquieting about Apollo's response to the nymph's transformation. His calm detachment indicates the gap between gods and mortals:

> Although thou canst not be
> The wife I wished, yet shalt thou be my tree,
> Our quiver, harp, our tresses never shorn,
> My laurel, thou shalt ever more adorn. (Sandys, p. 13)

Returning finally to the Ode's most quoted lines I would suggest that an Apollonian speaker renders their portentous vacuity comprehensible. In Allott's summary of various critics' opinions of the lines she defines Eliot's judgement as 'meaningless and therefore a blemish'. I would agree that they are meaningless but not that they are a blemish. They constitute a fitting conclusion to a poem which deals, at least in part, with the terrible inhumanity of divinity, the same inhumanity which, as we have seen, troubled so many other English Ovidians.

I suggested earlier that poetry might provide a final, fourth way of attaining immortality. The urn does not exist outside the words of the ode; its indestructible beauty is the gift of a literary rather than a visual artist. The *Metamorphoses*, like the ode, is concerned with the idea of intransience. If Keats did indeed make this identification between the possible immortality of his poem and the permanence of its subject matter he might have been inspired by the more forthright connection implied in the final lines of Ovid's masterpiece which suggest that the poet, like Augustus or Romulus, will undergo apotheosis into an immortal by virtue of his art:

> And now the work is ended, which, Jove's rage,
> Nor fire, nor sword shall raze, nor eating age.
> Come when it will my death's uncertain hour,
> Which of this body only hath a power:
> Yet shall my better part transcend the sky,
> And my immortal name shall never die.
> For, where-so-ere the Roman eagles spread
> Their conquering wings, I shall of all be read:
> And, if we poets true presages give,
> I, in my fame eternally shall live. (Sandys, p. 510)

9

Embedded Ovidianism: Beddoes' 'Pygmalion' and Browning's *The Ring and the Book*

Ovid's proud boast of his own poetic immortality, quoted at the end of the previous chapter, might seem to have been placed at the least appropriate place in this study. Ovid's reputation is generally perceived as having reached its nadir in the Victorian period. Norman Vance opens his essay 'Ovid in the nineteenth century' with a quotation from Hermann Fraenkel, who asserts that 'it was only in the nineteenth century that Ovid's prestige fell as low as it stands today' (Vance, p. 215). Vance does not take issue with this position very strenuously, although he does discuss various examples of poets, notably Swinburne, who owe a debt to the *Metamorphoses*. I wish to suggest that the Ovidian 'line' does not almost die out in the nineteenth century, only re-emerging with the birth of Modernism. But it does appear to be true that the Victorian reception of Ovid was characterised by a particular sort of unease.

The second half of this chapter is devoted to *The Ring and the Book*, a major work by one of the century's most celebrated poets and testimony to the fact that Ovidianism – even Ovid – continued to be a vital force within the Victorian mainstream. 'Pygmalion', on the other hand, is a little known work by a comparatively obscure poet, Thomas Lovell Beddoes. Although his was not a greatly influential voice, 'Pygmalion' repays attention, partly because of its intrinsic interest as a rare nugget of thoroughgoing nineteenth-century Ovidianism, partly because its treatment of the myth provides a missing link between Dryden's subtly skewed translation and a whole range of more decidedly disturbing responses to the story in twentieth-century literature. Beddoes and Browning exemplify two different aspects of embedded Ovidianism. In 'Pygmalion' we see that even the most apparently clearcut 'allusions' to the *Metamorphoses* can be reconfigured in terms of intertextuality; in other words rather than adducing Ovid as Beddoes' source we might invoke those 'unnumbered sounds' that Keats describes in the sonnet quoted in Chapter 1:

and thousand others more
That distance of recognizance bereaves,
Make pleasing music, and not wild uproar.

Ovid is a more fraught intertext in *The Ring and the Book*, invoked rather as Milton invoked pagan motifs – to be snubbed. But Vance's observation that 'the poetry and the poet drifted apart in popular awareness' (p.216) is particularly true in the case of Browning's Ovid, for the *Metamorphoses* has insinuated its way into the poem, embedding itself in the text as a far more potent presence than Browning himself appears to have recognised.

We may safely assume that a nineteenth-century poet who attended Charterhouse (where he won the Latin theme prize in 1818) and Oxford, who made a study of Arabic and used a German/Greek dictionary as an aid to learning German, had at least a passing knowledge of the *Metamorphoses*. But Thomas Lovell Beddoes, Pound's 'prince of morticians', does not appear to have absorbed Ovid in the fashion of poets such as Shakespeare and Milton. His passion was for earlier English literature, and works such as *Death's Jest Book* caused him to be seen as a Neo-Elizabethan rather than a Romantic poet. So the fact that he composed 'Pygmalion', a poem as profoundly Ovidian as any considered hitherto, should perhaps be ascribed to his immersion in the works of his Renaissance predecessors rather than the *Metamorphoses* itself. An examination of 'Pygmalion' reveals that Ovidianism by this time had become an almost autonomous phenomenon, no longer dependent upon a first hand knowledge of his work. (Although I assume Beddoes knew Ovid, I don't believe he *needed* to have read him in order to have written 'Pygmalion'. The story would, presumably, have been sufficiently well known for Beddoes to have read it in a summary elsewhere or derived it from a conversation.) As an imitation of the *Metamorphoses* 'Pygmalion' is striking, even more so perhaps if we consider that it may be an imitation (at least in part) at several removes.

The divergences from Ovid seem, at first reading, to be so substantial as to suggest that Beddoes, after being initially spurred on by the suggestive possibilities of the tale, abandoned *Metamorphoses* X as his source. Yet, as with *The House of Fame*, these ostensible departures from Ovid paradoxically draw him closer to the original. Ovidian features, only adumbrated in Book X, are strongly visible in Beddoes' poem, making it a distillation of certain facets of the *Metamorphoses* as a whole rather than a loose retelling of a single tale. One of the *Metamorphoses*' most pervasive preoccupations is with the unstable nature of all the apparently fixed boundaries which divide different orders of creation from one another, and the ease with which such

156

boundaries may be collapsed. The opening section of Beddoes' poem is a compelling attestation to his own fascination with this topic.

The focus of the description of Cyprus is constantly shifting; artefact and natural object merge into one another in a series of elisions which provide a fitting backdrop for the story of a statue who becomes a woman. The lack of any specific source in the *Metamorphoses* for this ecphrasis should perhaps heighten rather than diminish our sense of Beddoes' responsiveness to Ovid, suggesting as it does that Beddoes was suffused with the patterns of Ovidian and neo-Ovidian ecphrasis. Simply reproducing an original, it could be argued, does not signal the same depth of engagement as does an accomplished variation on a recurring theme. It might be indebted to a number of analogous moments in the *Metamorphoses* such as the description of Diana's grotto (III 155-62) and the doors of the Palace of the Sun (II 1-30) as well as passages from the work of earlier English Ovidians, such as Spenser's account of the Bower of Bliss or the opening of 'Upon Appleton House':

> There stood a city along Cyprus' side
> Lavish of palaces, an arched tide
> Of unrolled rocks; and, where the deities dwelled,
> Their clustered domes pushed up the noon, and swelled
> With the emotion of the god within,
> As doth earth's hemisphere, when showers begin
> To tickle the still spirit at its core,
> Till pastures tremble and the river-shore
> Squeezes out buds at every dewy pore. (Beddoes, vol. I, 1-9)

The phrase 'arched tide' aligns architecture with nature, merging the coastal buildings with the sea, and the description goes on to deconstruct further the divide between animate and inanimate, art and nature. The swelling of the domes is presented as a natural process – we are perhaps put in mind of some strange crop of mushrooms, and this hint at organic form is strengthened when Beddoes aligns the structures with burgeoning life more generally. The somatic vigour of the trembling and perspiring earth suggests sexual as well as simply vegetable generation. The parturient force of Earth's involvement with the creation of animals in Book VII of *Paradise Lost*, itself perhaps inspired by Ovid's account of the men who sprang up from dragons' teeth (III 104-14), might be adduced as a parallel:

> The earth obeyed, and straight
> Opening her fertile womb teemed at a birth
> Innumerous living creatures, perfect forms,
> Limbed and full grown: ...
> The grassy clods now calved, now half appeared
> The tawny lion, pawing to get free
> His hinder parts, ...

157

> the swift stag from underground
> Bore up his branching head: scarce from his mould
> Behemoth biggest born of earth upheaved
> His vastness: fleeced the flocks and bleating rose,
> As plants ... (VII 453-73)

And Pope's *The Temple of Fame* is another possible intertext:

> There might you see the lengthening spires ascend,
> The domes swell up, the widening arches bend,
> The growing towers like exhalations rise,
> And the huge columns heave into the skies. (89-92)

Beddoes' occlusion of the differences between various methods of generation, including, of course, artistic creation, may be seen in his allusion to the birth of Venus a little later in the poem:

> Cyprus's city-crown and capital
> Ere Paphos was, and at whose ocean-wall
> Beauty and love's paternal waves do beat
> That sprouted Venus ... (31-4)

We are reminded that the statue's nominal animator herself had a rather peculiar genesis – according to Hesiod Aphrodite (Venus) sprang from the severed parts of the god Uranus after he was castrated by his son Cronus.

Beddoes' description continues to evade definitive interpretation:

> And there were pillars, from some mountain's heart,
> Thronging beneath a wide, imperial floor
> That bent with riches; and there stood apart
> A palace, oft accompanied by trees,
> That laid their shadows in the galleries
> Under the coming of the endless light,
> Net-like ... (10-16)

The pillars, we assume, have been quarried from the mountain and incorporated into the structure of the palace. Yet as Beddoes says that they are beneath a floor rather than upon one, it may be that these pillars are only metaphorical and are in fact still within the mountain, helping to form the palace's foundations. This awareness of a latent, alternative state, already potentially present in a being or object is, as we have already seen, a hallmark of the *Metamorphoses*. Marvell's pun on 'imbark' is a pertinent example, and a reminder that Beddoes' 'Ovidianism' was probably not derived exclusively from Ovid.

The reference to the palace 'oft accompanied by trees', as though they were not always present, is curious; the shadows cast by these trees have an almost physical impact, being 'laid' rather than simply 'cast' and becoming tangible, 'net-like', an epithet which is made more emphatic by its isolated position at the opening of the line. This presentation is appropriate in a poem where, as we shall see, the *limen* between shadow and substance is more than usually unstable.

The palace contains a number of statues, described so as to foreshadow the central incident in the story:

> There stood, and sate, or made rough steeds their throne,
> Immortal generations wrung from stone,
> Alike too beautiful for life and death,
> And bodies that a soul of mortal breath
> Would be the dross of. (25-9)

The idea of being wrung from stone suggests that the statues possess a yielding, organic quality which, in conjunction with the next lines, creates an effect of tremulous poignancy rather than solidity. The next line and a half, almost Shakespearean in manner, are lovely but ambiguous. Their literal meaning alone contributes to the statues' apparent 'life' in that Beddoes says that human souls are as dross to them – an extraordinary assertion in that the word 'dross' suggest heaviness, inertia and indeed everything which we would generally ascribe to statues, not to human beings. The slightly convoluted nature of the statement may make it difficult to deduce what is being said straight away, but even on the most immediate and instinctive level Beddoes' poetry manages to involve humanity and stone statues together in preparation for the tale's climax.

The character of Pygmalion is now introduced:

> Whose fiery chisel with creation fed
> The shipwrecked rocks; who paid the heavens again
> Diamonds for ice; who made gods who make men. (37-9)

In his use of this supremely Ovidian trope (the association of artists with gods) Beddoes, yet again, is made to seem more Ovidian through departing from the Pygmalion story as it is told in the *Metamorphoses*. These lines are more particularly reminiscent of Mulciber or Arachne (for their artistry is described in a way which echoes the opening description of the creation) than Pygmalion, whose godlike qualities are only implicit in Ovid. The cumulative effect of having read the account of the creation, and then noted its affinities with both Mulciber's and Arachne's artistry, would encourage the reader of the *Metamorphoses* who had arrived at Book X to pick up on this subtext in the Pygmalion story without Ovid having to spell it out. In effect, Beddoes has recreated the experience of reading Ovid's Pygmalion in context by incorporating a theme which is diffused throughout the *Metamorphoses*.

The rocks from which Pygmalion carves his statues are made to seem less static and monolithic through being described as shipwrecks, reminding us that, for all their apparent permanence, they are not immobile. The meaning of the statement that Pygmalion 'paid the heavens again/ Diamonds for ice' is elusive yet it contributes to the general slipperiness of the divide between hard and soft, transient and permanent in the poem.

As Beddoes begins to describe Pygmalion's progress through the streets, one of the poem's most distinctive concepts, the idea of the mind having a physical reality, even independent of the thinker, finds its first expression. This emphasis on the power of the mind is intimately connected with Pygmalion's ability to bring Galatea to life and distinguishes Beddoes' conception of this miracle from Ovid's; he had stressed the power of artistry rather than simply intellect. Human intellect is perhaps a potentially more destructive force than artistic genius. Beddoes would have been forcibly impressed with this fact had he read the recently published *Frankenstein*, and his reception of Pygmalion might well have been affected by Mary Shelley's powerful story of a very different creator of life. Even before he has carved his Galatea, Pygmalion's genius seems to trouble rather than impress his countrymen. The crowds sense the force of Pygmalion's 'thinking breast' and

> left a place,
> A sun-room for him, that his mind had space
> And none went near; none in his sweep would venture ... (44-6)

Pygmalion's mind seems to require a physical space, outside his body, in which to operate; a little later the sculptor is described as 'walking his thoughts' (58).

Another important distinction between Beddoes' and Ovid's Pygmalions is that whereas the latter's distaste for his countrywomen is made to seem sympathetic because it follows an account of the prostitute Propoetides who were turned to stone, the former's rejection of the girls of Cyprus, who are described in tender and languishing terms, might strike the reader as unreasonable. We are given no hint that the women are depraved or unworthy, and they look on Pygmalion with respect:

> As he went along
> The chambered ladies silenced the half-song,
> And let the wheel unheeded whirl and skim,
> To get their eyes blest by the sight of him.
> So locks were swept from every eye that drew

Sun for the soul through circles violet-blue,
Mild brown, or passionate black.

                    Still, discontent,
Over his sensual kind the sculptor went,
Walking his thoughts. Yet Cyprus' girls be fair;
Day-bright and evening-soft the maidens are,
And witching like the midnight, and their pleasure
Silent and deep as midnight's starry treasure.
Lovely and young, Pygmalion yet loved none.
His soul was bright and lovely as the sun,
Like which he could create ... (50-65)

There is an ambiguity in the phrase 'over his sensual kind', for kind might be glossed 'nature' and thus refer to the sculptor himself rather than the women. (The idea of Pygmalion escaping from his own sexuality was also hinted at by Dryden.) Yet again Pygmalion's misogyny is potentially Narcissistic, for Beddoes emphasises the youthful beauty which makes his self-sufficiency particularly incongruous. Even the apparently positive comparison of the sculptor to the sun is undercut by the words 'like which he could create'.

The conception of Galatea is described as an epiphany and, not surprisingly in a poem where boundaries are so easily traversed, she seems more like a god than a created object:

Daytime and dark it came; like a dim mist
Shelt'ring a god, it rolled, and, ere he wist,
It fell aside, and dawned a shape of grace,
And an inspired and melancholy face,
Whose lips were smile-buds dewy: into him
It rolled like sun-light till his sight was dim,
And it was in his heart and soul again,
Not seen but breathed. (70-7)

The identification of Galatea and Pygmalion, the sense that she possesses him, acquires greater significance as the poem reaches its ambiguous climax.

Then follows an ecphrasis of place (78ff) similar to several in the *Metamorphoses*, in particular Narcissus' pool:

                    There was a grassy plain,
A pasture of the deer – Olympus' mountain
Was the plain's night, the picture of its fountain:
Unto which unfrequented dell and wood
Unwittingly his solitary mood
Oft drew him. In the water lay
A fragment of pale marble, which they say
Slipped from such fissure in the agued moon,
Which had caught earth-quake and a deadly swoon

161

When the sun touched her with his hilly shade ...
            ... How smooth the touch! It felt
Less porous than a lip which kisses melt,
And diamond-hard. (78-87, 95-7)

The mysterious aetiology which is provided for the fragment of marble
is a typically Ovidian motif, but the debt to Ovid must be perceived as
having been filtered through the mediating pens of (at least) Spenser,
(the enervating fountain in Book I which nearly defeats the Red Cross
Knight), Keats (the mysterious provenance of *Lamia*) and Shakespeare
(the little Western flower). The apostrophe to the stone is written within
a structure of language appropriate to rapture, yet a second reading
reveals that Pygmalion's criteria of excellence are unusual. The hard
immobility of marble is not generally compared favourably with the
human body although we might praise a sculptor for using the appar-
ently unrelenting medium of stone to evoke even the softness of skin.
The sculptor's character grows steadily more ambiguous, a process
which is carried further by the description of the marble as 'this
dripping quarry' (99). (Compare Maynwaring's use of the same pun.)
This piece of cleverness must be differentiated from the skilful fusion of
animate and inanimate in the opening lines of the poem because the
comparison of what will be Galatea with a dead deer is unpleasantly
disquieting, as though she, like Frankenstein's monster, were in some
way a reanimated corpse. In the *Metamorphoses* the objects of male lust
such as Daphne and Philomela are compared to a whole array of hunted
animals, and this analogue with legendary rape victims seems signifi-
cant as Beddoes makes considerably more of the potential for prurience
in this tale than Ovid did in his delicate version of what was originally
a far more salacious narrative. Pygmalion's creative urge is expressed
in explicitly sexual terms. He

            fed on sight of summer, till the life
Was too abundant in him; and so, rife
With light creative, he went in alone,
And poured it warm upon the growing stone.
The magic chisel thrust, and gashed, and swept,
Flying and manifold; no cloud e'er wept
So fast, so thick, so light upon the close
Of shapeless green it meant to make a rose ... (110-17)

Beddoes again identifies Pygmalion with a god in the following lines,
preceding the invocation to Venus:

            Who could help a sigh
At seeing a beauty stand so lifelessly
But that it was too beautiful to die?
Dealer of immortality,

Greater than Jove himself, for only he
Can such eternize as the grave has ta'en,
And open heaven by the gate of pain,
What art thou now, divine Pygmalion?
Divine! gods counting human. (134-42)

Although the sense is not immediately apparent, Beddoes appears to be saying that Pygmalion is greater than Jove because the god can only give immortality to people who have already died whereas Pygmalion can give immortality to those who have never lived. Yet these lines appear to contradict the description of Galatea as one who is 'too beautiful to die' for this suggests that she *is* alive.

Whereas Ovid goes to great pains to associate Galatea's miraculous transformation into a woman with Pygmalion's extraordinary artistic powers, Beddoes seems equally insistent that the statue is made almost in spite of the sculptor:

He carved it not; nor was the chisel's play,
That dashed the earthen hindrances away,
Driven and diverted by his muscle's sway.
The winged tool, as digging out a spell,
Followed a magnet wheresoe'er it fell,
That sucked and led it right: and for the rest,
The living form, with which the stone he blest,
Was the loved image stepping from his breast. (148-55)

The last line of this description harks back to the reference to Pygmalion's 'thinking breast' suggesting that Galatea has been fashioned from the sculptor's thoughts and thus implying that some part of him has been lost in order to create her. The curious verb 'sucked' perhaps suggests that his soul has been sucked out of him. His lack of volition in the actual act of creation, the impression of forces beyond his control, distinguishes Beddoes' Pygmalion from Ovid's more assertive artist. He appears to be in thrall to Galatea who is herself presented in a disturbingly negative way:

And therefore loves he it, and therefore stays
About the she-rock's feet, from hour to hour,
Anchored to her by his own heart ... (156-8)

At this point comes his prayer to Venus, which differs from its equivalent in the *Metamorphoses* in that it begins with a request that he may be spared death:

Goddess, that made me, save thy son, and save
The man, that made thee goddess, from the grave. (160-1)

The taut Ovidian chiasmus again makes curious reference to Pygmalion as a creator of gods. But despite the sculptor's apparent power he feels sure he will die without Venus' intervention. The agonized desperation of Pygmalion's speech has a Faustian intensity. He begs Venus to save him from the grave:

> Thou knowst it not; it is a fearful coop
> Dark, cold, and horrible – a blinded loop
> In Pluto's madhouse' green and wormy wall. (162-4)

He appears to share Faustus' vanity, 'Let me not die, like all;/ For I am but like one' (165-6), as well as his despair, 'My eyes are wet/ With the thick dregs of immature despair' (167-8). The earlier suggestion that Galatea's own vitality is vampirically dependent upon Pygmalion is upheld by the sculptor's depiction of himself as a mere husk of a man:

> With bitter blood out of my empty heart.
> I breathe not aught but my own sighs for air,
> And my life's strongest is a dying start.
> No sour grief there is to me unwed;
> I could not be more lifeless being dead. (169-73)

The last line in particular hints that he may in some sense be made of stone, and this stoniness may be perceived either as the result of Galatea having stolen away his vitality or as an inherent character defect, betrayed through his lack of sensibility to normal women and his lascivious attitude towards the statue. The strangeness of this passion is highlighted when he addresses her as 'my sweet rock, my only wife' (180) – we might recall 'Thou wall, O wall, O sweet and lovely wall' (*A Midsummer Night's Dream* V.i.172). As his speech progresses Pygmalion betrays the flaws in his character still further. His attitude towards his fellow human beings is coldly disdainful with unpleasantly eugenic overtones:

> Fool! I love the stone.
> Inspire her gods! oft ye have wasted life
> On the deformed, the hideous, and the vile ... (177-9)

The analogy with Faustus becomes yet more insistent:

> I do not ask it long: a little while,
> A year, a day, an hour, let it be!
> For that I'll give you my eternity.
> Or let it be a fiend, if ye will send
> Something, yon form to humanize and bend,
> Within those limbs – and, when the new-poured blood
> Flows in such veins, the worst must turn to good. (181-7)

It seems appropriate that Pygmalion should refer to Galatea in terms which recall the devil who impersonates Faustus' Helen, for the statue, like Marlowe's apparition, seems to have sucked forth his soul. Faustus, like Pygmalion earlier in the poem, uses the word dross in a way which might seem ironic or inappropriate, 'all is dross that is not Helena' (V.i.103). Clearly Ovid, whose presence was so strongly felt in the opening of *Pygmalion*, is not the only trace in this most intertextual of poems. Of course Marlowe and Ovid have their own intertextual relationship, and we may find in Faustus' Helen yet another figure of Galatea, suggesting that Marlowe anticipated the darkening of Pygmalion's story in later centuries. (Though perhaps *Dr Faustus* only becomes implicated in the reception of Pygmalion after Beddoes has fused the two narratives together.)

The same palindromic effect of woman:statue/statue:woman which Ovid achieved by following the tale of the Propoetides with that of Pygmalion is reproduced by Beddoes in an allusion to another petrified woman whose story is, of course, told at length in the *Metamorphoses*:

Twas Niobe thou drov'st from flesh to stone:
Shew this the hole she broke, and let her follow
The mother's track of steps and eyelid rain,
Treading them backwards into life again. (190-3)

Once again Beddoes has duplicated an Ovidian effect by following his source selectively. As Niobe's fate is far better known than that of the petrified prostitutes, Beddoes has only to allude to it to create the same kind of palindrome which Ovid achieved by narrating two tales back to back. The analogy with Ovid's use of language in the Narcissus episode of the *Metamorphoses* may of course be a chance connection yet, as we have already seen, the tale has a certain affinity with Beddoes's Pygmalion whose 'she-rock' seems even more closely connected with the artist's self than Ovid's statue with her creator. A few lines after his allusion to Niobe Pygmalion asks, 'Is there not gone/ My life into her which I pasture on?' (194-5). Furthermore, Beddoes' Pygmalion is, like Narcissus, or at least like the later reception of his legend, far more unpleasantly self-absorbed than Ovid's. His lust comes over still more strongly and disagreeably in his final address to the statue:

Live, thou dear marble, or I shall go wild.
I cover thee, my sweet; I leave thee there,
Behind this curtain, my delicious child ... (197-9)

Within the context of the sculptor's apparently rapacious desire the sexual meaning of 'cover' is inescapably present. The hint that the statue is his child provides yet another example of the way this poem has been enriched – even unconsciously or indirectly – by the *Metamor-*

phoses as a whole. The story of Pygmalion's incestuous descendants, Cinyras and Myrrha, reflects back uneasily on the sculptor's love for his own creation, and in Beddoes' version the link is further reinforced.

As Galatea gradually appears to come to life, the colour on her cheeks glows like a new dawn; conversely, Pygmalion's fire seems to be dying out. Yet again it seems as if the sculptor must, like Oscar Wilde's nightingale, pay a heavy price for the statue's rosy glow:

> There was a fleshy pink, a dimple wrought
> That trembled, and the cheek was growing human
> With the flushed distance of a rising thought,
> That still crept nearer – yet no further sign!
> And now, Pygmalion, that weak life of thine
> Shakes like a dewdrop in a broken rose,
> Or incense parting from the altar-glows. (207-13)

Ovid's palindrome seems to have been worked out in yet another new guise for Pygmalion is described as though death had made him turn to stone:

> His foot is stretching into Charon's barge.
> Upon the pavement ghastly is he lying,
> Cold with the last and stoniest embrace ... (217-19)

Yet at the very end of the poem he appears to have been given a reprieve:

> And then – O sight of joy and placid wonder!
> He lies, beside a fountain, on the knee
> Of the sweet woman-statue, quietly
> Weeping the tears of his felicity. (231-4)

Although commentators generally claim that Pygmalion dies at the moment of the statue's animation (Thompson, p. 99; Bush, p. 194), both these assumptions are doubtful. The ending is too oblique to allow of certain interpretation, but the sculptor is apparently weeping happily at the end of the poem. And although 'woman statue' may be a more pleasant term than 'she-rock' it does not signify a greater degree of humanity or animation, except perhaps in him who names her. The poem began by collapsing the boundaries between various types of creation, whether animal, vegetable, or mineral, yet seems to end by denying this possibility for change. We might ask whether it was not Pygmalion, rather than the statue, who needed to be turned from stone (of a sort) and become human. The final line 'weeping the tears of his felicity' certainly suggests a gentler, more human Pygmalion than the cavorting lecher, careless of his soul, who displayed himself so revealingly in his address to Venus. Ovid used the idea of a woman becoming stone as a warning against hard-heartedness in the tale of Anaxarete, and in Book II of *The Faerie Queene* Spenser makes the same connection in the aetiology of the stone fountain that will not allow its waters to be defiled by blood (II ii 9). Perhaps Beddoes is disguising a moral miracle under the guise of a more dramatic metamorphosis. He does, after all, describe whatever has happened at the poem's indeterminate ending as a 'placid wonder', suggestive of an interiorised and unmagical transformation. In the same way Hermione's 'animation' at the end of *The Winter's Tale* is only an illusion – the softening of Leontes' heart is the true metamorphosis.

Tracing the *Nachleben* of Pygmalion allows us to see Ovidianism as a complexly cumulative phenomenon. The doubts sown by Dryden are far more glaringly manifest in Beddoes' poem; the myth's tensions emerge still more strongly in the works of Joyce, and, as we shall see in the final chapter, the story continues to trouble today's imitators of Ovid.

*

In the poetry of Browning we can identify 'embedded' Ovidianism still more clearly than in Keats' 'Ode on a Grecian Urn' or Beddoes' 'Pygmalion'. Ovid is directly invoked in *The Ring and the Book*, but only in a way which seems to confirm the falling off of his reputation in the Victorian period. Far more indicative of Browning's true debt to Ovid – or at least to Ovidianism – are the poem's allusions to stories from the *Metamorphoses*, whether concealed or overt. As well as being inherently Ovidian, these allusions operate in a manner which is itself typical of the *Metamorphoses*, to call attention to the fictiveness of Browning's text and to hamper our efforts to interpret it 'correctly'.

The Ring and the Book is a long and complex poem in which Browning offers twelve different insights into a long forgotten Italian scandal. The perspectives of all the protagonists as well as various bystanders (these latter including the poet himself) are imaginatively reconstructed through a series of dramatic monologues. These combine to shape our view of events leading up to the murder of a young woman, Pompilia, as well as both her parents, by Pompilia's middle aged husband Count Guido Franceschini. As well as named individuals Browning includes monologues spoken by 'Half-Rome' and 'The Other Half-Rome'; these represent the adherents of Guido and Pompilia respectively. They are followed by 'Tertium Quid', a supposedly impartial voice. Each speaker gives his own version of the story; although no one seeks to deny the guilt of Guido, who is tried and executed for his crime, there is still plenty of room left for debate. The main uncertainties focus around the figure of Pompilia and the young priest, Caponsacchi, who attempted to rescue her from her miserable marriage. Whereas some assume the two were involved in an adulterous liaison, and thus excuse

Guido's actions, others, including Caponsacchi and the dying Pompilia, insist that the relationship was innocent, and that Guido attempted to engineer the 'elopement' for his own ends, even forging letters between the 'lovers'. Critical opinion has tended towards Pompilia's side, almost beatifying her in the process, although some dissenters have argued that, at the very least, she is not so artless as she appears. These questions or choices – although it is difficult to resist them – perhaps tend towards an inappropriate reification of the poem. This might seem to be a predictably 'modern' standpoint, yet we need not filter *The Ring and the Book* through the works of Derrida to arrive at such a conclusion – Ovid will do just as well.

The Ring and the Book might be said to typify the Victorian reception of the *Metamorphoses* in that 'Ovid' and 'Ovidianism' have become estranged. He is a surprisingly visible presence on the surface of the poem, confirming Norman Vance's assertion that the nineteenth century dismissed the poet as a frivolous degenerate. The dandified young priest, Caponsacchi, is a largely positive force in the poem, but his doubtful conduct in the Franceschini affair leads to his 'relegation', milder than exile but intended as a reprimand. Ovid too suffers *relegatio*, and Browning does not omit to point out the similarity (II 1220-1). Guido reinforces the affinity by describing the 'lovers' as:

A brisk priest who is versed in Ovid's art
More than his Summa, and a gamesome wife
Able to act Corinna without book ... (V 1357-9)

Yet the real importance of Ovid in *The Ring and the Book* belies Browning's evocation of the poet as a licentious trifler; the *Metamorphoses*, rather than the love poetry, is the poem's true Ovidian subtext. Here again I would take issue with Norman Vance (see above, p. 11) who suggests that the presence of interposing texts and pictures muddies the water of nineteenth-century Ovidianism. And in any case there is plenty in Browning to remind us that such 'distractions' were at work long before the Victorian period, and were certainly well underway by the time of the Franceschini affair. Browning describes the care taken by a possessive husband to shelter his wife from worldly knowledge by hiding Correggio's elegantly perverse 'Leda and the Swan' – one of a whole series of Ovidian canvasses by the artist – behind a curtain. The first gossiping monologues take place before Bernini's statue of the Triton, directly derived from *Metamorphoses* I:

Where the old Triton, at his fountain-sport,
Bernini's creature plated to the paps,
Puffs up steel sleet which breaks to diamond dust,
A spray of sparkles snorted from his conch ... (I 898-901)

The use of 'steel' and 'diamond' to evoke the contrast between a dense mass of water and the dispersed spray almost suggests that they are carved from these substances, when in fact real water is of course being dispensed; yet again metamorphosis slides into metaphor. Correggio and Bernini were just two of the mediating artists who would affect (as well as effect) Ovid's reception.

Browning describes his creation of *The Ring and the Book* out of the bare bones of his source in terms which might recall the Pygmalion myth, although the analogues which he explicitly mentions are Faust and Elisha:

> then write my name with Faust's!
> Oh, Faust, why Faust? Was not Elisha once? –
> Who bade them lay his staff on a corpse face.
> There was no voice, no hearing ...
> ... the flesh waxed warm ... (759-62,768)

But what [Browning] discovered was not that the facts could speak for themselves; he discovered that, like Michelangelo's David, they lay dead within their stony silence and could speak only after release into a living shape by a profoundly conscientious, imaginative craftsman willing thus to release them and let them have an autonomous life both in themselves and in the sensitized imaginative judgment of the individual viewing them. (Buckler, p. 12)

When he first buys his only source for the poem, the 'Old Yellow Book', it is:

> A book in shape but, really, pure crude fact
> Secreted from man's life when hearts beat hard,
> And brains, high-blooded, ticked two centuries since. (I 86-8)

Browning's fancy – the 'fiction which makes fact alive' (706) – is needed to animate the book's raw material, 'I fused my live soul and that inert stuff' (I 469):

> This that I mixed with truth, motions of mine
> That quickened, made the inertness malleolable
> O' the gold was not mine ... (I 701-3)

Browning refers to this process as 'mimic creation, galvanism for life' (I 740). The thrust of these passages is curiously to suggest that the truth requires an admixture of fiction in order to become animated. Although he muses 'Is fiction which makes fact alive, fact too' (I 705), such statements at the very least problematise our response to what follows.

The poem's heroine, as well as the poem itself, is a type of Galatea. This repetition reminds us that the one is as much a construct as the other – despite being an historical figure, in *The Ring and the Book* Pompilia is created by the language of all the men around her, and ultimately by Browning himself, author of her 'own' monologue. Most strikingly her husband (if we believe Pompilia's account) forges letters from her to Caponsacchi that his illiterate wife could never have written. Yet Guido is incapable of bringing Pompilia to life, and she adopts a statuesque stoniness as a defensive response to her intolerable position:

> Life means with me successful feigning death,
> Lying stone-like, eluding notice so … (VII 1004-5)

When the Franceschini's maid meets Caponsacchi, she tells him that 'my mistress is a stone' (VII 1108) and bids him 'leave the stone its cold' (1117). Guido describes her in the same way; she is 'cold and pale and mute as stone/ Strong as stone also' (XI 1311-12). In this context she is like a parody of the animated Galatea for her accedence to Guido's wishes is a function of stony indifference rather than womanly responsiveness:

> 'Speak!' she obeys, 'Be silent!' she obeys,
> As brood-bird when you saunter past her eggs.
> Departed, just the same through door and wall
> I see the same stone strength of white despair. (1319-22)

Here, as in Dryden's 'Pygmalion and the Statue', stoniness can be rebellious as well as passive:

> And blow redoubles blow, – his wife, the block.
> But, if a block, shall not she jar the hand
> That buffets her? (IX 406-8)

Not surprisingly it is the young priest who seems to emulate Pygmalion's miracle. When rebutting the very idea that she could be anything other than totally pure, Caponsacchi invokes Pompilia's resemblance, not to the virgin, but to one of Raphael's paintings of her – she is a *picta* as well as a *scripta puella*. Thus by extension her acknowledgement of his friendship takes on the quality of a Pygmalion-like miracle:

> Pictured Madonna raised her painted hand,
> Fixed the face Rafael bent above the Babe,
> On my face as I flung me at her feet … (VI 913-15)

But the emphasis on artifice detracts from our sense of her autonomy, for Caponsacchi seems to perceive her encouragement as a miracle shrouded in mystery rather than as a clue that his interest in her is reciprocated.

The Pygmalion myth is well calculated to draw attention to any text's artistry. Allusions to other Ovidian characters, used in subtle combinations, contribute to the same effect. By contrast with Ovid's use of real metamorphoses, Browning employs metamorphic imagery to obfuscate as well as clarify the characters of his protagonists, rather as Keats does in *Lamia*. Whereas Lycaon's transformation into a wolf is an unambiguous signal, matters are rarely so straightforward in *The Ring and the Book*:

> And trim the balance, and detect at least
> A touch of wolf in what showed whitest sheep,
> A cross of sheep redeeming the whole wolf ... (I 655-7)

Although these lines, referring to contemporary reactions to the case, appear to reflect Browning's scorn for the wavering populace, they also look forward to the poem's ambiguous subtleties. Line 656 is more apt than 657 – it is hard to find excuses for the thoroughly repulsive Guido, but misleading to exonerate completely the engaging Caponsacchi or even Pompilia, admirable though she (apparently) is. *The Ring and the Book* shares with the *Metamorphoses* a marked openness or readerliness, a susceptibility to differing interpretations. We tend to find our own prejudices and preferences reflected in these texts more clearly than either Browning's or Ovid's.

In Pompilia's own narrative she describes in veiled terms the horror of her marriage:

> When friends broke in, held up a torch and cried
> 'Why, you Pompilia in the cavern thus,
> How comes that arm of yours about a wolf?
> And the soft length, – lies in and out your feet
> And laps you round the knee, – a snake it is!' (VII 123-7)

The reference to her outstretched arm makes it possible to be wrong-footed by the opening of the next line, and think that 'soft length' is a further reference to her arm. 'Soft' suggests some pleasing object, rather than a serpent. Although ostensibly distancing Pompilia from the unpleasantness that surrounds her, these lines hint that she may be in some way implicated in the intrigue, not merely an innocent victim. The effect of this local ambiguity is matched by the more pervasive dubiety which emerges in the complex of Ovidian allusion surrounding Pompilia.

Pompilia manifests herself as several characters from the *Metamorphoses*. One of these is Daphne. The court responds leniently to her attempted elopement, recommending a change of scene:

> our best step to take with her,
> On her own showing, were to shift her root
> From the old cold shade and unhappy soil
> Into a generous ground that fronts the south ... (II 1188-91)

She is next figured as a tree in a peculiar passage which describes her parents as two walls circling a garden:

> Where a chance sliver, branchlet slipped from bole
> Of some tongue-leaved eye-figured Eden tree,
> Filched by two exiles and borne far away,
> Patiently glorifies their solitude ... (III 234-7)

It is Pompilia herself though who makes the link explicit, when describing how she and a childhood friend tried to trace resemblances between themselves and figures on a tapestry. Tisbe is like Diana, Pompilia Daphne:

> '– And there are you, Pompilia, such green leaves
> Flourishing out of your five finger-ends,
> And all the rest of you so brown and rough:
> Why is it you are turned a sort of tree?'
> You know the figures never were ourselves
> Though we nicknamed them so. (VII 193-8)

That Tisbe, although a child, can address her friend as though Pompilia really were Daphne, illustrates the ease with which we learn to speak metaphorically. The firmly stated, and apparently superfluous, reminder that the girls and the tapestry figures are not truly identical in a sense casts doubt on Browning's whole network of imagery and allusion. This is apparently a lesson which Caponsacchi has not mastered – to say that Pompilia is like a Raphael Madonna is to say that she really is both holy and a painting, as his rhetorical response to the suggestion that she might after all have written the overencouraging letters he received reveals:

> Learned Sir,
> I told you there's a picture in our church.
> Well, if a low-browed verger sidled up
> Bringing me, like a blotch, on his prod's point,
> A transfixed scorpion, let the reptile writhe,
> And then said, 'See a thing that Rafael made –
> The venom issued from Madonna's mouth!' –
> I should reply, 'Rather, the soul of you
> Has issued from your body, like from like,
> By way of the ordure-corner!' (VI 667-77)

The lawyer Bottinius offers a timely reminder of the pitfalls involved in putting faith in such a chance resemblance when he imagines the processes involved in painting the Holy Family:

> Is it a young and comely peasant-nurse
> That poseth? (be the phrase accorded me!)
> Each feminine delight of florid lip,
> Eyes brimming o'er and brow bowed down with love,
> Marmoreal neck and bosom uberous, –
> Glad on the paper in a trice they go
> To help his notion of the Mother-Maid ... (IX 49-55)

He explains that the initial studies taken from life require a further input of spirit, the artist's genius, in order to produce a masterpiece. This turns out to be the prelude to his comparison between Pompilia and a painting as part of his attempt to exonerate her:

> No more of proof, disproof, – such virtue was,
> Such vice was never in Pompilia, now!
> Far better say 'Behold Pompilia!' – (for
> I leave the family as unmanageable,
> And stick to just one portrait, but life-size) (IX 160-4)

As if his own earlier account of the disparity between appearance (Mary) and reality (peasant), and his consequent reminder that the artist rather than the subject creates a work of art, weren't enough to make this strategy dubious, he then invokes the example of Phryne, the Greek courtesan who won a lawsuit by revealing her breasts at the climax of the speech in her defence. The effect is doubly unsettling because Bottinius' account of the process of painting echoes Browning's own description of the poem's creation whereby the raw material is fused with genius and fancy. The complementary passages are mutually disruptive of the reader's attempts to navigate his way around the poem.

The allusions to Daphne, chaste and victimised, appear to work in Pompilia's favour. But Browning invites us to view the apparent affinity from another perspective. When Pompilia consults the Archbishop about her situation she begs to be allowed to embrace the life of a nun. He replies that the state of virginity, glorious in Mary, would have been a sin in Eve, destined to be the mother of mankind – our circumstances may make the same actions either vicious or virtuous:

> Had Eve, in answer to her Maker's speech
> 'Be fruitful, multiply, replenish earth'-
> Pouted 'But I choose rather to remain
> Single' – why, she had spared herself forthwith
> Further probation by the apple and snake,
> Been pushed straight out of Paradise! (VII 761-6)

Eve's damnable answer is of course the same as that given by Daphne to her own 'maker' Peneus when he bids her give him grandchildren. At the end of Pompilia's monologue her thoughts turn to Caponsacchi; it is clear to the reader if not to herself that her feelings for him are amorous, even though she firmly rejects the idea of marriage with him, knowing that as a priest this would be forbidden. The dangerous direction in which her thoughts are leading, towards a proscribed love, is suggested by the imagery she uses:

> He is ordained to call and I to come!
> Do not the dead wear flowers when dressed for God?
> Say, – I am all in flowers from head to foot!
> Say, – not one flower of all he said and did,
> Might seem to flit unnoticed, fade unknown,
> But dropped a seed has grown a balsam-tree
> Whereof the blossoming perfumes the place
> At this supreme of moments! (VII 1814-21)

The apparent arbitrariness of metamorphosis in Ovid, the fact that the deserving and the wicked meet similar fates, means that a subtle shift in Browning's allusive framework hints at a quite different Pompilia from the virginal Daphne figure. Despite being presented as a rapturous epiphany this allusion to metamorphosis into a balsam-tree is potentially disquieting, for it is possible to trace a resemblance between the image and Myrrha's fate. She, like Pompilia, is the victim of a forbidden (incestuous) love, and is transformed into a similarly fragrant and exotic plant. Balsam, like myrrh, is perceived to weep. This initially tenuous link is reinforced by Bottinius, who works on Pompilia's behalf not by exonerating her from sin but by excusing her misdemeanours as the inevitable result of feminine frailty. He tries to brush aside Pompilia's supposed licentiousness by indelicately suggesting that it doesn't really rob Guido of pleasure:

> These are no household-bread each stranger's bite
> Leaves by so much diminished for the mouth
> O' the master of the house at supper-time:
> But rather like a lump of spice they lie,
> Morsel of myrrh, which scents the neighbourhood
> Yet greets its lord no lighter by a grain. (IX 321-6)

The last line is unfortunate, for Pompilia would certainly be 'lighter' – i.e. more wanton – were she really to behave in this way. The possibility that Browning aligns her forbidden passion with that of Myrrha is strengthened when Guido envisages the fate that might befall her after death:

> Only, be sure, no punishment, no pain
> Childish, preposterous, impossible,

174

But some such fate as Ovid could foresee, -
Byblis in fluvium, let the weak soul end
In water, *sed Lycaon in lupum*, but
The strong become a wolf for evermore!
Change that Pompilia to a puny stream
Fit to reflect the daisies on its bank! (XI 2046-53)

Buckler apparently assumes that the metamorphoses are in complete
contrast: 'Let Pompilia become the daisied stream of the pastoral poets;
let him become the prehuman wolf unhindered by the human half into
which the wolfman has grown' (p. 277). But any reader of Ovid will see
that the stream and the wolf are more alike than they at first seem. It
is unlikely that Browning uses the example of Byblis – guilty of inces-
tuous love for her brother – gratuitously, when the association between
Lycaon and Guido is so carefully worked out through a whole series of
passages in *The Ring and the Book*. Had Browning – or rather Guido –
merely wanted to express a sense of her weakness he could have
adduced the example of Arethusa or Clymene, blameless nymphs who
underwent a similar metamorphosis. But Byblis provides a curious
mirror image of Lycaon, both guilty of *impietas*, although the former
(like Myrrha) is a pathetic as well as an erring figure whereas Lycaon
is merely savage.

In addition to the Eve/Daphne parallel noted earlier, there is a more
prominent example of a Christian and a Pagan legend being fused
together by Browning. The parallel narratives of St George and the
Dragon and Perseus and Andromeda have long been identified as
having special significance for Browning. The myth of Perseus was
familiar to the young Pompilia as it too was represented on the tapestry.
Although it is Caponsacchi who is primarily associated with the hero,
the first reference to him is confused in its application:

And when next day the cavalier who came
(Tisbe had told me that the slim young man
With wings at head, and wings at feet, and sword
Threatening a monster, in our tapestry,
Would eat a girl else, – was a cavalier)
When he proved Guido Franceschini ... (VII 389-94)

Through the vague common denominator 'cavalier', Perseus is tempo-
rarily aligned with Guido, at least until Pompilia realises that he is old
and ugly. The syntactical confusion within the parenthesis perhaps
makes this less anomalous, for once again the reader may find himself
wrongfooted. The words 'would eat a girl else', within the logic of
grammar if not of narrative, seem at first to apply to Perseus. Only
when we reach 'was a cavalier' do we realise that 'who' must be under-
stood, referring back to the monster. Considering the way Guido blights

175

Pompilia's life, eventually destroying her, the momentary misreading is rather appropriate. It might have seemed more logical to construct a firmer, more permanent set of analogies – Caponsacchi, Guido, Pompilia: Perseus, monster, Andromeda. But Browning consciously rejects such an easy option, with the result that the 'truth' about the characters and their actions continues to elude us. In Caponsacchi's account of events hero and victim appear to change places, with the priest, like Andromeda, 'pinioned fast' by Guido's friends, and Pompilia assuming the active role:

> She sprung at the sword that hung beside him, seized,
> Drew, brandished it, the sunrise burned for joy
> O' the blade (VI 1544-6)

More disturbing are hints of a link with yet another of Perseus' adventures:

> Guido's, this last husband's-act.
> He lifts her by the long dishevelled hair,
> Holds her away at arms' length with one hand ... (IV 1384-6)

> Had I enjoined 'Cut off the hair!' – why, snap
> The scissors, and at once a yard or so
> Had fluttered in black serpents to the floor ... (XI 1363-5)

Tertium Quid's account of her head being held at arm's length and Guido's own disgusted perception of her hair as serpents combine to associate her with Medusa and her husband with Perseus. These allusions therefore work against the more prominent Perseus subtext which casts Guido as the monster. Significantly, this is not the only example of Pompilia being cast simultaneously as both the beloved and the enemy of a single hero. We have already seen the links between her and Daphne. In Book II, while describing Caponsacchi's relationship with Pompilia, Browning refers to the encounter which immediately precedes this tale, Apollo's victory over the Python:

> there posed he
> Sending his god-glance after his shot shaft,
> Apollos turned Apollo, while the snake
> Pompilia writhed transfixed through all her spires. (II 792-5)

As the speaker is Half-Rome, one of Guido's adherents, we should not be surprised that he compares Pompilia here and elsewhere to a snake, and it is equally predictable that his opponent, The Other Half-Rome, counters by insulting Guido in the same way (III 696). It is however curious that the latter speaker uses a similar image of Pompilia when he gives his account of the climactic meeting at Castelnuovo:

Guilt motionless or writhing like a worm?
No! Second misadventure, this worm turned,
I told you: would have slain him on the spot
With his own weapon ... (III 1288-91)

Tertium Quid uses the same unexpected simile in his own version of
events, saying that she 'sprang at him like a pythoness' (IV 1162). Most
surprising is its reoccurrence in Pompilia's own speech, highlighted by
the comparison between Guido and a serpent which immediately pre-
cedes it:

The serpent towering and triumphant – then
Came all the strength back in a sudden swell,
I did for once see right, do right, give tongue
The adequate protest: for a worm must turn
If it would have its wrong observed by God. (VII 1589-93)

One might argue that it is possible to discriminate between worms and
serpents even though the two words are often synonymous, but another
passage destroys the distinction:

While out of the poor trampled worm the wife,
Springs up a serpent! (X 698-9)

The speaker is one of Pompilia's most ardent supporters, the Pope.
  The problems of argument by allusion come to the fore later in
Bottinius' speech when he invokes yet another variant on the Perseus
myth, the tale of Hesione rescued from the sea monster by Hercules. He
first imagines the way his adversary will choose to smirch Pompilia's
reputation:

But thither she picked way by devious path
Stands dirtied, no dubiety at all! (IX 952-3)

Bottinius seeks to neutralise this argument by making the metaphorical
language refer to literal fact; he describes how Hesione covered herself
with pitch in order to delay the attack of 'the purblind monster' (976).
Clearly this way of being 'dirtied' is morally irreproachable, but the lawyer
exposes his own sophistry when he again dextrously transfers this literal
stain to the 'real' narrative, apparently answering his adversary, but in fact
making no attempt to refute the accusation of moral turpitude:

            What you take for pitch,
Is nothing worse, belike, than black and blue,
Mere evanescent proof that hardy hands
Did yeoman's service, cared not where the gripe
Was more than duly energetic. (1002-6)

177

Unfortunately for the lawyer this explanation hardly works in the couple's favour; bruises – such as those Pygmalion fears he has left on the statue – could be the result of amorous enthusiasm.

In a final neat example of allusive confusion – here taken from the Bible rather than Ovid – Bottinius invokes the story of virtuous Judith, patriotic slayer of Holofernes:

> Pompilia took not Judith's liberty,
> No faulchion find you in her hand to smite, –
> No damsel to convey the head in dish,
> Of Holophernes, – style the Canon so –
> Or is it the Count? (IX 570-4)

But the image of a woman carrying a head on a dish recalls a very different Biblical character, Salome the destroyer of John the Baptist. Bottinius' stumbling confusion of two opponents, Count and Canon, draws attention to the ambiguity. Pompilia's equivocal allusive positioning between Judith and Salome operates in the same way as Pygmalion's suspension between Deucalion, creator of life out of stone, and Cinyras who couples with his own creation.

The metamorphoses – like those in 'Upon Appleton House' – are invoked as a series of possibilities rather than as decisive moments of change, and are thus in a sense unOvidian. This results in a shifting, contradictory picture which mirrors the ambiguity of *The Ring and the Book*. Allusion cannot be used as a definitive interpretative tool – instead it reminds us that all readings are simply that, just as the allusions (as Pompilia points out) are themselves only readings. We cannot describe the monologues as evidence, merely as Browning's readings of a document which is itself only a reading.

Browning explores the indeterminacy of 'facts' and 'reality' using an image previously employed by Chaucer in *The House of Fame* (787-806) when describing how a sound is multiplied, that of ripples caused by a stone falling in the water. Browning's more subtle and elaborate variation on this simple idea is as relevant to both Chaucer and Ovid's conception of Fame's continual mutations of news and narrative as it is to his own poem:

> First the world's outcry
> Around the rush and ripple of any fact
> Fallen stonewise, plumb on the smooth face of things;
> The world's guess, as it crowds the bank o' the pool,
> At what were figure and substance, by their splash:
> Then, by vibrations in the general mind,
> At depth of deed already out of reach. (I 839-45)

Truth is elusive, and the spectators, whom Browning goes on to identify as his variously partial narrators, must deduce the stone's position from ambiguous signs. The vibrations of the water are transferred to the watchers' minds, further suggesting the near impossibility of arriving at the 'truth' of any matter, entirely unmediated by one's own prejudices and point of view – we may recall the way Ovid blurs the boundary between rumours and those who spread them. Browning, as well as his narrators, is implicated in this process, for we may compare the stone, invisible except via the ripples it creates in the water, with the *Metamorphoses*, more potent as an undercurrent in *The Ring and the Book* than as a visible presence. One of the 'ripples' which mediates between Ovid and Browning is of course Chaucer's *House of Fame*. A little later Browning explicitly invokes Chaucer while describing the past in terms of a landscape:

> A novel country: I might make it mine
> By choosing which one aspect of the year
> Suited mood best, and putting solely that
> On panel somewhere in the House of Fame,
> Landscaping what I saved, not what I saw ... (I 1348-52)

'Saved' apparently means 'selected'; again Browning, like Chaucer's dreamer, presents himself as a potentially partial narrator. As he is the archnarrator of the entire poem, Browning thus problematises our instinctive sense that if we weigh up the evidence carefully all the answers will be forthcoming.

As if in anticipation of the reader's possible assumption that he at least can assess the biases of each side and deduce what 'really happened', the supposedly impartial speaker 'Tertium Quid' is as blinkered as 'Half-Rome' and 'The Other Half-Rome'. In fact Browning explicitly ascribes to him a 'critical mind, in short: no gossip-guess' (I 926). Browning's critics themselves are no more authoritative than Tertium Quid, and to read any selection of literature on *The Ring and the Book* is a little like rereading the poem, for both experiences offer a spectrum of viewpoints rather than the 'truth'. 'Of the making books there is no end' (X 9) as Browning's Pope reminds us in a line which echoes Ecclesiastes 12:12 via the first line of *Aurora Leigh*. At the very end Browning mockingly tells his readers what the message of his poem has been:

> So, British Public, who may like me yet,
> (Marry and amen!) learn one lesson hence
> Of many which whatever lives should teach:
> This lesson, that our human speech is naught,
> Our human testimony false, our fame
> And human estimation words and wind. (XII 831-6)

We are not of course bound to take him at his word.

10

Scriptae puellae: Pygmalion in Eliot, Joyce and H.D.

·Modernist writers such as Pound and Eliot were greatly influenced by classical writings, not least by the *Metamorphoses*. Indeed it is such an obviously informing presence in their work that it might no longer seem necessary to speak of an 'embedded' Ovidianism – here surely we have the real thing. But by this stage a readiness to return to Ovid's own writings was not enough to give a poet unmediated access to the *Metamorphoses*. Far too many influential voices – including all those discussed here – had intervened, collectively working to help shape and determine what kind of 'Ovid' a modern reader encountered when he opened Ovid. Certain stories, for example, would stand out in greater relief, as it were, because they had already informed the works of countless other Ovidians. It is scarcely surprising to find that Pygmalion is a prominent presence in so many modernist texts, for the myth's *Nachleben* had confirmed its status as a key episode in the *Metamorphoses*. Additional factors strengthened the story's appeal for, particularly when taken in conjunction with the complementary narrative of Narcissus, Pygmalion's story adumbrates a number of tropes and preoccupations which – while not being exclusive to this period – characterised the work of Modernist writers. These include ideas of division or separation within the self – consider Baudelaire's remarks about being both murderer and executioner (p. 175) – a related but more general focus on temporal and spatial as well as psychological fragmentation and indeterminacy reflected in the use of collage and montage effects, the conception of a split between word and referent, and particularly the polarisation of male and female principles, often figured in terms of language and discourse, which frequently resulted in the aestheticisation of woman as art-object.

The modernist response to Pygmalion is distinguished by a preoccupation with Galatea as a textual as much as a sculpted artefact, an emphasis which serves to underline the affinity between the fictional artist and the writer who created him. The identification between writers such as Joyce and their own artist characters suggests a connection with those earlier writers who were fascinated by the same Ovidian motif. But modernist texts seem to be free of the anxiety manifest in,

181

for example, the *Faerie Queene* where we saw how Spenser sought to dissociate himself from Acrasia and Busirane whilst revealing a guilty bond with their evil art. Indeed Joyce drew attention to the way the character of one of his Galatea figures, Gerty Macdowell, might only have been a figment of Bloom's imagination, thus fusing him and Joyce together as her joint progenitors (Power, p. 6). Hilda Doolittle (H.D.) is equally happy to acknowledge her affinity with Pygmalion, although her sex adds a further level of complexity to the relationship, and her own reception of the story reflects her preoccupation with gender issues.

Pygmalion is only an occluded presence in A Game of Chess (the second section of *The Waste Land*), but this is the modernist text which in some ways most strongly reflects the degree of affinity between Ovid's art and that of the sculptor he created. Whereas Joyce and H.D. create characters who function as Pygmalions, the hidden Pygmalions in A Game of Chess are Eliot's poetic predecessors including Ovid himself. The woman Eliot describes – sometimes associated with his first wife Vivien – is (like the poem itself) a compound of fragments, many cannibalised from earlier works of literature, making her the textual equivalent of one of Galatea's collateral descendants, Frankenstein's monster, who was similarly cobbled together from a variety of sources. As one of these sources is the *Metamorphoses* itself she is in a sense as much a product of Ovid's art as the original Galatea. These earlier poets are artists manipulated, ventriloquised, by the controlling pen of Eliot in the same way in which Ovid drove the chisel of his Pygmalion. Collectively the fragments combine to strengthen the aura of artificiality which surrounds the woman by drawing attention to the constructedness of the poem and to Eliot's unconcealed reliance on the words of others. And taken individually the quotations confirm this effect of unreality, each in some way mirroring the same transgression of the divide between art and nature exemplified by Pygmalion's miracle. The first and most famous quotation is of course taken from Shakespeare rather than Ovid:

> The Chair she sat in, like a burnished throne,
> Glowed on the marble, where the glass
> Held up by standards wrought with fruited vines
> From which a golden Cupidon peeped out
> (Another hid his eyes behind his wing)
> Doubled the flames of sevenbranched candelabra
> Reflecting light upon the table ... (77-83)

In Enobarbus' original speech the effect of Cleopatra's breathtaking splendour is created by its very inexpressibility – it can only be suggested by describing her appurtenances and her effect on her environment. In A Game of Chess, Eliot similarly avoids describing the woman herself, and this indirection is heightened by the curious focus on the mirror reflecting the contents of the room rather than the room itself, an apt enough strategy for a poem which is itself an echo or reflection of earlier tropes and texts. (And we should remember here that Shakespeare's account of Cleopatra is itself a quotation, being closely modelled on North's Plutarch.) The woman is evoked through the harsh glitter of jewels and synthetic perfumes – the mirror itself seems almost more alive because of the curious phrase 'wrought with fruited vines'. 'Fruited' is a particularly striking adjective, with a verbal force suggesting that the grapes have grown on the vine rather than been carved by an artist. The fact that 'fruited' is an emendation, replacing the more congruous 'golden' of Eliot's original version suggests that the word was chosen with some care. Although there is no direct link between the opening lines and any part of the *Metamorphoses* it is possible to situate their shifting instabilities – like those of the Bower of Bliss or Beddoes' Cyprus – within the wider Ovidian tradition. Far more directly derived from the *Metamorphoses* – Eliot provides us with the line reference in his endnotes – is the allusion to Philomela:

Above the antique mantel was displayed
As though a window gave upon the sylvan scene
The change of Philomel, by the barbarous king
So rudely forced; yet there the nightingale
Filled all the desert with inviolable voice
And still she cried, and still the world pursues,
'Jug Jug' to dirty ears. (97-103)

Here too we hover on the threshold between art and reality. The picture is so skilfully done that it resembles a view seen through a window – yet this supposedly realistic landscape is described as a 'sylvan scene' – the Miltonic phrase (again signalled by Eliot in the notes) works against the discourse of nature and reality, and draws attention to the whole poem's craftedness. The painting's subject itself contributes to the poem's ambiguities, for Philomela famously wove her own story into a tapestry. Despite its verisimilitude the picture above the mantel might be a reflection at two removes, a depiction of a depiction just as Eliot's description is itself constructed at two removes – as a collage of Milton, Shakespeare and Ovid. This 'chinese box' effect is of course also extensively used by Ovid. But looked at another way the passage enhances rather than dilutes Philomela's claim to 'reality' for there is an impression of narrative development in these lines which works against this pictorial quality; the metamorphosis itself, the rape, and the continuing existence of the nightingale are all evoked in turn.

Eliot alludes to further images 'told upon the walls' which he describes as 'other tales, from the old stumps and bloody ends of time' (104), suggesting that he was thinking of *Titus Andronicus* whose heroine, Lavinia, has her hands cut off so that she cannot resort to Philomela's stratagem for revealing her rapists' guilt. This tacit reference to a text which is directly derived from Ovid's tale of Philomela suggests that whereas we attempt to visualise Eliot's fragmentary description somehow fitting together in a physical space – a room – what we are in fact reading is a verbal construct, a written artifact where the relationship between 'objects' takes place within the literary tradition. 'Told' suggests verbal rather than pictorial presentation, reminding us that everything we 'see' in the poem is in fact the creation of Eliot's language. The strange description of the woman's hair which 'Spread out in fiery points/ Glowed into words' (108-9) is not after all so bizarre; her body, like everything else in the poem, exists only on paper.

A verbal tic associates the woman with Ovid's Echo, making her an auditory as well as a visual reflection:

> 'My nerves are bad to-night. Yes, bad. Stay with me.
> 'Speak to me. Why do you never speak? Speak.
> 'What are you thinking of? What thinking? What?
> 'I never know what you are thinking. Think.' (111-14)

The identification between the two is significant for she, like Echo, can only exist through words which have already been used by others, even though they may be recontextualised and thus gain new meaning. One of the most instantly recognisable of the quotations is Ovidian at one remove, 'Those are pearls that were his eyes' (125). This line again reminds us of the threshold between art and nature through invoking Ariel's description of a drowned body not decaying so much as metamorphosing into a work of art. The substitution of pearls and coral for eyes and bones gains an added significance in the context of a woman whose eyes seem to have been replaced by jewels that glitter and whose 'strange synthetic perfumes' are substitutes for her natural scent. The quotation thus contributes both to the artificiality of the woman – as one of the fragments of which she is a compound – and to the similar artificiality of the poem, itself composed of fragments on a larger scale. Even if we have not read *The Tempest* we too 'remember/ Those are pearls that were his eyes' for the line has already been quoted in the first section of *The Waste Land*. The reader's memory is jogged as well as the narrator's. As Stephen Hinds observes:

> Certain allusions are so constructed as to carry a kind of built-in commentary, a kind of reflexive annotation, which underlines or intensifies their demand to be interpreted *as* allusions (Hinds 1998, p. 1)

Eliot might seem to stand firmly outside the frame within which he has placed Ovid and the other poets he draws on. But *The Waste Land* – like the fragments which compose the woman in A Game of Chess –

184

possesses an ontological instability of its own. Eliot, as a poet who has created a Galatea and (in a sense) a Pygmalion within *The Waste Land*, might be aligned with Orpheus, another fragmented poet, who narrates the story of Pygmalion within the *Metamorphoses*, leaving the role of the ultimate creator, Ovid himself, to Ezra Pound, 'il miglior fabbro', who transformed and curtailed Eliot with the same kind of freedom which Eliot had already used in his appropriation of the poets whose voices we hear in *The Waste Land*.

Ovid's importance as a key influence on the poetry of Eliot has always been acknowledged. However, Joyce and Woolf also owed an important (though less obviously apparent) debt to the *Metamorphoses*. Their works testify to Ovid's capacity for endless renewal and metamorphosis; his disdain for boundaries certainly includes those of genre.

When he was just eighteen years old, the precocious Joyce wrote a lengthy review of Ibsen's *When We Dead Awaken* for *The Fortnightly Review*. The central character is a sculptor, Professor Rubek, who, after several years, is reunited with his mysterious former model, Irene, the inspiration for his greatest work, *The Resurrection Day*. Ibsen signals his affinity with Rubek, the text's Pygmalion figure, by making the name of the sculptor's greatest work a kind of echo of the title of the play itself. *When We Dead Awaken* draws on the potential for male/female conflict within the Pygmalion myth, and at the same time reinforces the peculiar affinity between the sculptor and Narcissus, implicit in Ovid's text, and suggestively enhanced by Dryden, Beddoes and Browning.

In a curious and apparently perverse comparison an acquaintance of Rubek's, the hunter Ulfheim, compares the sculpted stone with his own prey, echoing earlier writers' sense of a resistant Galatea – a submerged pun on 'quarry' (earlier exploited by Maynwaring and Beddoes) strengthens the link for English readers:

'Yes, for the stone has something to fight for too, I take it. It is dead, and determined with all its might not to be hammered into life.' (p. 35)

The act of slaughter might seem fundamentally opposed to the idea of a statue awakening to consciousness, yet in Ibsen and elsewhere, the art of Pygmalion may bestow death as well as life. Although we can loosely align any female statue with Galatea, Rubek's sculpture seems designed in some way to recall the feat of Pygmalion, for it is 'figured in the likeness of a young woman, awakening from the sleep of death' (p. 55). Even his motivation, idealistic and visionary, echoes that of Ovid's sculptor for 'it was to be the awakening of the noblest, purest, most ideal woman the world ever saw' (p. 55).[1] It is significant that the discovery

[1]Compare 'formamque dedit, qua femina nasci/ nulla potest', 'giving it a beauty more perfect than that of any woman ever born' (X 248-9).

of Irene postdates his conception of the sculpture. To quote another playwright of the *fin de siècle*, Nature here holds a mirror up to Art.

Ulfheim's suggestion that the sculpture resists its creator's animating touch is mirrored by the model's resentment of her own treatment, which she claims has deprived her of life – 'I gave you my young, living soul. And that gift left me empty within' (p. 58). In a nicely Ovidian reversal the statue's apparent awakening is paralleled by Irene's own transformation into a work of art. When Rubek asks how she has spent the past few years, Irene's enigmatic answer is that she has 'posed as a naked statue in living pictures' (p. 45). A woman need not be turned into a poem or a picture to become objectified in a male world. Even her appearance is statuesque, for she is draped in white garments and described several times as 'cold'. The sculptor's young wife Maia ensures that we haven't missed the point by referring to Irene as 'striding – like a marble statue'.

Rubek seems a callous, self-centred figure, openly admitting to Maia that he finds their four year marriage tedious, and apparently wishing to exploit Irene only for the impetus she might give his now enervated art. Whereas she had originally been the sole figure on the sculpture Rubek reveals that he later shifted her to a less prominent position (p. 110). We eventually learn what became of the new focus:

> 'Yes, but let me tell you, too, how I have placed myself in the group. In front, beside a fountain ... sits a man weighed down with guilt who cannot quite free himself from the earth-crust. I call him remorse for a ruined life. He sits there and dips his fingers in the purling stream – to wash them clean – and he is gnawed and tortured by the thought that he will never succeed. Never in an eternity will he attain to freedom and the new life. He will remain for ever prisoned in his hell.' (p. 112)

In his physical situation and remediless frustration Rubek resembles Narcissus. Even his apparent self-criticism is called into doubt by Irene who contemptuously claims that he is in fact endlessly self-forgiving.

Although Joyce's review of *When We Dead Awaken* cannot be said to anticipate his maturer genius, Ibsen's play still offers a useful starting point for a discussion of Joyce's own treatment of the Pygmalion legend. Although there is no doubt that he had independent first hand knowledge of Ovid – 'Et ignotas animum dimittit in artes' (VIII 188) is the epigraph for *A Portrait of the Artist as a Young Man* and Ovid is explicitly referred to elsewhere in this text as well as in *Finnegans Wake* and *Ulysses* – it is likely that a modern response to the legend by a writer whom Joyce particularly admired would have encouraged, if not initiated, his own reinvention of Pygmalion.

Joyce's first Pygmalion is Gabriel Conroy in 'The Dead' from *Dubliners* – the title itself seems to gesture back to Ibsen. Gabriel watches his wife Gretta as she leans on the banisters, listening to Bartell D'Arcy singing *The Lass of Aughrim*. He muses, not on her inner life, but on her appearance and symbolic significance:

> There was grace and mystery in her attitude as if she were a symbol of something. He asked himself what is a woman standing on the stairs in the shadow, listening to distant music, a symbol of. If he were a painter he would paint her in that attitude. Her blue felt hat would show off the bronze of her hair against the darkness and the dark panels of her skirt would show off the light ones. *Distant Music* he would call the picture if he were a painter. (p. 240)

Gabriel fails to realise that there may be some secret, private reason for her intensity of response, and persists in interpreting her enigmatic appearance in terms of something exterior to her self – even the proposed title for the painting takes her out of focus, rather as Rubek moves Irene to the background of his sculpture. This is another inversion of Pygmalion's miracle. Ovid's sculptor created his Galatea through art, Beddoes' statue is animated more by intellect, but Gabriel pushes the living Gretta back into both these boxes, recreating her as a work of art which is more a piece of intellectual symbolism than a representation of a real woman. Despite Gabriel's name he heralds not the word made flesh but the flesh made word.

The couple have arranged to spend the night at a hotel. Gabriel feels a sharp pang of desire for his wife but is irritated by her apparent distraction, and wishes that she would show some sign of reciprocal passion.

> If she would only turn to him or come to him of her own accord! To take her as she was would be brutal. No, he must see some ardour in her eyes first. He longed to be master of her strange mood. (p. 248)

He wishes that her thoughts would move in time to his and that she would yield at his bidding; the response he longs for is a mirror image of his own, and is thus both Narcissistic and Pygmalion-like. When she turns to kiss him, Gabriel is sure his wish has been granted:

> Just when he was wishing for it she had come to him of her own accord. Perhaps her thoughts had been running with his. Perhaps she had felt the impetuous desire that was in him and then the yielding mood had come upon her. (p. 249)

But his illusions are shattered when Gretta reveals that she was moved by the song because it reminded her of an old love, Michael Furey, who died while still a boy. Gabriel is thus reminded that Gretta has a mind and will of her own, independent of his. As if in ironic comment on his failure to find his own reflection in Gretta, Gabriel catches sight of himself in the cheval-glass at the very moment when she breaks down in tears (p. 249). If Gabriel is an inverse Pygmalion, perhaps it is Joyce who represents the positive aspect of the sculptor's art, bringing his heroine back to life as a thinking unit in her own right. But in a sense he is no different from Gabriel; for her creator as for her husband Gretta is ultimately a symbol, a vehicle for a message. Gretta is, after all, precisely the kind of Galatea Gabriel wants her to be, except that it is to her creator, Joyce, that she responds, rather than to her equally fictional husband.

Gabriel's misapprehensions spring from love, a subtler form of self-ishness than Rubek's, and he does not alienate the reader's sympathies. Stephen Daedalus is an altogether cooler and more self-conscious Pyg-malion figure for whom the aestheticisation of women is a way of furthering his development as an artist. Galatea's first incarnation in *A Portrait of the Artist as a Young Man* comes in the unexpected form of the Virgin Mary. Stephen ponders the significance of her litany, and the reasons Protestants made fun of it:

> *Tower of Ivory*, they used to say, *House of Gold*! How could a woman be a tower of ivory or a house of gold? Who was right then? (p. 37)

He follows in Pygmalion's footsteps by identifying the means – here metaphor rather than metamorphosis – whereby a woman can be created out of ivory and gold:

> Eileen had long white hands. One evening when playing tig she had put her hands over his eyes: long and white and thin and cold and soft. That was ivory: a cold white thing. That was the meaning of *Tower of Ivory*. (p. 37) ... Her fair hair had streamed out behind her like gold in the sun. *Tower of Ivory. House of Gold*. By thinking of things you could understand them. (p. 44)

The leap from a comprehension of simile to an understanding of meta-phor represents a relatively elementary stage in young Stephen's learning development. Later in the novel he moves beyond this reliance on affinities between an image, a metaphor, and what it connotes; he finds himself contemplating words 'in stolid wonder that they had been so silently emptied of instantaneous sense until every mean shop legend bound his mind like the words of a spell' (p. 193). He idly makes up a verse about the yellow ivy which 'whines upon the wall' and then questions his composition:

> Did any one ever hear such drivel? Lord Almighty! Who ever heard of ivy whining on a wall? Yellow ivy: that was all right. Yellow ivory also. And what about ivory ivy? (p. 182)

It seems that the phrase 'ivory ivy' came to him more because of the affinity of appearance and sound between the two words than because of any link between the two substances. (In *Finnegans Wake* Joyce encourages the reader to make the same connection when he refers to 'Saint Holy and Saint Ivory' (p. 556.) This effect is compounded when Stephen goes on to dissociate the word ivory from its meaning: 'The word now shone in his brain, clearer and brighter than any ivory sawn from the mottled tusks of elephants' (p. 182). Whereas in the *Metamorphoses* ivory ceases to be ivory, in *Portrait* 'ivory' ceases to be ivory. The reference to studying Ovid which follows seems prompted by the memory of learning a Latin tag, but is also significant as a reminder that words have connotations beyond their referents:

> *Ivory, ivoire, avorio, ebur.* One of the first examples that he had learnt in Latin had run: *India mittit ebur*; and he recalled the shrewd northern face of the rector who had taught him to construe the Metamorphoses of Ovid in a courtly English, made whimsical by the mention of porkers and potsherds and chines of bacon. (pp. 182-3)

The register of these words, rather than their meanings, Englishes and domesticates Ovid. The next apparently arbitrary memory is equally significant:

> He had learnt what little he knew of the laws of Latin verse from a ragged book written by a Portuguese priest.
>
> *Contrahit orator, variant in carmine vates.* (p. 183)

This may be translated: 'The orator summarizes; the poet-prophets transform (elaborate) in their verses.' Joyce is himself one of these *vates* who use language as a tool of metamorphosis, invoking his poetic inspiration as though it were the Annunciation. 'O! in the virgin womb of the imagination the word was made flesh' (p. 221). (In the *Oxen of the Sun* chapter of *Ulysses* the development of 1500 years of English prose parallels the growth of a foetus.) In a sense, as with Gabriel, the opposite is true, for Stephen rather transforms women into poetry than creates them out of poetry.

This can be seen in the novel's famous 'epiphany', when Stephen sees the wading girl on the beach. The description reflects Stephen's own sense of himself as a poet. Although we are told that 'she seemed like one whom magic had changed into the likeness of a strange and beautiful seabird' (p. 175), her birdlike aspect probably has as much to do with Stephen's own identification with his winged namesake as with her actual appearance. (As she is so very much his creation it is perhaps significant that her thighs are 'softhued as ivory' (p. 175).) This sense of the girl as a projection of Stephen's artistic faculty is strengthened in the description which follows:

Her long slender bare legs were delicate as a crane's and pure save where an emerald trail of seaweed had fashioned itself as a sign upon the flesh. Her thighs, fuller and softhued as ivory, were bared almost to the hips where the white fringes of her drawers were like featherings of soft white down. Her slateblue skirts were kilted boldly about her waist and dovetailed behind her. Her bosom was as a bird's soft and slight, slight and soft as the breast of some darkplumaged dove. But her long fair hair was girlish: and girlish, and touched with the wonder of mortal beauty, her face. (p. 175)

Up to a point the similes may be read as attempts to describe a real phenomenon – her birdlike appearance – accurately. Yet we are convinced more by the insistent use of an avian vocabulary than by any kind of visual impression of the girl. We *might* accept that her slender bare legs in the water recall those of a crane, and even that the fringes of her drawers are like down. But why should her bosom resemble that of a *dark*plumaged dove? The word 'dovetailed' is also problematic. Generally this word is not designed to evoke a real dove – indeed the phenomenon it describes is unlikely to put anyone especially in mind of this or any other bird – but here it is reinvested with its original inspiration and serves to enhance our sense that the girl is like a bird. Language can create as well as describe metamorphosis – Joyce has the power to weld a word and its referent back together as well as force them apart. Whereas Pygmalion carved a woman out of solid ivory, Joyce's women – the Virgin, Eileen, the birdgirl – are created (in part) by 'ivory' rather than ivory, by a discourse of metamorphosis, in other words, rather than by actual transformation – 'He spoke of the plastic monosyllable as a sculptor speaks about a stone' (Ellmann p. 432).

'Like Narcissus, Stephen has fallen in love with his projected self-image clothed in female garb' (Henke and Unkeless, p. 93). Henke's suggestion of an affinity between Stephen and Narcissus is apt, but might equally well be expressed in terms of Pygmalion and the statue, better, indeed, for he has created her in his image rather than found her in that state. The moment of contact between them, their mutual gaze, suggests that she is in some sense his mirror image, particularly because nothing separates their eyes within the structure of the sentence, 'She was alone and still, gazing out to sea; and when she felt his presence and the worship of *his eyes her eyes* turned to him in quiet sufferance of his gaze ...' (pp. 175-6). This moment also recalls the awakening of Pygmalion's statue:

> dataque oscula virgo
> sensit et erubuit timidumque ad *lumina lumen*
> attollens pariter cum caelo vidit amantem.

The maiden felt the kisses, blushed and, lifting her timid eyes up to the light, she saw the sky and her lover at the same time. (X 292-4)

Lumina might be translated 'his eyes' as easily as 'the light'.

The very style of the passage is a response, not to the girl, but to Stephen's preconceived literary tastes. The mannered cadences which bring this purple passage to a close reflect his fondness for 'the poise and balance of the period itself' (p. 171). He elaborates: 'Did he then love the rhythmic rise and fall of words better than their associations of legend and colour? Or was it that, being as weak of sight as he was shy of mind, he drew less pleasure from the reflection of the glowing sensible world through the prism of a language manycoloured and richly storied than from the contemplation of an inner world of individual emotions mirrored perfectly in a lucid supple periodic prose?' (p. 171). Although Stephen's birdgirl may seem like a quintessentially visual emblem, she is in fact precisely this – a figment of his inner life reflected in the language of the poet's maturing art. The description of her eyes meeting his is explicitly filtered through Stephen's own discourse. The effect of a mirror image reflects his prose style – 'poise and balance' – rather than reality. As for Gabriel, the woman represents both mirror and work of art for Stephen, making him both Pygmalion and Narcissus – but this time there is no jarring reminder of her inconvenient autonomy.

The principal Galatea in *Ulysses* is Gerty MacDowell, the focus of 'Nausicaa', and an object of erotic interest for Bloom. Critics have noted an ironic parallel between the birdgirl and Gerty, both in terms of their setting and the way they are perceived by Stephen and Bloom respectively. Both are clearly in part the creation of masculine desire.

In Chapter 7 we saw how Belinda seemed to appropriate Pygmalion's art to further her reinvention of herself, yet ultimately could never escape from the controlling pen of her creator, Pope. Gerty MacDowell is in a similar position. In a sense she writes her own chapter, for an impression of her discourse, as with Molly at the end of the novel, is reproduced by Joyce even though she is always referred to in the third person. Gerty reinscribes herself as a heroine of the type of romantic, sentimental novel she enjoys reading. She is introduced as 'in very truth, as fair a specimen of winsome Irish girlhood as one could wish to see' (pp. 285-6). But this is really her own hopeful estimate of her charms rather than the narrator's. What is apparently a move to increase Gerty's autonomy has the effect of reinforcing her fictionality, even to the extent of making her a sculptural as well as a literary artefact: 'The waxen pallor of her face was almost spiritual in its ivorylike purity though her rosebud mouth was a genuine Cupid's bow, Greekly perfect. Her hands were of finely veined alabaster with tapering fingers ...' (p. 286). This hint is introduced more strongly a little later: 'Gerty's lips parted swiftly to frame the word but she fought back the sob that rose to her throat, so slim, so flawless, so beautifully moulded it seemed one an artist might have dreamed of' (p. 297).

191

She aspires to the beauty of a girl in a picture of young love which is displayed in the MacDowell lavatory: 'She often looked at them dreamily when she went there for a certain purpose and felt her own arms that were white and soft just like hers ...' (p. 291). It should not surprise us that Gerty's favourite poem is entitled 'Art thou real, my ideal?' (p. 298). It is equally appropriate that she should associate herself with the Virgin Mary, another of Joyce's Galateas. Gerty has four sets of underclothes with different coloured ribbons: 'She was wearing the blue for luck, hoping against hope, her own colour and lucky too for a bride to have a bit of blue somewhere on her ...' (p. 288). The context might perhaps suggest that 'her own colour' means that blue suits Gerty's complexion. But Joyce's characters' musings are frequently elliptical, and we are surely meant to think of the Virgin Mary, with whom the colour blue was particularly associated. This confusion between the two reflects Gerty's own identification with Mary whom she describes as one 'who is in her pure radiance a beacon ever to the stormtossed heart of man' (p. 284). This is precisely how the idealistic young girl would like to be perceived by her beloved.

Gerty's inability to escape from a male discourse of creation is highlighted when, for example, she is described as 'a radiant little vision, in sooth, almost maddening in its sweetness' (p. 295). She cannot help seeing herself through the eyes of (as she thinks) Bloom and (more accurately) male novelists, and thus sees herself as an object of sexual desire. Her supposed response to masculine attention intensifies her attraction as an erotic spectacle more than it conveys her own sexual feelings:

> Her woman's instinct told her that she had raised the devil in him and at the thought a burning scarlet swept from throat to brow till the lovely colour of her face became a glorious rose. (p. 295)

It might be argued that Gerty regains control of her own narrative because she cannot help letting her real thoughts slip through, in other words because of *lack* of control. Little vulgarisms – 'swank' (p. 297), 'snottynosed' (p. 296), 'rossies' (p. 299) – have no place in her rose-tinted romancings, but enliven Gerty's preferred discourse of elevated cliché. Yet we are always aware of Joyce's highly wrought art controlling our reception of Gerty's voice just as he controls our reception of Bloom's. Midway through the chapter we are handed back to Bloom, and see events from his quite different perspective. His name, withheld up till now because unknown to Gerty, the scene's focaliser, is finally introduced, even though Gerty's voice still predominates:

> Then all melted away dewily in the grey air: all was silent. Ah! She glanced at him as she bent forward quickly, a pathetic little glance of piteous protest, of shy reproach under which he coloured like a girl. He

was leaning back against the rock behind. Leopold Bloom (for it is he) stands silent, with bowed head before those young guiltless eyes. What a brute he had been! At it again? A fair unsullied soul had called to him and, wretch that he was, how had he answered? (p. 300)

The explicit reference to Bloom disrupts the narrative. The melodramatic 'for it is he' might seem in keeping with Gerty's breathless style, but is clearly an interjection from Joyce, for only he and the reader, not Gerty, are already familiar with Bloom's name. By appropriating Gerty's discourse within the wider narrative of the novel as a whole, Joyce reestablishes his own control over it – and her. Another little detail – 'at it again' – is a further sly reminder that Gerty is not really in charge of what we are being told. The reference is to Gerty's exhibitionism which has just brought Bloom to orgasm. She is fully aware of what is going on, but distinguishes his actions from those of the lodger in a friend's house who 'had pictures cut out of papers of those skirt-dancers and highkickers and ... used to do something not very nice that you could imagine sometimes in the bed' (pp. 299-300). But for Bloom, Joyce and the reader the encounter with Gerty is just one in a whole series of extraconjugal emissions, and 'at it again' reflects this.

It has been suggested – by Joyce himself among others – that Gerty's interior as well as her exterior is no more than a figment of Bloom's self-serving imagination. But to do him justice, a Galatea is precisely what Bloom does *not* want:

Whew! Girl in Meath street that night. All the dirty things I made her say. All wrong of course. My arks she called it. It's so hard to find one who. Aho! If you don't answer when they solicit must be horrible for them till they harden. And kissed my hand when I gave her the extra two shillings. Parrots. Press the button and the bird will squeak. (p. 303)

Bloom's memories of encounters with prostitutes blend Galatea with her mirror image, the Propoetides. Although sharing the latter's profession – even being described as 'hardened' – the girl's response is as dutiful as Galatea's, for she exists to reflect her client's wishes. She is even likened to a parrot, just as the statue is (implicitly at least) by Dryden.

Bloom is to manifest himself as Pygmalion once again in the 'Circe' chapter. One of the strange cast of Nighttown is the nymph whose picture hangs over the Blooms' bed: 'Given away with the Easter number of *Photo Bits*: splendid masterpiece in art colours' (p. 53). She has already prompted Bloom's misleading definition of metempsychosis – 'they used to believe you could be changed into an animal or a tree, for instance. What they called nymphs, for example' (p. 53) – a phenomenon which she now exemplifies (for Bloom is clearly getting muddled with metamorphosis) by effecting a Galatea-like transformation, described in a stage direction:

> Out of her oakframe a nymph with hair unbound, lightly clad in teabrown artcolours, descends from her grotto and passing under interlacing yews stands over Bloom. (p. 444)

Bloom's earlier treatment of her parodies Pygmalion's response to his statue, blending artistic creativity and eroticism. She reminds him how he 'set me above your marriage couch. Unseen, one summer eve, you kissed me in four places. And with loving pencil you shaded my eyes, my bosom and my shame' (p. 445). After complaining about the sights she has been forced to witness, including soiled items of underwear and Molly using the commode, the nymph reveals her kinship with the Greek statues in which Bloom took a prurient and anatomically specific interest when he visited the museum: 'We immortals, as you saw today, have not such a place and no hair there either. We are stonecold and pure' (p. 449). But eventually, after Bloom has torn off her veil, the nymph appears to join the world of humanity, here evoked as a far more sordid condition than in Ovid:

THE NYMPH
(with a cry flees from him unveiled, her plaster cast cracking, a cloud of stench escaping from the cracks)

In a sense the two Galateas come together in 'Circe' for Gerty makes another appearance in Nighttown, showing Bloom 'her bloodied clout' (she is menstruating) in place of the scented handkerchief she waved at him earlier. Whereas Stephen's birdgirl remains a work of art, Bloom's Galateas come to life in that they escape from the trammels of aesthetic idealisation of Woman (trammels which are partly self-imposed in Gerty's case) and become 'real' human beings.

Pygmalion is a still more complex presence in *Finnegans Wake*. The book's female characters – essences or principles might be more accurate terms – are multiply metamorphic, being figured as trees and rivers as well as stones. Just as in Ovid, linguistic play is the instrument by which different orders of creation are merged together. Whereas *Ulysses* is full of metamorphoses – Bloom's sex change in the Circe chapter, the transformation of language from Anglo-Saxon to modern in *The Oxen of the Sun* – and invitations to see one thing in terms of another – Shakespeare as God ('Shapesphere'), Molly as Penelope – in *Finnegans Wake* the process is taken one step further because the different states or identities are present simultaneously:

> It was in a fairly fishy kettlekerry, after the Fianna's foreman had taken his handful, enriched with ancient woods and dear dutchy deeplinns mid

194

which were an old knoll and a troutbeck, vainyvain of her osiery and a
chatty sally with any Wilt or Walt who would ongle her as Izaak did to the
tickle of his rod ... (p. 76)

The river's personification as a vain female encourages the reader to
extend osiery (pertaining to osiers, reeds) to hosiery, a more conven-
tional focus for feminine pride. Similarly, although ongle suggests
'angle' because Isaak is obviously Isaak Walton, author of *The Compleat
Angler*, 'ogle' might also be implied, particularly as the phrase 'tickle of
his rod' is clearly susceptible of a sexual interpretation.

Later in the book a bilingual pun further involves water and a woman
in the parenthetical exclamation '(tha lassy! tha lassy!)' (p. 328). This
echoes the exclamation 'Thalassa! Thalassa' (or 'Thalatta! Thalatta!),
'The sea! The sea!' from Xenophon's *Anabasis*. Joyce's strange metamor-
phosis of the Greek is a reprise of an association made by Buck Mulligan
at the very beginning of *Ulysses*, '*Thalatta! Thalatta!* She is our great
sweet mother' (p. 5). In *Finnegans Wake* Joyce uses a kind of montage
effect to incorporate Mulligan's gloss into the phrase itself, by deforming
and feminising it. Further metamorphoses are effected during the
course of the *Wake*. Anna Livia Plurabelle is addressed as 'Galata!
Galata!' (p. 547) involving the sea, already associated with femininity,
with Pygmalion's statue. This takes us back to the novel's first rear-
rangement of the Greek phrase:

The letter! The litter! And the soother the bitther! Of eyebrow pencilled,
by lipstipple penned.... From dark Rasa Lane a sigh and a weep, from
Lesbia Looshe the beam in her eye ... (p. 93)

This typically opaque little passage evokes the same phenomenon of the
scripta puella, discussed earlier in Chapter 7. As the letter is written by
ALP we may take the articles of makeup to be substitute writing
implements, but there is also the suggestion of a woman created (both
painted and written) by makeup – the idea of a woman being *written* by
makeup becomes less obscure if we recall Gerty, as much a product of
the discourse of makeup as of makeup itself. The two women, Rasa Lane
and Lesbia Looshe, are aptly named, for *rasa* is the feminine past
participle of *rado*, to erase, and Lesbia is of course the most famous
scripta puella of them all. The letter is a recurrent motif, and the paper
on which it is written is described earlier in the novel, 'For that (the rapt
one warns) is what papyr is meed of, made of, hides and hints and
misses in prints' (p. 20). The last words should apparently be contracted
to 'misprints', thus in a sense exemplifying the statement. But of course
this is more than mere error; by drawing out the 'miss' in misprint Joyce
suggests woman's textuality. We may compare a later reference to a
man who 'wanna git all his flesch nuemaid motts truly prural and
plusible' (p. 138). There could hardly be a more concise encapsulation of

195

the *scripta puella*. As we read 'nuemaid' we understand 'newmade' yet in the light of the polyglot *Wake* the word could also be glossed 'naked maid'. The apparent use of French here (nue) may affect the way the reader responds to 'motts'. The French 'mots' (words) is perhaps more readily available than the word's English meaning – it is an obsolete colloquialism for girl (also spelled 'mort' or 'mot'). So within these two words we have two competing paths of interpretation, 'newmade word' and 'naked maid girl', which are of course liable to merge together. Although 'flesch' suggests flesh, it is possible that in conjunction with 'newmade', 'fresh' may also be suggested. It might at first seem that Joyce's strange neologisms 'prural' and 'plusible' (plural and plausible, prurient and extensible?) strengthen the 'word' rather than the 'girl' resonances, but by this stage in the book we are used to hearing all kinds of echoes and distortions of 'Anna Livia Plurabelle', the novel's universal woman. There is no unifying context, no stable frame of reference, to help us decide between the two strands of meaning, just as the lack of a dependable authorial voice prevents us from aligning Pompilia entirely with Daphne or with Myrrha. We have seen how Pygmalion's Galatea and her various descendants are all creations of the poet's language as much as the sculptor's art, and here Joyce welds together still more closely the creation of language and of woman, taking the process begun in the birdgirl epiphany and continued in 'Nausicaa' a stage further.

*

Joyce was not the only Modernist writer to make use of the story of Pygmalion. The myth had a special importance for the Imagist poet and novelist Hilda Doolittle and acquired an extra complexity in her writings because her sex linked her with the statue rather than the sculptor. The myth's paradigm of male creativity and wish fulfilment becomes problematic when employed by a female writer who is debarred from total identification with Pygmalion despite being herself an artist. H.D.'s response to the story manifests a confusion, an edginess, which is missing in the work of a male artist such as Joyce. It is often possible to identify Joyce with his various Pygmalions – Stephen, Bloom, and Gabriel are all portraits of the artist to some degree. Thus although his male and female characters are equally fictional, Joyce's men are far less likely to seem constructed. And when men are Pygmalions and women Galateas this tendency for the female characters to seem more fictional, more constructed, is increased. The Pygmalion motif spilled over into Joyce's life, for he tried to mould Nora into his own image; in a letter written while the couple were living in Trieste he expresses irritation and even betrayal when her thoughts fail to mirror his own. She at first refused to admit to sharing his own repulsion and disgust at the sight of a priest who passed them in the street, and then compounded this perceived disloyalty through her reluctance to listen to Joyce talk of his ambitions and ideas after he had returned from a café late at night (Ellmann, p. 304). Joyce displays his selfishness and solipsism with unconscious humour which makes the reader wonder how far his Pygmalions are ironised. His wounded response when Nora declines to echo his own prejudices against priests resembles that of Gabriel when Gretta also refuses to dance to his tune. And it is hardly surprising that Nora, mother of two small children, did not particularly want to be woken up to listen to her husband's effusions.

But if Joyce is Pygmalion, Doolittle has a particular affinity with Galatea. Her namesake, Shaw's Eliza Doolittle, is the statue's most famous descendant, and the poet found her own Professor Higgins in Ezra Pound, who in a sense constructed her by devising her curious penname, H.D. (Pound was equally ready to help mould male poets, of course.) She had herself photographed naked, creating images which resembled 'popular turn-of-the-century photographs of naked nymphs lying prone on the earth or perched in trees' (Gilbert and Gubar, p. 168). She is thus the real life equivalent of Bloom's nymph, and indeed of Gerty, for H.D. is always conscious of the voyeur's gaze.

She might be said to anticipate the response of Amy Richlin to the problems posed by Ovid to his female readers:

A woman reading Ovid faces difficulties. In the tradition of Western literature his influence has been great, yet even in his lifetime critics found his poetry disturbing because of the way he applied his wit to unfunny circumstances, Is his style a virtue or a flaw? Like an audience watching a magician saw a lady in half, they have stared to see how it was done. I would like to draw attention to the lady. (Richlin 1992, p. 159)

Most Galatea-like are the photographs of stone statues on which H.D. superimposed her own face. Her poem 'Pygmalion' is written from the sculptor's point of view, but questions his relationship with the art he produces, suggesting both his identity with it:

Which am I,
the stone or the power
that lifts the rock from the earth? (p. 49)

and, after affirming his superiority to his work with a *hubris* reminiscent of Beddoes' sculptor, his subordination to the statues he produces:

I made god upon god
step from the cold rock,
I made the gods less than men
for I was a man and they my work ... (p. 49)

197

each of the gods, perfect,
cries out from a perfect throat:
you are useless,
no marble can bind me,
no stone suggest. ...
each from his marble base
has stepped into the light
and my work is for naught. (p. 50)

In coming to life the statues seem to negate rather than affirm the sculptor's power. Although the statues ostensibly represent divinity rather than femininity, the original subject of the legend is sufficiently well known for the reader to import questions of gender and sexuality into the poem. This is certainly the focus of H.D.'s most sustained response to Pygmalion, her novel *Her.* H.D. calls attention to the novel's autobiographical nature by calling the heroine after yet another manifestation of Galatea, Hermione from *The Winter's Tale.* Even the abbreviation, Her, presses the point further, inscribing her as a permanent object within the text. Hermione's Shakespearean provenance is made explicit in the book, and the play's significance for H.D. is apparent in the name she gave her own daughter, Perdita. In a sense this naming is already a kind of reinvention of the legend – one Galatea has manufactured another in her mirror image, Narcissus-like. Within the novel a succession of variations is played on the narratives of both Narcissus and Pygmalion within the context of Her's relationships with George Lowndes (modelled on her mentor and former fiancé Pound) and another woman, Fayne Rabb.

Her intriguingly refers to the way her Shakespearean namesake 'later froze into a statue' (p. 66). We normally focus on the way this process is reversed, when the 'statue' comes to life and proves to be the real Hermione who has remained concealed for the past fifteen years. Her is presumably thinking of Leontes' jealous anger, responsible for her deathlike swoon and thus indirectly for her apparent petrifaction. Thus a new slant is put on Shakespeare's ostensibly positive treatment of the myth, and a hint is given that man's 'creation' of woman is potentially destructive. In the context of her relationship with George, Her is often presented as a kind of reflection. As she muses on their relationship we are told that 'her two hands reached toward George like the hands of a drowned girl', as if she were in a pool of water with him looking on as at an image of himself. 'She wanted George to pull her out, she wanted George to push her in, let Her be drowned utterly' (p. 63). In keeping with her scepticism about *The Winter's Tale,* Lowndes' caresses seem to turn her into stone rather than make her come to life. Yet again stoniness is a response to male attention (compare Dryden and Browning) rather than a state which may be softened away by a lover's embrace: 'Kisses forced her into soft moss. Her head lay marble

198

weight in cushion of forest moss. ... The kisses of George smudged out her clear geometric thought ...' (p. 73). The comparison is repeated insistently, 'The back of marble head pressed down into moss ... The back of her head in the moss was pressed out, rounded out, round marble-polished surface in the soft moss' (p. 74). As with the Rasa/Lesbia pairing in *Finnegans Wake*, the Galatea figure must apparently be erased before being recreated, 'George like a sponge had smudged her smooth face with kisses, had somehow, now she recalled it, smudged out something' (118).

Her's refutation of her mother's casting of George as Pygmalion in his sinister Svengali aspect is not entirely convincing:

> 'George Lowndes is teaching you, actually *teaching* you words, telling you what to say.' 'George isn't. He never tells me what to say. I never say anyhow what anyone ever tells me to say. Do you think I have so little spunk, so little character that I would repeat (like a foul parrot) words, words, words out of someone else's mouth ...' (p. 95)

But Her has already received intimations of an escape route from George, and finds herself thinking not of his grey green eyes, but of Fayne's eyes, which are like sapphires. Her's strangely fragmented self-image makes her perceive her head as a kind of mirror which she now turns inward:

> The front of her head turned and looked into the back of her head as a child may do, astonished to find things turned round in a mirror. (p. 75)

> She did not think this for her mind was too astonished to perceive how she could turn, perceive as a mirror the whole of the fantasy of the world reversed and in that mirror a wide room opening. (p. 76)

In her introduction to the Virago edition of *Her*, Helen McNeil refers to Her's relationship with Fayne in terms of a 'rewrite of the romantic "other" into a homoerotic mirroring' (p. vii). Instead of being Lowndes' helpless drowned reflection she now partakes of a mirror relationship where the parties are apparently more equal. When George looked at her he saw himself because, like Stephen and Gabriel, he treated her as a mirror, Narcissistically self-absorbed. But within a homoerotic context Her can look at Fayne and see a true reflection of herself. The closeness between self and other possible in a lesbian relationship is suggested when Her says, ' "Anyhow I love – I love Her, only Her, Her, Her." And he said, "Narcissus in the reeds, Narcissa" ' (p. 170). But George's scoffing admonition is unfair; Her is of course also her, Fayne.

Her's first glimpse of Fayne figures her as a Galatea – 'she was stonily incarnated' (p. 50). Yet this apparent kinship between her and Her is contradicted when Fayne takes the part of Pygmalion in a

199

tableau. But there seems to be no question of the relationship between the two women merely replicating the power relations of Her's previous heterosexual liaison. They meet after the tableau:

> 'And I – I'll make you breathe, my breathless statue.' 'Statue? You – *you* are the statue.' (p. 163)

As if to emphasise their parity, both are Pygmalion, both Galatea; it is impossible to infer from the context who speaks first. Yet although Pygmalion and Narcissus are used as a way of privileging lesbianism, the narrative ultimately works against the dynamic of the mythical matrix for it transpires that Fayne and Lowndes are themselves involved in some sort of liaison, a revelation which drives Her to mental breakdown. Although the novel ends on a note of possible reconciliation – in the last sentence Her is informed by the maid that Fayne is waiting for her upstairs – the effect is open and equivocal rather than celebratory. But *Her* does not represent the last word in the rather recherché category of feminist, modernist Ovidianism. In Virginia Woolf's *Orlando*, which appeared just one year after *Her*'s composition, myth is used to analyse and deconstruct relations between the sexes, and in particular women's need to escape objectification, in a far more confident way.

11

Intersexuality: Virginia Woolf's
Orlando

Woolf's dialogue with Ovid, like H.D.'s, is a gendered one. Well-established Ovidian stories and tropes acquire an additional edge when reappropriated by a self-consciously female voice. Ovid continues to inspire unease (and applause) in feminist critics, and it is hardly surprising that Woolf found Ovidianism a problematic discourse. Her views could be seen as typically twentieth-century, but she was not the first to find the Ovidian universe disquieting; luckily the *Metamorphoses* was as amenable to appropriation by a feminist novelist as by a Christian poet such as Milton.

Orlando's affinity with the *Metamorphoses* lies in its shape, in its entirety, as much as in its use of particular stories. In both texts a complex narrative charts the events of several centuries, disdaining boundaries of periodisation, gender (more especially species in the case of Ovid) and genre. *Orlando* is a mock biography complete with illustrations and an index, wittily mocking the form in which it is written in a manner which Sandra Gilbert terms 'metabiographical' (p. xxix) in her introduction to the Penguin edition of the novel. This generic uncertainty is also of course a key feature of the *Metamorphoses*.

In some ways Woolf and Ovid stand in a similar relation to their respective literary environments. Ovid has been perceived as less serious, less important than other classical poets, most notably Virgil. *Orlando* has met with similar criticisms; Virginia Woolf herself referred to the novel as a 'freak', calling it 'child's play' (Woolf, p. xxxiii). (Damning one's own most Ovidian works may be a recurring theme – Beddoes called his 'Pygmalion' 'considerable trash' (Bush p. 194).) The kind of language used by critics even to praise it – 'charming', 'witty' – somehow consigns it to a lower level of consideration than her 'serious' novels, such as *To the Lighthouse*. It is a *jeu d'esprit* or a *tour de force* but not a masterpiece.

Both *Orlando* and the *Metamorphoses* open with a set piece describing a profound upheaval in the natural world. Woolf's depiction of the Great Frost has much in common with Ovid's influential account of the deluge. There is the same accumulation of vivid startling detail, combining the fantastic and mysterious with the everyday in a gallery of surreal arrested moments. Woolf, like Ovid, uses transformations and boundary changes with at least some basis in nature or fact to foreshadow the more magical metamorphosis which is to follow:

> Occupat hic collem, cumba sedet alter adunca
> et ducit remos illic, ubi nuper arabat:
> ille supra segetes aut mersae culmina villae
> navigat, hic summa piscem deprendit in ulmo.
> figitur in viridi, si fors tulit, ancora prato,
> aut subiecta terunt curvae vineta carinae;
> et, modo qua graciles gramen carpsere capellae,
> nunc ibi deformes ponunt sua corpora phocae.
> mirantur sub aqua lucos urbesque domosque
> Nereides, silvasque tenent delphines et altis
> incursant ramis agitataque robora pulsant.

Here one man seeks a hill-top in his flight; another sits in his curved skiff, plying the oars where lately he has plowed; one sails over his fields of grain or the roof of his buried farmhouse, and one takes fish caught in the elm-tree's top. And sometimes it chanced that an anchor was embedded in a grassy meadow, or the curving keels brushed over the vineyard tops. And where but now the slender goats had browsed, the ugly sea-calves rested. The Nereids are amazed to see beneath the waters groves and cities and the haunts of men. The dolphins invade the woods, brushing against the high branches, and shake the oak-trees as they knock against them in their course (I 293-303).

The Great Frost was, historians tell us, the most severe that has ever visited these islands. Birds froze in mid-air and fell like stones to the ground. At Norwich a young countrywoman started to cross the road in her usual robust health and was seen by the onlookers to turn visibly to powder and be blown in a puff of dust over the roofs as the icy blast struck her at the street corner. The mortality among sheep and cattle was enormous. Corpses froze and could not be drawn from the sheets. It was no uncommon sight to come upon a whole herd of swine frozen immovable upon the road. The fields were full of shepherds, ploughmen, teams of horses, and little bird-scaring boys all struck stark in the act of the moment, one with his hand to his nose, another with the bottle to his lips, a third with a stone raised to throw at a raven who sat, as if stuffed, upon the hedge within a yard of him. The severity of the frost was so extraordinary that a kind of petrifaction sometimes ensued; and it was commonly supposed that the great increase of rocks in some parts of Derbyshire was due to no eruption, for there was none, but to the solidification of unfortunate wayfarers who had been turned literally to stone where they stood. (p. 24)

An intermediate moment – perhaps even a mediating source – between Ovid and Woolf can be found in Marvell's 'Upon Appleton House' where a topsy-turvy flood anticipates more serious disruptions in a poem which shares both generic uncertainty and metamorphic fluidity with

11. Virginia Woolf's Orlando

Orlando and the *Metamorphoses*. The evocation of the Frost as a time of mysterious transformation paves the way for the more dramatic metamorphosis which lies at the heart of Virginia Woolf's novel. The young Orlando – young despite having already lived for a century or so – is inexplicably transformed into a woman while serving as an ambassador in Constantinople. Among the hundreds of metamorphoses in Ovid's long poem several involving a change of sex may be found: Salmacis and Hermaphroditus fuse together to form a single androgynous being, Iphis is transformed into a man on the eve of her wedding to Ianthe, and Tiresias is famously turned from a man into a woman and then back again. But although precedents for Orlando's sex change may be found in the *Metamorphoses*, this incident in itself does not justify calling Woolf's novel Ovidian. Yet in some ways it has an affinity with Ovid which is not exceeded even by such consciously classicised, poetic products of modernism as *The Waste Land* or the Cantos.

Two very different Ovidian subtexts operate in *Orlando*: Daphne and Apollo and Salmacis and Hermaphroditus. The first tale emphasises and exaggerates the division between the sexes, in the second they merge together. Yet these characteristics of the two tales, and their apparent opposition to one another, are complicated in *Orlando*, for here the two legends combine to form a contrapuntal framework which deconstructs the divisions between subject and object, male and female, poet and poem. Although I am happy to assume Woolf's first hand knowledge of the *Metamorphoses*, much of her Ovidianism may be traced back through various mediating pens, such as those of Marvell and Shakespeare. If we trace a trajectory from the *Metamorphoses* to *Orlando* one intermediate text where both subtexts make a brief appearance is *The Taming of the Shrew*.

As we have already seen, the tale of Apollo and Daphne is one of conflict, opposition and division. A brief allusion to the tale in *The Taming of the Shrew* reinforces the gulf between Apollo and Daphne, the sense that they inhabit different worlds. As part of the elaborate joke played upon Sly he is promised all sorts of luxuries, including wonderful paintings depicting mythological figures. One portrays Daphne:

> Or Daphne running through a thorny wood,
> Scratching her legs, that one shall swear she bleeds;
> And at the sight shall sad Apollo weep,
> So workmanly the blood and tears are drawn. (Induction ii.55-8)

Logically, there is surely no causal link between the painter's praiseworthy verisimilitude and the fact that Apollo is weeping – the god's tears are one of the things the artist has depicted with especial skill. Yet the folio punctuation and the force of 'so' contrive to suggest that Apollo is responding to the tapestry rather than part of it. 'Drawn' may be glossed 'depicted'; however, an alternative reading, 'drawn forth', is also possible. (This confusion perhaps looks forward to the way layers of fictionality are used in the play. Sly is no more 'real' than the characters in the play he watches, and the 'play within a play', the main story, breaks free of its confines at the end, for there is no reprise of the Sly framing device.) In the *Metamorphoses* Apollo simply seemed to belong in a different genre to Daphne -- erotic comedy as opposed to tragedy -- but here the disparity is even sharper for he appears to inhabit a different level of reality from Daphne, to be a connoisseur of her as a beautiful artwork, rather than as a woman, almost as though he were playing Pygmalion to her Galatea. This gulf between the two is implicit in the original legend, for Daphne is not immortal, and she turns into a non-sentient organism.

The story of Apollo and Daphne is the key Ovidian subtext of *Orlando*. This might at first appear strange -- that a novel which is so concerned with deconstructing the boundaries between male and female, wooer and wooed, should foreground a tale where the gulf between the different experiences of its participants is presented in such an exaggerated form. But for Woolf the figure of Daphne is a tool which may be used to interrogate rather than reinforce gender roles. She offers one answer to a question posed by Amy Richlin:

> But we must ask how we are to read texts, like those of Ovid, that take pleasure in violence -- a question that challenges not only the canon of Western literature but all representations. (p. 158)

The first covert reference to the tale in the novel comes on the very first page, but it is as yet unidentifiable. The young Orlando is practising his sword play on the mummified head of a Moor. We are told that 'the green arras with the hunters on it moved perpetually' (p. 11). Not until page 76 do we find out who these hunters are. We are now in the seventeenth century -- Orlando is still a young man, and has returned to his country mansion:

> And when it was evening and the innumerable silver sconces were lit and the light airs which for ever moved about the galleries stirred the blue and green arras, so that it looked as if the huntsmen were riding and Daphne flying; when the silver shone and lacquer glowed and wood kindled; when the carved chairs held their arms out and dolphins swam upon the walls with mermaids on their backs ... (p. 76)

As in *The Taming of the Shrew* the tale appears on a tapestry whose verisimilitude is emphasised. The mounted huntsmen are placed in apposition to Daphne each time the arras is mentioned, making them, rather than Apollo (who is apparently absent), seem to be her pursuers.

The significance of its subject matter does not really emerge until after the novel's central metamorphosis. Then the relationship between the sexes is foregrounded by the tension between continuity and discontinuity experienced by Orlando after she has become a woman.

Shortly after the transformation, Orlando muses on her changed circumstances in terms which recall the Daphne narrative, but, through emphasising the pleasure to be found in both states, transform Daphne's pain and terror into a kind of 'sweet, reluctant, amorous delay': 'Then she had pursued, now she fled. Which is the greater ecstasy? The man's or the woman's? And are they not perhaps the same? No, she thought, this is the most delicious ... For nothing', she thought, '... is more heavenly than to resist and to yield; to yield and to resist' (p. 109). The opposition between the man and the woman is mirrored by a parallel opposition within the woman. Her experience of contradictory impulses – resisting and yielding – is made to seem like a continual pulse through repetitive chiasmus, and there is no sense of real inner conflict. This harmony also seems to operate within the 'battle' *between* the sexes, for pursuit and flight are associated with ecstasy rather than distress.

We are briefly reminded of the tapestry when Orlando returns home as its mistress for the first time and 'observed the arras, how it swayed; watched the huntsmen riding and Daphne flying' (p. 121). More significant is its final, fourth appearance at the very end of the novel after her marriage to the similarly epicene Shelmerdine:

> Ah, but she knew where the heart of the house still beat. Gently opening a door, she stood on the threshold so that (as she fancied) the room could not see her and watched the tapestry rising and falling on the eternal faint breeze which never failed to move it. Still the hunter rode; still Daphne flew. The heart still beat, she thought, however faintly, however far withdrawn, the frail indomitable heart of the immense building. (p. 218)

This passage reinforces the sense that Daphne's story is being reinvented as an emblem of complementary harmony between the sexes. The movement of the tapestry, aligned by Woolf with a beating heart, is what creates the dynamic of the chase upon the arras – the original bitter conflict is here associated with the seat of life itself. Orlando, appropriately enough seen hovering on a boundary, a threshold, represents a meeting point between male and female experience where the similarities between the two are asserted as well as the differences:

> Yet through all these changes she had remained, she reflected, fundamentally the same. She had the same brooding meditative temper, the same love of animals and nature, the same passion for the country and the seasons. (p. 163)

Earlier writers had also read the legend against the grain in various ways, most obviously by associating Daphne with lust rather than chaste virginity. (A poem by Thomas Brown says that she 'flew like a whore from a constable freed' ('The Fable of Daphne and Apollo', line 36), and Aphra Behn compares Chloris fleeing Lysander with Daphne – she is distressed by his untimely flaccidity rather than his lust ('The Disappointment', line 122).) But in contrast to such largely unsubtle reflexes of reversal Woolf has metamorphosed the myth more radically by suggesting that the relationship between the two might in some strange way be used to suggest mutuality, reciprocity, a sameness as well as a difference. The movement of both pursuer and pursued is triggered by the same event, the 'eternal faint breeze', rather than by opposed wills. When Ovid's Apollo promises Daphne that he will match his pace to hers it is no more than a cruel joke. On Orlando's tapestry the promise is fulfilled, for the two figures must always move at the same speed, in time with one another. As well as comprising a male/female partnership, Orlando and her husband each contain masculine and feminine elements within their makeup. This means that the tapestry can be aligned with either of them as individuals as well as with their marriage.

Ovid's account of the tale's climactic moment is eloquent of the disparity between its two participants. The dramatic and final alteration of Daphne's whole being simply provides Apollo with a plant whose leaves will crown the poetic achievements which are his province. In Orlando the poet's calling and the possibility of metamorphosis into a tree are strangely blended, reflecting her participation in both male and female experience. A few pages into the novel, immediately before he first meets Queen Elizabeth, Orlando flings himself under an oak tree and feels his heart tugging at his side:

> To the oak tree he tied it and as he lay there, gradually the flutter in and about him stilled itself; the little leaves hung, the deer stopped; the pale summer clouds stayed; his limbs grew heavy on the ground; and he lay so still that by degrees the deer stepped nearer and the rooks wheeled round him and the swallows dipped and circled and the dragon-flies shot past, as if all the fertility and amorous activity of a summer's evening were woven web-like about his body. (p. 15)

'Flutter' serves to associate the little leaves with Orlando's heart, and the increasing heaviness and stillness of his body, which seem mirrored in his environment, as well as the other creatures' lack of fear, suggest that he has become one with the oak tree. In another reversal of the Daphne story Orlando has a tendency to be more treelike during his encounters with women. The following description occurs immediately after he realises to his joy that the Russian princess is a woman and not, as he first suspected, a boy:

206

Orlando stared; trembled; turned hot; turned cold; longed to hurl himself
through the summer air; to crush acorns beneath his feet; to toss his arms
with the beech trees and the oaks ...' (p. 27)

Later Sasha says he is 'like a million-candled Christmas tree (such as
they have in Russia) hung with yellow globes' (p. 39). Earlier the
Queen's possessive love for Orlando also brought with it a hint of
Orlando's metamorphosis: 'He was to be the son of her old age; the limb
of her infirmity; the oak tree on which she leant her degradation' (p. 19).
The oak may be the garland of civic rather than poetic achievement, but
there is still an association between Orlando's dendrification and his
literary output. Although Orlando writes scores of plays and poems it is
The Oak Tree to which he continually returns and which eventually
wins her recognition in the twentieth century. Whereas the myth served
to shore up the divide between masculine creativity and feminine
applause, Orlando, appropriately enough considering his uncertain
gender, partakes of both sides of the equation, being both poet and tree,
and, through the subject matter of his poem, further emphasises the
link rather than the division between these two sides.

But Apollo and Daphne is not the only Ovidian subtext in *Orlando*.
In contrast with allusions to this tale of a male pursuer and a reluctant
maid, echoes of the story of Salmacis' unrequited passion for the beau-
tiful Hermaphroditus may be traced in the novel, the two contradictory
narratives comprising a chiasmus, itself a favoured Ovidian trope,
which reflects the shifts and contradictions within the life of the
hero/ine. Again, I want to use an apparent allusion to the tale in *The
Taming of the Shrew* as my starting point.

Salmacis' rapturous address to Hermaphroditus is imitated by
Shakespeare in a scene which emphasises gender fluidity. As part of her
taming, Kate is forced to address an aged man as though he were a
beautiful girl:

> Young budding virgin, fair, and fresh, and sweet,
> Whither away, or where is thy abode?
> Happy the parents of so fair a child;
> Happier the man whom favourable stars
> Allots thee for his lovely bedfellow. (IV.v. 36-40)

>   puer o dignissime credi
> esse deus, seu tu deus es, potes esse Cupido,
> sive es mortalis, qui te genuere, beati,
> et frater felix, et fortunata profecto,
> si qua tibi soror est, et quae dedit ubera nutrix;
> sed longe cunctis est, si quam dignabere taeda.

> O youth, most worthy to be believed a god, if thou art indeed a god, thou
> must be Cupid; or if thou art mortal, happy are they who gave thee birth,

blest is thy brother, fortunate indeed any sister of thine and thy nurse who gave thee suck. But far, oh, far happier than they all is she , if any be thy promised bride, if thou shalt deem any worthy to be thy wife. (IV 320-6)

The fact that Kate is harking back to a passage which, although typical of the language of male courtship, is in fact addressed by a woman to a man adds an additional layer of irony to the gender confusion.

Virginia Woolf addresses her hero/ine employing the same rhetorical structure as both Salmacis and Kate.

> Happy the mother who bears, happier still the biographer who records the life of such a one! Never need she vex herself, nor he invoke the help of novelist or poet. From deed to deed, from glory to glory, from office to office he must go, his scribe following after, till they reach whatever seat it may be that is the height of their desire. (p. 12)

Salmacis appropriated male language when courting a man who is shortly to amalgamate with her to form an androgyne, Kate (herself originally acted by a boy) addresses a man as though he were a woman, and Woolf adds to the inherited gender confusion by assuming the guise of a male biographer who needs no help from creative writers when she is in fact both a woman and a novelist. The object of the address already shares an instability of gender with both the old man and Hermaphroditus – by beginning *Orlando* with the words, 'He, for there could be no doubt of his sex ...', Woolf immediately raises just such doubts. By substituting biographer for lover, and describing their relationship in terms of pursuit and climax, Woolf hints at the eroticism of her own relationship with her subject, an eroticism which is unconventional in that it places the woman in the active role, and, in so far as Orlando will shortly herself be a woman, because it is a lesbian love based on Woolf's own relationship with Vita Sackville-West. This is not the only passage where biography shades into amorous pursuit:

> For that was the way his mind worked now, in violent see-saws from life to death, stopping at nothing in between, so that the biographer must not stop either, but must fly as fast as he can and so keep pace with the unthinking passionate foolish actions and sudden extravagant words in which, it is impossible to deny, Orlando at this time of his life indulged. (p. 32)

Here again, it is the female who is the hunter and the male who flees.

In Queen Elizabeth Orlando finds another Salmacis, although she perhaps resembles more closely Salmacis' direct descendant, the Venus of Shakespeare's *Venus and Adonis*. Like Hermaphroditus, Orlando is abashed by her admiration:

pueri robor ora notavit;
nescit, enim, quid amor; sed et erubuisse decebat ...

But the boy blushed rosy red; for he knew not what love is. But still the blush became him well. (IV 329-30)

The young man withstood her gaze blushing only a damask rose as became him. (p. 18)

Both Salmacis and Elizabeth inspire disgust by their ardour:

denique nitentem contra elabique volentem
inplicat ut serpens, quam regia sustinet ales
sublimemque rapit: pendens caput illa pedesque
adligat et cauda spatiantes inplicat alas;
utve solent hederae longos intexere truncos,
utque sub aequoribus depresnsum polypus hostem
continet ex omni dimissis parte flagellis.

At length, as he tries his best to break away from her, she wraps him round with her embrace, as a serpent, when the king of birds has caught her and is bearing her on high: which, hanging from his claws, wraps her folds around his head and feet and entangles his flapping wings with her tail; or as the ivy oft-times embraces great trunks of trees, or as the sea-polyp holds its enemy caught beneath the sea, its tentacles embracing him on every side. (IV 361-7)

At the height of her triumph when the guns were booming at the Tower and the air was thick enough with gunpowder to make one sneeze and the huzzas of the people rang beneath the windows, she pulled him down among the cushions where her women had laid her (she was so worn and old) and made him bury his face in that astonishing composition – she had not changed her dress for a month – which smelt for all the world, he thought, recalling his boyish memory, like some old cabinet at home where his mother's furs were stored. He rose, half suffocated from the embrace. 'This', she breathed, 'is my victory!' – even as a rocket roared up and dyed her cheeks scarlet. (pp. 18-19)

One of Orlando's relationships partakes of both mythical subtexts. Towards the end of his male manifestation he inspires the love of the eccentric Archduchess Harriet, who is over six feet two inches tall, and grotesque and startling both in manner and appearance. Her wooing, like that of both Salmacis and Queen Elizabeth, is associated with a voracious and animalistic lust from which the more refined young man recoils in disgust. As if to underline the unnaturalness of her position as a female predator she is compared to 'a hare whose timidity is overcome by an immense and foolish audacity; a hare that sits upright and glowers at its pursuer with great, bulging eyes' (p. 78). The hare is typically used to suggest the helplessness of a woman – Philomela,

209

Arethusa, and indeed Daphne, are all compared to hares. Her relation-ship with Orlando provides yet a further twist to the book's network of androgyny and transsexuality, for after Orlando has become a woman the Archduchess reveals that he was in fact Archduke Harry all along, and only disguised his sex to further his suit. If their relationship began by echoing the narrative of Salmacis and Her-maphroditus, the reversals each undergoes make the pair more like Daphne and Apollo, except that Orlando is never in much danger from her rather pathetic suitor. This relationship may be aligned with that between Orlando and his creator, who as female novelist hiding behind the mask of male biographer, also in a sense partakes of both sexes.

The novel's final gender confusion is Orlando's marriage to Shelmer-dine.

> 'You're a woman, Shel!' she cried.
> 'You're a man, Orlando!' he cried. (pp. 174-5)

During the walk which precedes their meeting she glimpses 'a silver pool, mysterious as the lake into which Sir Bedivere flung the sword of Arthur' (p. 170). More than one of Ovid's tales begins with such a setting, and Orlando does indeed seem on the verge of metamorphosis rather than marriage. After falling and breaking her ankle, she lies down on the moor and rejects the idea of union with a man, saying she will be 'nature's bride', and dreams of a Daphnean stasis:

> 'I have found a greener laurel than the bay. My forehead will be cool always ... My hands shall wear no wedding ring ... the roots shall twine about them.' (p. 170)

In a twist to the Daphne theme, Orlando (who was, after all, once a man), stumbles on the word husband, 'my hyacinth, husband I mean' (p. 199). In Ovid the hyacinth springs from the blood of Hyacinthus, object of Apollo's *homosexual* desire.

*

As we have already seen, one of the hallmarks of the *Metamorphoses* is its preoccupation with various kinds of artists, and the nature of the art they produce. Both Woolf and Ovid associate their own artistry with that of their creations, and share an alertness to the way the relation-ship between metaphor and metamorphosis suggests the transformative power of poetic art. This can be seen most clearly in the *Metamorphoses* where so many more different types of transformation are possible than in *Orlando*:

ille cavis velox adplauso corpore palmis
desilit in latices alternaque bracchia ducens
in liquidis translucet aquis, ut eburnea si quis
signa tegat claro vel candida lilia vitro.

He, clapping his body with hollow palms, dives into the pool, and swim-
ming with alternate strokes flashes with gleaming body through the
transparent flood , as if one should encase ivory figures or white lilies in
translucent glass. (IV 352-5)

The things with which Hermaphroditus is compared – lilies, ivory – are
precisely the same kind of objects into which people are prone to
metamorphose in this poem. As a poet, Ovid is invested with the same kind
of powers as the gods in his own poem who transform both others and
themselves into different substances. When describing how the power of
Venus causes Pygmalion's statue to become a woman, he compares its
softening to malleable wax – his metaphor evoking Galatea's metamorpho-
sis, yet also contradicting it by seeming to deny that she is now flesh and
blood. The same move which underlines Ovid's power as a poet simultane-
ously flatters Pygmalion's power as a sculptor by suggesting that the
statue is somehow sculpted into life. The way the metaphor is superim-
posed on to the metamorphosis thus draws together the gods, the sculptor
and Ovid himself. Orlando also uses metaphors which chime with the
novel's 'real' metamorphoses so as to suggest an imaginative bond with her
creator. 'She compared the flowers to enamel and the turf to Turkey rugs
worn thin. Trees were withered hags, and sheep were grey boulders.
Everything, in fact, was something else' (p. 101). Although her comparisons
are ostensibly fantastic, earlier we were told that, at the time of the Frost,
sheep were rumoured to have turned into boulders.

At the beginning of the novel Woolf offers a description of her hero,
where the most conventional, not to say novelettish, comparison be-
tween his eyes and 'drenched violets' is extended until it acquires
something of the peculiar quality of the description of the submerged
Hermaphroditus, lapidary, vegetable and liquid at once:

> ... we must admit that he had eyes like drenched violets, so large that the
> water seemed to have brimmed in them and widened them; and a brow
> like the swelling of a marble dome pressed between the two blank
> medallions which were his temples.' (p. 12)

Orlando the poet employs the same strategies as his creator, and a few
pages later uses similar metaphors to describe Sasha, causing her to
undergo a virtual metamorphosis in the reader's mind:

> Images, metaphors of the most extreme and extravagant twined and
> twisted in his mind. He called her a melon, a pineapple, an olive tree, an
> emerald, and a fox in the snow all in the space of three seconds... (p. 26)

Although Orlando's urge to describe the Russian princess makes him replicate the conventional pattern whereby the male subject objectifies the female through metaphoric – and metamorphic – language, the gender divide is subverted because the images echo the female author's account of her own male creation. Orlando's dismissive view that 'girls were roses, and their seasons were short as the flowers' (p. 20) is undermined because only a page earlier Woolf likened her blushing hero to a damask rose himself. Yet he reasserts his 'masculine' capacity for Pygmalion-like creative authority to combat the one woman over whom we would expect him to have no power, his author.

The distinction between Woolf's use of metaphor and Orlando's becomes increasingly blurred, as though he were taking over the writing of the novel:

> Every single thing, once he tried to dislodge it from its place in his mind, he found thus cumbered with other matter like the lump of glass which, after a year at the bottom of the sea, is grown about with bones and dragon-flies, and coins and the tresses of drowned women.
> 'Another metaphor by Jupiter!' he would exclaim as he said this (which will show the disorderly and circuitous way in which his mind worked and explain why the oak tree flowered and faded so often before he came to any conclusion about Love ... (pp. 69-70)

Orlando is self-critical about his – and Woolf's – metaphor.

> 'A figure like that is manifestly untruthful', he argued, 'for no dragon-fly, unless under very exceptional circumstances, could live at the bottom of the sea.' (p. 70)

Some time later, it becomes clear that Woolf/Orlando has profited by this advice, for the image resurfaces, with the dragonflies safely on dry land.

> Among the hurry of these thoughts, however, there now rose, like a dome of smooth, white marble, something which, whether fact or fancy, was so impressive to her fevered imagination that she settled upon it as one has seen a swarm of vibrant dragon-flies alight, with apparent satisfaction, upon the glass bell which shelters some tender vegetable. (p. 116)

It is not apparent for some time what the object is that resembles a white marble dome. For Orlando it recalls the forehead of Shakespeare – another sign of her imaginative affinity with her author, for we have already seen that Woolf compared Orlando's forehead with a swelling marble dome in her first description of him. Eventually it turns out that the apparent metaphor was simple reality – Orlando has caught her first glimpse of the dome of St Paul's. This convergence of Woolf and Orlando in metaphor is further complicated if we remember that the early description of Orlando underneath the oak tree also involved dragon-flies in an image of encirclement.

Like Apollo in *Shrew* Orlando resists confinement within the bounds of an artwork. Books about writing books are hardly novel, yet there is a particular subtlety in the way Woolf blurs the distinction between herself and her creation. This element in the novel is Ovidian both in terms of broad strategy and detail. The fantastic image of the metamorphosed lump of glass, like the description of Orlando's violet eyes, may be aligned with the description of Hermaphroditus, as well as mediating sources such as 'Full fathom five', which comes of course from another text which seems to be 'written' by its central character.

Even though Pygmalion is not invoked by Woolf her relationship with her creation may be contrasted with male writers' use of the myth. Unlike a narrator with a stable masculine identity who employs a surrogate male Pygmalion figure to create and control an objectified Galatea, Woolf and Orlando are unstably gendered and toss the roles of creator and created back and forth between them. Thus the divergent methods of Joyce and H.D. come together in an androgynous synthesis.

Although both Daphne and Salmacis do of course metamorphose, Orlando's own transformation may be aligned with the phenomenon of Ovidian metamorphosis more generally. Ovid's interest in emphasising the continuity between one's original being and one's new, post-metamorphosis form, becomes in *Orlando* a continuity between male and female states. When Orlando is transformed, like Callisto, like Actaeon, he both is and is not the same.

> We may take advantage of this pause in the narrative to make certain statements. Orlando had become a woman – there is no denying it. But in every other respect, Orlando remained precisely as he had been. The change of sex, though it altered their future, did nothing whatever to alter their identity. Their faces remained, as their portraits prove, practically the same. (p. 98)

The use of 'their' contradicts the statement that the male and female Orlandoes are identical – 'The change of sex, though it altered their future, did nothing whatever to alter their identity'. The word 'identity' is teasingly ambiguous. It might be glossed 'personality, selfhood', or else 'exact similarity'. If the latter is true, then the two Orlandoes, however close, cannot be absolutely one – 'their' is a genuine plural.

Callisto is in a similar predicament when she is metamorphosed into a bear and she too hovers between a dual and a single identity, 'mens antiqua tamen facta quoque mansit in ursa', 'still her human feelings remained, though she was now a bear' (II 485). The shifts in the line's meaning reflect the tensions within Callisto. The first four words seem to suggest that her mind has been transformed along with her body – they might be translated 'her old mind however was made ...' – but as

213

we continue reading it becomes clear that her mind remains the same. However, it seems that Callisto's mind is not so secure as the line in its entirety implies and that our 'misreading' is therefore not totally mistaken, because, unlike Aesop's bat who can switch between his two aspects as policy suggests, she seems stuck with the worst aspects of both bear and woman:

> a! quotiens per saxa canum latratibus acta est
> venatrixque metu venantum territa fugit!
> saepe feris latuit visis, oblita quid esset,
> ursaque conspectos in montibus horruit ursos
> pertimuitque lupos, quamvis pater esset in illis.

> How often was she driven over the rocky ways by the baying of hounds and, huntress though she was, fled in affright before the hunters! Often she hid at sight of the wild beasts, forgetting what she was; and though herself a bear, shuddered at sight of other bears which she saw on the mountain-slopes. She even feared the wolves, although her own father, Lycaon, ran with the pack. (II 491-5)

The confusion of Callisto, afraid of her own species, may be compared to the predicament of Orlando after she has become a woman:

> 'Heavens!' she thought, 'what fools they make of us – what fools we are!' And here it would seem from some ambiguity in her terms that she was censuring both sexes equally, as if she belonged to neither; and indeed, for the time being, she seemed to vacillate; she was man; she was woman; she knew the secrets, shared the weaknesses of each. It was a most bewildering and whirligig state of mind to be in. ... She was a feather blown on the gale. (p. 113)

It is impossible to tease out the terms of her opening criticism. Is she speaking as a man, lamenting the devious ways of women and men's foolish readiness to fall for their tricks? Or is she already thinking in accordance with her changed sex, deploring the way men treat women, but also condemning women for their capitulation? It is also possible that she adjusts her thinking as she speaks – 'they' and 'we' are both women. For Orlando, as for so many of Ovid's characters, metamorphosis represents a destabilisation of one's selfhood as well as a physical transformation.

This phenomenon is well illustrated by the case of Actaeon. When he introduces the tale Ovid tells us that 'alienaque cornua fronti/ addita', 'upon whose brow strange horns appeared' (III 139-40). As *alienus* means belonging to someone else the implication is that Actaeon undergoes the superimposition of an alternative identity onto his existing one rather than an integral change. The suggestion is compounded by the information that after seeing his reflection in a pool, 'lacrimaeque per

214

ora/ non sua fluxerunt', 'and tears course down his changeling cheeks' (III 202-3). The position of the line ending adds to the surprise we experience in learning that Actaeon's tears fall on cheeks which are not merely strange, but are specifically not his own. It is as if the metamorphosis takes place even as the words are read, particularly as the verb *fluo* may mean to vanish or change. The word *ora* which ends the line may thus contain an appropriate hint of liminality as it is also the nominative form of the word for extremity or margin.

Ovid's transsexuals are few compared to his host of characters who change far more dramatically into an animal, a stone, a plant or a star. Whereas the *Metamorphoses* cumulatively weakens and questions the reader's sense that boundaries between different orders of creation are fixed and stable, Woolf's more narrow focus makes her readers aware of the fluidity and artificiality of gender roles. But just as there would be no horror in Daphne's story and no delight in Pygmalion's success if there were really no difference between women, stones and trees, so it is Orlando's ability to bridge the boundaries between male and female which makes her unique and mysterious in a gendered world. As Amy Richlin says of Ovid's own participation in the play of gender reversal:

> The cross-sex fantasy model offers no exit from gender hierarchy. The female is still the site of violence, no matter what the location of the subject. Even if the magician and the lady change places, *he* is still taking *her* place. (p. 178)

Orlando's spontaneous sex change is as fantastic as Woolf's reinvention of Daphne's fate as a positive experience; the novel is a space for play which, like the wood of *A Midsummer Night's Dream*, we can only visit for a few short hours.

12

Carmen perpetuum: Ovid today

It would be possible to trace the Ovidian line's continuation into a great deal of twentieth-century culture – such a project might include the discourses of psychoanalysis and postmodernism as well as artistic developments such as surrealism and magic realism. The *Metamorphoses* has been described as a cinematic text, and there is certainly room for an investigation of Ovid and film, which might focus on works with an avowed debt to myth, such as Cocteau's *Orphée*, or perhaps on more diffused Ovidian motifs – Pygmalion as a subtext in *Vertigo* for example. Until very recently such an approach, continuing the move away from direct influence already initiated in the previous chapters, might have provided the most obvious conclusion to this study; however the last decade has produced an unexpected flowering of fully conscious Ovidianism. Christoph Ransmayr's dreamlike novel of exile *The Last World*, a (very) free translation of the *Metamorphoses* by David Slavitt, *After Ovid* – a modern Garth – and, most recently, Ted Hughes' *Tales from Ovid*, are among the most notable examples of this development.

Critics and teachers may take some of the credit for this welcome resurgence of interest in the *Metamorphoses* among creative writers. Long marginalised by the academy, Ovid has finally been reabsorbed into the mainstream. The rehabilitation of the *Metamorphoses* can be traced back to L.P. Wilkinson's *Ovid Recalled* (1955), and then to a steadily increasing number of important critical studies, including such diverse volumes as Galinsky's *Ovid's Metamorphoses* and Solodow's *The World of Ovid's Metamorphoses*. Critics whose concerns might loosely be termed 'theoretical' have responded with particular enthusiasm to Ovid, having discovered that the poet who could be allegorised, euhemerised and moralised is equally amenable to being politicised, psychoanalysed and deconstructed – or indeed received.

Hughes celebrates Ovid's 'relevance' to a twentieth-century audience in his introduction to *Tales from Ovid*. He reminds us that the *Metamorphoses* was written at the time of Christ's birth, when Rome was waiting for a new religion to fill the gap left by the decay of the old Pantheon:

> For all its Augustan stability, it was at sea in hysteria and despair, at one extreme wallowing in the bottomless appetites and sufferings of the gladiatorial arena, and at the other searching higher and higher

for a spiritual transcendence – which eventually did take form, on the crucifix. (p. xi)

Hughes then invites us to align this state of mind with the imminent millennium, implying a special bond between our own age and Ovid's – for gladiators and crucifixes read Tarantino and the X Files. Such a claim is dubious; it is debatable how much impact the death of an obscure Jew would have had on a sophisticated Roman. And although Hughes implies that ours is an age with a peculiar affinity with Ovid his translations continually remind us that he comes at the end of a venerable Ovidian tradition.

The modern reader may be inclined to overestimate Hughes' daring, for reasons which are implicit in a thoughtful review of the volume by Allan Massie:

> All this is admirably Ovidian. If he fails, for me anyway, where Dryden and Golding succeed, it is for a reason that has nothing to do with his rendering. The truth is that, although they translate Ovid into the poetic language of their own day, just as Hughes does, time has given their versions a sheen of age which makes them more like Ovid than any translation into modern idiom can. (*The Daily Telegraph*, 24 May, 1997)

There is a telling slippage in Massie's claim that Dryden and Golding are 'more like Ovid' than Hughes. Obviously the glamour of antiquity was itself once absent from Ovid – as Pope's 'The First Epistle of the Second Book of Horace Imitated' would remind us. There is certainly plenty in Hughes to jar on the reader in search of classical remoteness. When Jove prepares to destroy Phaethon rather than allow the earth to be incinerated, 'He soared to the top of heaven,/ Into the cockpit of thunder' (p. 42). Still more strikingly anachronistic is Hughes' description of Jove's appearance before Semele in his full divine glory:

> He chose
> A slighter manifestation
> Fashioned, like the great bolts, by the Cyclops
> But more versatile – known in heaven
> As the general deterrent. ...
>
> In that splinter of a second,
> Before her blazing shape
> Became a silhouette of sooty ashes
> The foetus was snatched from her womb. (p.99)

The vocabulary of nuclear warfare – 'general deterrent' is reinforced by the evocation of Semele's ghostly trace, the silhouette of a Hiroshima victim.

But as we saw in this book's very first example of Ovidianism,

12. Carmen perpetuum: Ovid today

Chaucer's *House of Fame*, to depart from the letter of the *Metamorphoses* can bring one closer to its spirit. The precise details used by Hughes were obviously not available to Ovid, but the effect is directly paralleled in various anachronistic touches in the *Metamorphoses*, such as when Venus is described consulting the 'archive office' (XV 810), a ploy which was not lost on Ovid's earlier translators, and particularly the contributors to Garth's edition of the *Metamorphoses*.

Indeed many of Hughes' stylistic quirks would, one feels, have appealed to Ovid. The inappropriately jaunty zeugma of Venus' punishment of the Propoetides – 'She stripped off their good names/And their undergarments' (p. 145) – has a parallel at an equally 'serious' moment in the original. When Apollo begs Phaethon to reconsider his choice of boon he pleads that he should 'take my counsel, not my chariot', 'consiliis, non curribus utere nostris!' (II 146). The punning description of Callisto's fear of Diana after being seduced by Jove will make the same readers who are alienated by Keats' wordplay in the last stanza of 'Ode on a Grecian Urn' squirm with annoyance:

> Callisto's
> Jumpy terror of Diana's likeness
> Grabbed with electric hands, and she bolted – (p. 48)

In another uneasy pun Adonis (the son of Cinyras and Myrrha) is described as 'the meaty fruit her father implanted' (p. 129). This is just one of a number of unpleasant touches from the author of *Crow* which might seem to owe little to Ovid's famous urbanity and elegance. Yet 'implanted' performs precisely the same function as *medulla*, invoking Myrrha both as tree and woman. In a similarly ingenious vein Hughes' Venus cautions Adonis not to 'stake my heart in a fool's gamble' (p. 131) – the pun is absent in the original of course, but is in many ways typical of a poet often censured for his self-consciously clever wordplay. For Hughes as well as for Ovid, words, not just objects, are subject to metamorphosis.

In his creative fidelity to the original Hughes is guilty of some inconsistency. In the introduction to *Shakespeare's Ovid*, an earlier volume containing a selection of the later *Tales*, Hughes suggests that he subscribes to an outmodedly limited view of Ovid, ascribing to his work the epithets 'romantic' and 'superficial' and concluding that 'the outline of the mural cartoon is Ovid's, and I stick to it: the colouring is my own' (Hughes 1995, p. ix). But if Hughes underestimates the degree to which he has been influenced by the spirit of Ovid, he is at least in good company, for we may remember that an earlier Poet Laureate was equally scornful of Ovid's 'boyisms' and yet did them more than justice in his own translations. In a more specific instance Hughes may be said

219

to resemble Dryden, for both poets appear to have responded with particular intensity to the tale of Pygmalion.

Pygmalion's misogyny, subtly tainted by Dryden and made more decidedly problematic in Beddoes' version (which omits the Propoetides), is here unambiguously pathological:

> The spectacle of these cursed women sent
> Pygmalion the sculptor slightly mad.
> He adored woman, but he saw
> The wickedness of these particular women
> Transform, as by some occult connection,
> Every woman's uterus to a spider. (p. 145)

As in Beddoes' 'Pygmalion' (and unlike in Ovid) the sculptor has a vision of the statue which predates the carving itself. But whereas Beddoes' Galatea comes to him like a beautiful if mysterious epiphany, inspiring his greatest work of art, Hughes describes a disembodied shade, as dubious as Keats' Lamia:

> a spectre, sick of unbeing,
> That had taken possession of his body
> To find herself a life. (p. 146)

In a further negative intensification of a process begun by Beddoes, the statue's creation is itself controlled by this vampiric female. We may recall that in Beddoes the sculptor seemed in the grip of a nameless external force, whereas Ovid emphasises his conscious artistry:

> She moved into his hands,
> She took possession of his fingers
> And began to sculpt a perfect woman. (p. 146)

Like Pope's Belinda and H.D., this is a Galatea in at least partial control of her own creation.

Hughes' Pygmalion is less unequivocally solicitous than Ovid's, who is anxious lest he has bruised the statue; he 'half wanted to bruise her/ into a proof of life' (147). The line ending is poised so that we must wait to learn that his strange wish is in some way justified, and the hint of sadism still lingers. Similarly the sculptor's placing of the statue on his bed, a tender if erotic moment in Ovid, gains an additional salaciousness in Hughes through the sexual force of two ambiguous verbs – 'He *laid* her on his couch,/ *Bedded* her in pillows' (p. 148).

As we saw in Chapter 7, Dryden was particularly alert to the connections between the stories of Pygmalion and Myrrha, his great-granddaughter. Significantly, when Hughes describes the latter's metamorphosis, he allows a third possible form to hover between the obvious ones of woman and tree, 'she swayed/ Living statuary on a tree's foundations' (p. 128). This curious detail might seem designed to remind us of Galatea, and perhaps nudge the reader into reflecting that both Pygmalion and Myrrha fall in love with their 'creations'. Certainly Hughes, like so many Ovidian writers before him, seems attuned to all the more disturbing possibilities within this ostensibly positive tale.

Michael Longley offers a still more unusual version of the story in 'Ivory and Water'. The retelling remains reasonably faithful – though truncated – up to the vital moment of animation when the metamorphosis is itself metamorphosed:

> And her veins pulse under your thumb to the end of the dream
> When she breaks out in a cold sweat that trickles into pools
> And drips from her hair dissolving it and her fingers and toes,
> Watering down her wrists, shoulders, rib-cage, breasts until
> There is nothing left of her for anyone to hug or hold. (*After Ovid*, p. 240)

Galatea's mollification doesn't stop at flesh; she softens further into water. Although we might expect a certain amount of similarity between quite independent accounts of girls changing into streams, it does seem possible to discover traces of both Cyane and Arethusa's metamorphoses in Longley's poem – the former is changed into a fountain out of shock at Proserpina's rape, and the latter is herself metamorphosed to avoid being ravished:

> post haec umeri tergusque latusque
> pectoraque in tenues abeunt evanida rivos ...
> restatque nihil, quod prendere possis.

> Next after these, her shoulders, back and sides and breasts vanish into thin watery streams ... and nothing is left that you can touch. (V 434-5, 437)

> occupat obsessos sudor mihi frigidus artus,
> caeruleaeque cadunt toto de corpore guttae,
> quaque pedem movi, manat lacus, eque capillis
> ros cadit

> Cold sweat poured down my beleaguered limbs and the dark drops rained down from my whole body. Wherever I put my foot a pool trickled out, and from my hair fell the drops ... (V 632-5)

These troubling intertexts invite us to view Pygmalion's attraction to the statue as predatory and rapacious rather than loving and miraculous. Even if the transformation into a stream did not recall other victims of male lust, the picture is still a negative one, suggesting disintegration and a loss of stable selfhood rather than, as we might expect, a dawning personality. Longley's treatment of Pygmalion thus

221

seems to align itself with H.D.'s similarly barbed response to the legend. Alternatively, if we recall that Pygmalion can be seen as a Narcissus figure and the statue as an extension of his fantasy life, the pulsing veins under his thumb and subsequent dreamy liquefaction might lead the reader to a rather more mundane interpretation of the poem. Unpleasantly twentieth-century as such a reading might seem, it should be remembered that Beddoes' Pygmalion also appears almost to ejaculate Galatea into being.

*

It is difficult to respond in an entirely novel way to a poem which has been read, imitated and appropriated constantly for two thousand years. David Slavitt certainly tries to inject fresh life into his recent translation of the *Metamorphoses*, giving us plenty of reminders that his is a response grounded in the late twentieth century: Jove uses a 'thick duvet of cloud' (I 600) to conceal his liaison with Io from Juno, and Actaeon's dogs include 'Valley Girl', 'Tenzing' and 'Damned Spot (who always wants to go out)'. For sheer breathtaking banality it is hard to beat Slavitt's fancy that a gouged out eyeball sticks on an antler tine 'like a cocktail cherry' (XII 262) – unless of course we turn to Ovid's account of the same incident (the battle between the lapiths and the centaurs) when he likens brains oozing through a shattered skull to sieved cottage cheese (XII 436-8).

Still more audacious are Slavitt's own comments and interjections, which are incorporated seamlessly into the body of the text. After introducing the story of Byblis and Caunus for example:

> This story, a somewhat mannered performance,
> is one of those nice rhetorical set pieces Ovid loved
> To dazzle with. He could put his lawyer's training to use
> as he made up elaborate speeches for his characters to declaim. (IX 441-4)

He takes even greater liberties with the story of Medea, alluding briefly to her dealings with Creusa, not mentioned by Ovid, and then continuing:

> But the point is that Ovid avoids it, gives us
> instead a bizarre catalogue in the effete Alexandrian style
> of references we're supposed to get and respond to, pointless
> except for the way they obscure what is uppermost in his mind
> and ours, too. In dreams, we find ourselves sometimes engaged
> in this kind of repression, distortion, transmogrification ... (VII 369-74)

But we might align this daring, postmodern metatranslation with one of the earliest and (to modern eyes) least attractive treatments of Ovid,

222

the *Ovide Moralisé* which also incorporates comment, interpretation and judgment within the translation itself. Slavitt himself acknowledges the influence of mediating Ovidians upon his work. His two acknowledged debts are perhaps surprising, for they are not derived from the most fashionable or revered Ovidians – Eliot and Shakespeare for example – but from Sandys and Gay. Slavitt reproduces Gay's rendition of Polyphemus' song verbatim in Book XIII and uses the same rhyme scheme as Sandys for the last dozen lines of his poem. With this act of homage we may compare Kenneth Koch's bizarre *Io*, written (apparently in tribute to Golding) in rebarbative fourteeners – the redundant padding in the following couplet, if not the diction, is certainly authentic:

> The King of Gods espying her, in her bodacious tresses,
> Desired for to fuck with her beside the watercresses ... (*After Ovid*, p. 59)

Slavitt responds sensitively to Ovid's interest in the ontology, the psychology of metamorphosis. As Actaeon begins to metamorphose:

> His ears are sharpening into pointed
> excrescences, while his hands are pointing, becoming hoofs,
> and his arms are turning to forelegs. His skin is a hide,
>   and his heart
> is cold with terror. (III 184-7)

The catalogue of change cheats us into expecting that Actaeon's heart has also become something different. The line ending intensifies the shock of remembering that his consciousness remains that of a suffering human. This is the key to the tale's horror – the hunter fully shares the reader's awareness of his fate's terrible irony. A line break is used to similar effect in Slavitt's account of Pygmalion:

>   One, especially lovely,
> he fashioned out of a piece of snowy ivory flesh
> could never have duplicated. No skin was as smooth and clear ... (X 246-8)

We are reminded of the resemblance between Pygmalion's statue and a poet's *scripta puella* – each equally a construct. Ivory might as easily be an adjective qualifying flesh as a noun, and only as our eye travels to the next line do we realize we have been wrongfooted. We may remember that Dryden played precisely the same trick on his readers in his translation of the Wife of Bath's tale. A suggestive refinement, hinting at the idea of nature imitating art, is introduced in the way Slavitt translates 'formamque dedit, qua femina nasci/ nulla potest', 'giving it a beauty more perfect than that of any woman ever born' (X 248-9). Slavitt's version implies that the statue sets the standard which mere flesh can only aspire to duplicate, and thus draws out the unnatural, fetishising aspect of Pygmalion's love. Again, this modification of Ovid was anticipated by Dryden:

> And carved in ivory such a maid, so fair,
> As nature could not with his art compare,
> Were she to work; but in her own defence
> Must take her pattern here and copy hence. (7-10)

Beddoes also describes souls as mere 'dross' compared to beautiful statues.

Hughes is equally engaged by the idea of being two things at once. Of Actaeon he writes, 'Human tears shone on his stag's face' (p. 108). As well as evoking the split between mind and body, Hughes replicates the impression of a metamorphosis taking place even as we read, discussed at the end of the previous chapter. The tears which left his eyes when they were human have not yet dried although his metamorphosis is now complete. Sometimes Hughes provides us with an extra reminder of a character's double identity. Arethusa, the nymph who is transformed into a stream, describes to Ceres how she became aware of Proserpina's presence in the underworld:

> As I slid through the Stygian pool
> In the underworld, I felt myself
> Reflecting a face that looked down on me. (p. 62)

In the original Arethusa simply sees Proserpina; the embellishment is, however, entirely in keeping with Ovid's own acute awareness of the phenomenology of metamorphosis.

*

Strictly speaking Christoph Ransmayr's *The Last World* falls outside this book's brief, being the work of an Austrian rather than an English Ovidian; nevertheless this complexly textured and richly imaginative response to the *Metamorphoses* deserves some attention. Once again we have come full circle, for Ransmayr's subject is Ovid's banishment to Tomi refracted through the distorting lens of his *Metamorphoses* – a move anticipated by Ovid in the metamorphic world of his own exile poetry.[1] The poet is presumed dead at the beginning of the novel, which is narrated by his friend Cotta who arrives in Tomi to find it peopled by characters from the *Metamorphoses*, albeit strangely altered – Tereus is the local butcher and Fama keeps a grocery store. Ransmayr's

---

[1] Ovid's exile is also the inspiration for David Malouf's *An Imaginary Life*, although his handling of the subject is far less interestingly 'Ovidian' (in my opinion) than Ransmayr's.

Philomela does not weave her dreadful tidings but points to Tereus' house, 'a blank wall framed in ivy and wild grape' (p. 169), as though creating, if not a picture, a kind of *tabula rasa* on which Procne can project her own worst fears – only the border is yet in place. Like Hughes, Ransmayr seeks to bring our world closer to Ovid's, for the decaying Roman outpost is arbitrarily infected by twentieth-century paraphernalia to produce a confusing montage of anachronisms; the effect is typical of late twentieth-century fiction – of magic realism, for example – but at the same time true to the spirit of Ransmayr's original source, for Ovid also combines the remote and miraculous with practical, humdrum detail. Even in metamorphosing Ovid, Ransmayr replicates his effects; the process which transforms Arachne, for example, into the deaf-mute weaver of Tomi, engages the reader in the same identification of sameness and difference as does one of Ovid's metamorphoses. The eventual metamorphosis of Tomi itself as it becomes overrun with unruly vegetation mirrors the contest between art and nature fought over Diana's grotto:

> It was impossible to tell if a weather-cock or a gable ornament was still in place or had long since fallen apart under the embracing branches. The rioting green mimicked the forms it enclosed, playfully, mockingly at first, but then, obeying its own law of form and beauty, went on relentlessly to obliterate all signs of human handiwork. (p. 165)

The evocation of nature initially imitating the forms of art – or architecture – might be compared with Stanley Spenser's *The Resurrection in Cookham Churchyard* where the vegetation similarly follows the precise lines of the church gable.

Much of what seems new and daring in these postmodern – or even millennial – *Metamorphoses* can be traced back either to Ovid's many imitators or to Ovid himself. The erotic charge of Fred D'Aguiar's 'Thisbe to Pyramus' might read like a modern accretion:

> Your wet blade's sweet tip
> Is hardly in me;
> Already the fruit
> Turn red on the tree. (*After Ovid*, p. 113)

but the imagery of penetration is matched by Ovid's own ejaculatory evocation of Pyramus' wound:

> ut iacuit resupinus humo, cruor emicat alte,
> non aliter quam cum vitiato fistula plumbo
> scinditur et tenui stridente foramine longas
> eiaculatur aquas atque ictibus aera rumpit.

> As he lay stretched upon the earth the spouting blood leaped high; just as

225

when a pipe has broken at a weak spot in the lead and through the small
hissing aperture sends spurting forth long streams of water, cleaving the
air with its jets. (IV 121-4)

Some of the contributors to *After Ovid* opt for full-scale modernisations.
Lawrence Joseph recasts Pyreneus (who offered the Muses shelter from
the rain and then tried to rape them) as an American gangster:

> Two of his boys drove up, told us
> to get in out of the rain. Took us
>
> to the villa. Into an inner room.
> From his rococo chair upholstered
>
> with silk he arose, arms extended,
> to greet us. Designer blue jeans,
>
> T-shirt, yellow linen jacket. (p. 138)

And William Logan offers a strange version of Niobe, where Apollo and
Diana are transformed into inbred homicidal rednecks, and Niobe
herself into the wife of a Wall Street banker with a Hermès handbag
and a brownstone off Park Avenue. But even these Ovidian improvisa-
tions are merely the latest in a line of modernised Ovids. At the
beginning of the tradition we find Chaucer's Manciple's Tale, a retelling
of Apollo's revenge on the unfaithful Coronis (II 542-632), reinventing
the god as a cuckold straight out of fabliau tradition. The tell tale crow
who betrays Coronis is a free agent in Ovid but a domestic caged bird
in Chaucer, and Coronis herself is described as Apollo's 'wyf'; like May
and Alisoun, she knows how to take advantage of a husband's absence:

> And so bifel, when Phebus was absent,
> His wyf anon hath for hir lemman sent. (203-4)

Even this rather vague circumstantial detail, suggesting the need to
plan an intrigue within defined spatial and temporal constraints, is
missing in Ovid's more lofty version.

Matthew Prior's 1715 version of Apollo and Daphne is just as freely
and irreverently modernised. It takes the form of a dialogue between
god and nymph; whereas the former's speeches uphold the subtitle's
claim to have 'faithfully translated' from *Metamorphoses* I, Daphne has
been metamorphosed from a trembling victim into a pert Augustan
miss:

> A. What is to come by certain art I know.
> D. Pish, Partridge has as fair pretence as thou.
> A. Behold the beauties of my locks – [D] a fig,
>   That may be counterfeit a Spanish wig ...

226

12. Carmen perpetuum: Ovid today

A. I sing – [D] that never shall be Daphne's choice.
   Syphacio had an admirable voice. (15-18, 21-2)

(Partridge was a well known astrologer, Syphacio a castrato.) Daphne does soften so far as to suggest that Apollo might like to amuse her father by reading the 'Courant' with him – this was a contemporary newspaper, but Prior is also making a punning reference to Peneus' watery provenance.

Modernisation seems to be one of the many constants running through the Ovidian tradition – although it would certainly be dangerous to assume that Chaucer and Prior wrote with precisely the same intentions or achieved the same effect as today's modernisers, or that the same impulses which drove Medieval illuminators to present Narcissus and Apollo *et al.* in the costume of their own day inspired Cocteau to substitute a posse of hit-and-run bikers for the snake which killed Eurydice.

To end this book with a study of the last decade's Ovidianism emphasises the way the reception of the *Metamorphoses*, as well as the poem itself, is a *carmen perpetuum*, not only because Ovid's influence on English literature is an ongoing process, but also because, like *Finnegans Wake*, the end of the story in a sense takes us right back to where we started – and indeed to everywhere we've been along the way:

In nova fert animus mutatas dicere formas
corpora; di, coeptis (nam vos mutastis et illas)
adspirate meis primaque ab origine mundi
ad mea perpetuum deducite tempora carmen!

My mind is bent to tell of bodies changed into new forms. Ye gods, for you yourselves have wrought the changes, breathe on these my undertakings, and bring down my song in unbroken strains from the world's very beginning even unto the present time. (I 1-4)

227

Bibliography

This is a bibliography of items cited in the text, as well as a selection of other items consulted in the preparation of this book, rather than an exhaustive bibliography of the topic.

Abrams, Richard, 'The Tempest and the Concept of the Machiavellian Playwright', English Literary Renaissance 8 (1978) 43-66.

Ahl, F.M., Metaformations: Sound and Wordplay in Ovid and Other Classical Poets (Ithaca, NY: Cornell University Press) 1985.

Altick, Richard D. & Loucks, James F., Browning's Roman Murder Story: A Reading of The Ring and the Book (Chicago & London: University of Chicago Press) 1968.

Anderson, J.J., 'The Narrators in The Book of the Duchess and The Parliament of Fowles', Chaucer Review 26 (1992) 219-35.

Anderson, W.S., 'Multiple Change in the Metamorphoses', Transactions of the American Philological Association 94 (1963) 1-27.

Arathoon, Leigh A., ed., Chaucer and the Craft of Fiction (Michigan: Solaris Press Inc.) 1986.

Armitage, David, 'The Dismemberment of Orpheus: Mythic Elements in Shakespeare's Romances', Shakespeare Survey 39 (1987) 123-33.

Attridge, Derek & Ferrer, Daniel, Post-structuralist Joyce: Essays from the French (Cambridge: Cambridge University Press) 1984.

Baldwin, T.W., William Shakespeare's Small Latin and Lesse Greeke, 2 vols (Urbana: University of Illinois Press) 1944.

Barber, C.L., Shakespeare's Festive Comedy: A Study of Dramatic Form and its Relation to Social Custom (Princeton: Princeton University Press) 1959.

Barkan, Leonard, 'Diana and Actaeon: The Myth as Synthesis', English Literary Renaissance 10 (1980) 317-59.

Barkan, Leonard, ' "Living Sculptures": Ovid, Michelangelo and The Winter's Tale', ELH 48 (1981) 639-67.

Barkan, Leonard, The Gods Made Flesh: Metamorphosis and the Pursuit of Paganism (New Haven & London: Yale University Press) 1986.

Barthes, Roland, S/Z, trans. Richard Miller (New York: Hilland Wang) 1974.

Bate, Jonathan, Shakespeare and Ovid (Oxford: Clarendon Press) 1993.

Baudelaire, Charles, My Heart Laid Bare and Other Prose Writings, trans. Norman Cameron (London: Soho Book Company) 1986.

Bauer, George, Bernini in Perspective (New Jersey: Prentice-Hall Inc.) 1976.

Beddoes, T.L., The Poetical Works, 2 vols (London: J.M. Dent and Co.) 1890.

Behn, Aphra, Poems upon Several Occasions (London: Tonson) 1684.

Beja, Morris and Norris, David, Joyce in the Hibernian Metropolis (Columbus: Ohio State University Press) 1996.

Bibliography

Bender, John B., *Spenser and Literary Pictorialism* (Princeton: Princeton University Press) 1972.

Bennett, J.A.W., *Chaucer's Book of Fame: An Exposition of The House of Fame* (Oxford: Clarendon Press) 1968.

Beressem, Hanjo, 'The Letter! The Litter! The Defilements of the Signifier in *Finnegans Wake*', *European Joyce Studies* 6 (1990) 139-64.

Berger, Harry, 'Busirane and the War between the Sexes: An Interpretation of *The Faerie Queene* III xi-xii', *English Literary Renaissance*, vol. 1 no. 2 (1971) 99-121.

Beyette, Kent, 'Ovid and Pope's *Rape of the Lock*', *CEA Critic*, vol. 37 no. 2 (1975) 23-4.

Blake, William, *The Poems*, ed. C.H. Stevenson (London: Longman) 1971.

Bloom, Harold, *A Map of Misreading* (Oxford: Oxford University Press) 1975.

Bloom, Lillian D., 'Addison as Translator: A Problem in Neo-Classical Scholarship', *Studies in Philology*, vol. 46 no. 1 (1949) 31-53.

Boitani, P., *Chaucer and the Imaginary World of Fame* (Cambridge: D.S. Brewer) 1984.

Bowen, Zack & Carens, James F., *A Companion to Joyce Studies* (Connecticut: Greenwood Press) 1984.

Braden, Gordon, *The Classics and English Renaissance Poetry: Three Case Studies* (New Haven & London: Yale University Press) 1978.

Brady, Ann P., *Pompilia: A Feminist Reading of Robert Browning's The Ring and The Book* (Athens: Ohio University Press) 1988.

Braudy, Leo, *The Frenzy of Renown: Fame and its History* (New York & Oxford: Oxford University Press) 1986.

Brinkley, Robert A., 'Spenser's *Muiopotmos* and the Politics of Metamorphosis', *English Literary History*, vol. 48 no. 4 (1981) 668-76.

Brivic, Sheldon, *Joyce the Creator* (Madison: University of Wisconsin Press) 1985.

Brooke, N.S., 'C.S. Lewis and Spenser: Nature, Art and the Bower of Bliss', in A.C. Hamilton (1972) 13-28.

Brown, Richard, *James Joyce and Sexuality* (Cambridge: Cambridge University Press) 1985.

Brown, Susan, 'Pompilia: The Woman (in) Question', *Victorian Poetry*, vol. 34 no. 1 (1996) 15-37.

Brown, Thomas, *Works* (London: Sam Briscoe) 1715.

Browning, Robert, *The Ring and the Book* (London: Penguin) 1971.

Buckler, William E., *Poetry and Truth in The Ring and the Book* (New York & London: New York University Press) 1985.

Bullough, Geoffrey, *Narrative and Dramatic Sources of Shakespeare* (London & New York: Routledge & Kegan Paul) 1957-66.

Burrow, Colin 'Metamorphoses in *The Faerie Queene*', in Martindale (1988).

Burrow, Colin, *Epic Romance: Homer to Milton* (Oxford: Clarendon Press) 1993.

Burrow, John, 'Poems without Endings', *Studies in the Age of Chaucer* 13 (1991) 17-37.

Bush, Douglas, *Mythology and the Romantic Tradition in English Poetry* (Cambridge: Harvard University Press) 1937.

Bush, Douglas, *Mythology and the Renaissance Tradition in English Poetry* (New York: Norton) 1963.

Butler, Christopher, 'Joyce, Modernism and Post-Modernism' in *The Cambridge Companion to James Joyce*, ed. Derek Attridge (Cambridge: Cambridge University Press) 1990, 259-82.

Bibliography

Byatt, A.S., *Possession: A Romance* (London: Vintage) 1990.

Calabrese, Michael A., *Chaucer's Ovidian Arts of Love* (Gainesville: University Press of Florida) 1994.

Calderwood, James L., *Shakespearian Metadrama: The Argument of the Play in Titus Andronicus, Love's Labour's Lost, Romeo and Juliet, A Midsummer Night's Dream and Richard II* (Minneapolis: University of Minneapolis Press) 1971.

Campbell, Joseph, *Mythic Worlds, Modern Worlds: On the Art of James Joyce,* ed. Edmund L. Epstein (New York: HarperCollins) 1993.

Carroll, L.C., *The Metamorphoses of Shakespearean Comedy* (Princeton: Princeton University Press) 1985.

Chaucer, Geoffrey, *The Riverside Chaucer,* ed. Larry D. Benson (Oxford: Oxford University Press) 1988.

Childs, Donald, 'Metamorphoses, Metaphysics and Mysticism', *Classical and Modern Literature, a Quarterly,* vol. 13 no. 1 (1992) 15-29.

Clemen, Wolfgang, *Chaucer's Early Poetry,* trans. C.A.M. Synge (London: Barnes & Noble) 1963.

Clements, Patricia, ' "As in the Rough Stream of a Glacier": Virginia Woolf's Art of Narrative Fiction', in *Virginia Woolf: New Critical Essays,* ed. Patricia Clements & Isobel Grundy (London: Vision Press) 1983, 11-31.

Colie, Rosalie, *My Ecchoing Song: Andrew Marvell's Poetry of Criticism* (New Jersey: Princeton University Press) 1970.

Collett, Jonathan H., 'Milton's Use of Classical Mythology in *Paradise Lost*', *PMLA,* vol. 85 no. 1 (1970) 88-96.

Colvin, Sidney, *John Keats* (London: Macmillan) 1917.

Cooper, Helen, 'Chaucer and Ovid: A Question of Authority' in Martindale (1988) 71-81.

Crockett, Bryan, ' "The Wittiest Partition": Pyramus and Thisbe in Ovid and Shakespeare', *Classical and Modern Literature, a Quarterly,* vol. 12 no. 1 (1991) 49-58.

Curran, Leo C., 'Transformation and Anti-Augustanism in Ovid's *Metamorphoses*', *Arethusa* 5 (1972) 71-91.

Dane, Joseph A., 'Chaucer's Eagle, Ovid's Phaëton: a Study in Literary Reception', *Journal of Medieval and Renaissance Studies,* vol. 11 no. 1 (1981) 71-82.

Dante, *La Divina Commedia,* ed. Natalino Sapegno (Milan: Riccardo Ricciardi Editione) 1957.

Dante, *The Divine Comedy,* trans. C.H. Sisson (London: Pan) 1980.

Delaney, Sheila, *Chaucer's House of Fame: The Poetics of Skeptical Fideism* (Chicago and London: University of Chicago Press) 1972.

Deneef, A. Leigh, *Spenser and the Motives of Metaphor* (Durham N.C.: Duke University Press) 1982.

Desmond, Marilynn, 'Chaucer's *Aeneid*: The Naked Text in English', *Pacific Coast Philology,* vol. 19 (1984) 62-7.

Devlin, Kimberly, 'The Female Eye: Joyce's Voyeuristic Narcissists' in *New Alliances in Joyce Studies,* ed. Bonnie Kime Scott (London & Toronto: Associated University Presses) 1988, 135-43.

Donahay, Martin A., 'Mirrors of Masculine Desire: Narcissus and Pygmalion in Victorian Representation', *Victorian Poetry,* vol. 32 no. 1 (1994) 35-53.

Donnelly, Michael L., 'With Cunning Hand Pourtrahed: Mural Decoration in Spenser, Ovid and the Middle Ages', in *Spenser and the Middle Ages* ed. David A. Richardson (Cleveland: Cleveland State University Press) 1976.

231

Bibliography

Doody, Margaret Anne, *The Daring Muse: Augustan Poetry Reconsidered*, (Cambridge: Cambridge University Press) 1985.

D'Orsay, W. Pearson, ' "Unkinde" Theseus: A Study in Renaissance Mythography', *English Literary Renaissance*, vol. 4 no. 2 (1974) 276-98.

Dryden, John, *The Poems of John Dryden,* 4 vols, ed. James Kinsley (Oxford: Clarendon Press) 1980.

Due, O.S., *Changing Forms: Studies in the Metamorphoses of Ovid* (Copenhagen: Gyldendal) 1974.

DuRocher, Richard J., *Milton and Ovid* (London & Ithaca NY: Cornell University Press) 1985.

Dwyer, Warren F., *Profit, Poetry and Politics in Augustan Translation: A Study of the Tonson-Garth Metamorphoses of 1717*, Ph.D. Diss., University of Illinois, 1969.

Eliot, T.S., *Selected Essays* (London: Faber & Faber) 1932.

Eliot, T.S., *The Waste Land*, ed. Valerie Eliot (London: Faber & Faber) 1971.

Elliott, Alison Goddard, 'Ovid and the Critics: Seneca, Quintilian and "Seriousness" ' *Helios*, vol. 12 no. 1 (1985) 9-20.

Ellmann, Richard, *James Joyce* (Oxford: Oxford University Press) 1982.

Elsner, J., *Art and Text in Roman Culture* (Cambridge: Cambridge University Press) 1996.

Empson, William, *The Structure of Complex Words* (London: Chatto & Windus) 1951.

Erzgraber, Willi, 'Common Traits of Chaucer's and Joyce's Narrative Art', in Lehmann, E. & Lenz, B. eds, *Telling Stories: Studies in Honour of Ulrich Broich* (Amsterdam: B.R. Grüber) 1992, 188-204.

Feeney, D.C., *The Gods in Epic: Poets and Critics of the Classical Tradition* (Oxford: Clarendon Press) 1991.

Fielding, Henry, *Amelia* (Oxford: Clarendon Press) 1983.

Findlay, L.M., 'Taking the Measure of Différance: Deconstruction and *The Ring and the Book*', *Victorian Poetry*, vol. 29 no. 4 (1991) 401-14.

Fowler, Rowena, 'Browning's Metamorphoses' (unpublished paper).

Fraenkel, Hermann, *Ovid: A Poet Between Two Worlds* (Berkeley & Los Angeles: University of California Press) 1945.

Fraunce, Abraham, *The Third Part of the Countesse of Pembrokes Yuychurch: entituled Amintas Dale* (London: Thomas Woodcocke) 1592.

Friedman, Susan Stanford, 'Portrait of the Artist as a Young Woman: H.D.'s Rescriptions of Joyce, Lawrence and Pound', in Writing the Woman Artist: Essays in Poetics, Politics, and Portaiture, ed. Suzanne W. Jones, (Philadelphia: University of Pennsylvania Press) 1991, 23-42

Fritz, Antonia, 'Oviditties in "Ithaca" ', *European Joyce Studies* 6 (1994) 77-101.

Froula, Christine, *Modernism's Body: Sex, Culture and Joyce* (New York: Columbia University Press) 1996.

Fry, Donald, 'The Ending of *The House of Fame*', in *Chaucer at Albany,* ed. Rossell Hope Robbins (New York: Burt Franklin & Co, Inc.) 1975, 27-40

Fyler, John M., *Chaucer and Ovid* (New Haven & London: Yale University Press) 1979.

Gabbard, G.N., 'Browning's Metamorphoses', *Victorian Poetry* 4 (1966) 29-31.

Galinsky, G.K., *Ovid's Metamorphoses: An Introduction to the Basic Aspects* (Berkely & Los Angeles: University of California Press) 1975.

Garber, Marjorie B., *Dream in Shakespeare: from Metaphor to Metamorphosis* (New Haven & London: Yale University Press) 1974.

Garth, Sir Samuel, *Claremont* (London: J. Tonson) 1715.

Bibliography

Giamatti, A. Bartlett, *The Earthly Paradise and the Renaissance Epic* (Princeton: Princeton University Press) 1966.

Giamatti, A. Bartlett, *Play of Double Senses: Spenser's Faerie Queene* (New Jersey: Prentice-Hall Inc.) 1975.

Gilbert, Sandra M. & Gubar, Susan, *No Man's Land: The Place of the Woman Writer in the Twentieth Century*, vol. 3 *Letters From the Front* (New Haven & London: Yale University Press) 1994.

Robert Gittings, *The Odes of Keats and their Earliest Known Manuscripts* (London: Heinemann) 1970.

Golding, Arthur, *The Metamorphoses* (London: De la More Press) 1904.

Gordon, John, *James Joyce's Metamorphoses* (Dublin: Gill & Macmillan) 1981.

Gose, Elliot B. Jr, 'Joyce's Goddess of Generation' in *James Joyce: The Centennial Symposium*, ed. M Beja, P. Herring, M. Harmon & D. Norris (Urbana: University of Illinois Press) 1986, 158-69.

Greenblatt, Stephen, *Renaissance Self-Fashioning: From More to Shakespeare* (Chicago: University of Chicago Press) 1980.

Greenblatt, Stephen, *Shakespearean Negotiations: The Circulation of Social Energy in Renaissance England* (Oxford: Clarendon Press) 1988.

Greene, T.M., *The Light in Troy: Imitation and Discovery in Renaissance Poetry* (New Haven: Yale University Press) 1982.

Griffin, Alan H.F., 'Ovid's *Metamorphoses*', *Greece and Rome*, vol. 24 (1977) 57-70.

Gross, Kenneth, *The Dream of the Moving Statue* (Ithaca NY & London: Cornell University Press) 1992.

H.D., *Her* (London: Virago Press) 1984.

H.D., *Collected Poems 1912-44*, ed. Louis L. Martz (Manchester: Carcanet Press) 1984.

Hale, John K., 'Milton Playing with Ovid', *Milton Studies* 25 (1989) 3-19.

Hall, Anne D., 'The Actaeon Myth and Allegorical Reading in Spenser's "Two Cantos of Mutabilitie"', *The Sixteenth-Century Journal*, vol. 26 no. 3 (1995) 561-75.

Hamilton, A.C. 'Spenser's Treatment of Myth', *ELH*, vol. 26 no. 3 (1959) 335-54.

Hamilton, A.C., ed. *Essential Articles for the Study of Edmund Spenser*, (Connecticut: Archon Books) 1972.

Hamilton, Donna, *Virgil and The Tempest: The Politics of Imitation* (Ohio: Ohio State University Press) 1990.

Hammond, Paul 'Marvell's Sexuality', *The Seventeenth Century*, vol. 11, no. 1 (1996) 87-123.

Hanning, Robert W., 'Chaucer's First Ovid: Metamorphosis and Poetic Tradition in *The Book of the Duchess* and *The House of Fame*', in Arathoon, 121-63.

Hardie, Philip, ' "Why is Rumour here?" Tracking Virgilian and Ovidian *Fama*' (unpublished paper).

Harding, D., 'Milton and the Renaissance Ovid', *Illinois Studies in Language and Literature*, vol. 30 no. 4 (1945).

Harries, Byron, 'The Spinner and the Poet: Arachne in Ovid's *Metamorphoses*', *Proceedings of the Cambridge Philological Association*, no. 216 (1990) 64-82.

Hayward, Sir John, *David's Tears* (London: J. Bill) 1623.

Hazlitt, William, *The Complete Works of William Hazlitt in Twenty-One Volumes*, ed. P.P. Howe (London: Dent) 1930.

Henke, Suzette, *James Joyce and the Politics of Desire* (New York & London: Routledge) 1990.

233

Henke, Suzette & Unkeless, Elaine, *Women in Joyce* (Brighton: Harvester Press) 1982.

Hibbard, Howard, *Bernini* (London: Pelican) 1965.

Hinds, S.E., *The Metamorphosis of Persephone: Ovid and the Self-Conscious Muse* (Cambridge: Cambridge University Press) 1987.

Hinds, S.E., 'Generalising about Ovid', *Ramus* 16 (1987) 4-31.

Hinds, S.E., *Allusion and Intertext: Dynamics of Appropriation in Roman Poetry* (Cambridge: Cambridge University Press) 1998.

Hofmann, Michael & Lasdun, James, *After Ovid* (London: Faber & Faber) 1994.

Holland, Peter, 'Theseus' Shadows in *A Midsummer Night's Dream*', *Shakespeare Survey* 47 (1994) 139-51.

Hollander, John, 'The Poetics of Ekphrasis', *Word and Image*, vol. 4 (1988) 209-17.

Hollenberg, Donna Krolik, *H.D.: The Poetics of Childbirth and Creativity* (Boston: Northeastern University Press) 1991.

Homan, Sidney, '*The Tempest* and Shakespeare's Last Plays: The Aesthetic Dimension', *Shakespeare Quarterly*, vol. 24 no. 1 (1973) 69-76.

Hopkins, David, 'Dryden and Ovid's "Wit out of Season" ', in Martindale (1988) 167-90.

Howe, P.P., ed. *The Complete Works of William Hazlitt in Twenty-One Volumes*, (London: Dent) 1930.

Hughes, Ted, *Shakespeare's Ovid* (London: Enitharmon Press) 1995.

Hughes, Ted, *Tales from Ovid* (London: Faber & Faber) 1997.

Ibsen, Henrik, *When We Dead Awaken*, trans. William Archer (London: Heinemann) 1900.

Jack, Ian, *Keats and the Mirror of Art* (Oxford: Oxford University Press) 1967.

Johnson, Samuel, *A Dictionary of the English Language* (London, 1755).

Johnson, Samuel, *Lives of the English Poets*, ed. George Birkbeck Hill (Oxford: Clarendon Press) 1905.

Jones, Ellen Carol, 'The Letter Selfpenned to One's Other: Joyce's Writing, Deconstruction, Feminism', in *Coping with Joyce: Essays from the Copenhagen Symposium*, ed. Morris Beja & Shari Benstock (Columbus: Ohio State University Press) 1989, 180-94.

Jordan, Robert M., 'Lost in the Funhouse of Fame: Chaucer and Postmodernism', *Chaucer Review*, vol. 18 no. 2 (1983) 100-15.

Joyce, James, *Ulysses* (London: Bodley Head) 1986.

Joyce, James, *A Portrait of the Artist as a Young Man* (London: Jonathan Cape) 1964.

Joyce, James, *Finnegans Wake* (London: Faber & Faber) 1939; repr. 1971.

Joyce, James, *Dubliners* (London: Jonathan Cape) 1967.

Keach, William, *Elizabethan Erotic Narratives: Irony and Pathos in the Ovidian Poetry of Shakespeare, Marlowe and their Contemporaries* (London: Harvester Press) 1977.

Kean, P.M., *Chaucer and the Making of English Poetry*, 2 vols (London & Boston: Routledge & Kegan Paul) 1972.

Keats, John, *The Complete Poems*, ed. Miriam Allott (London: Longman) 1970.

Keats, John, *The Poems of John Keats*, ed. Jack Stillinger (London: Heinemann) 1978.

Kennedy, Duncan F., *The Arts of Love: Five Studies in Roman Love Elegy* (Cambridge: Cambridge University Press) 1993.

Kinsley, James and Helen, *Dryden: The Critical Heritage* (London & New York: Routledge) 1971.

Bibliography

Kittredge, G.L., 'Chaucer's Lollius', *Harvard Studies in Classical Philology*, vol. 28 (1917) 47-133.

Koonce, B.G., *Chaucer and the Tradition of Fame: Symbolism in The House of Fame* (Princeton: Princeton University Press) 1966.

Krier, Theresa M., *Gazing on Secret Sights: Spenser, Classical Imitation and the Decorums of Vision* (Ithaca & London: Cornell University Press) 1990.

Laird, Andrew, '*Ut Figura Poesis*: Writing Art and the Art of Writing in Augustan Poetry', in Elsner, 75-102.

Lamb, M.E., '*A Midsummer Night's Dream*: The Myth of Theseus and the Minotaur', *Texas Studies in Language and Literature*, vol. 21 no. 4 (1979) 478-91.

Lanham, R.A., *The Motives of Eloquence: Literary Rhetoric in the Renaissance* (New Haven: Yale University Press) 1976.

Lateiner, D., 'Mythic and Non-mythic Artists in Ovid's *Metamorphoses*', *Ramus* 13 (1984) 1-30.

Lawrence, Karen, 'Joyce and Feminism' in *The Cambridge Companion to James Joyce*, ed. Derek Attridge (Cambridge: Cambridge University Press) 1990, 237-58.

Leach, Eleanor W., 'Ekphrasis and the Theme of Artistic Failure in Ovid's *Metamorphoses*', *Ramus* vol. 3 no. 1 (1974) 102-42.

Leishman, J.B., *The Art of Marvell's Poetry* (London: Hutchinson) 1966.

Lewiecki-Wilson, Cynthia, *Writing against the Family: Gender in Lawrence and Joyce* (Carbondale: Southern Illinois University Press) 1994.

Lewis, C.S., *The Allegory of Love: A Study in Medieval Tradition* (Oxford: Clarendon Press) 1938.

Llewellyn, Nigel, *Illustrating Ovid*, in Martindale (1988) 151-66.

Longo, Joseph A., 'Myth in *A Midsummer Night's Dream*', *Cahiers Elisabéthains*, no. 18 (1980) 17-27.

Lotspeich, Henry Gibbons, *Classical Mythology in the Poetry of Edmund Spenser* (Princeton: Princeton University Press) 1932.

McDonald, Russ, 'Reading *The Tempest*', *Shakespeare Survey* 43 (1991) 15-28.

McDowell, Lesley, *The Feminine Fictions of James Joyce*, Ph.D. Diss., University of Glasgow, 1994.

MacCabe, Colin, *James Joyce and the Revolution of the Word* (London: Macmillan) 1978.

Maclure, Millar, 'Nature and Art in *The Faerie Queene*', in Hamilton, 171-88.

Mann, Thomas, *Lotte in Weimar*, trans. H.T. Lowe-Porter (London: Secker & Warburg) 1940.

Martindale, Charles, 'Paradise Metamorphosed: Ovid in Milton', *Comparative Literature*, vol. 37, no. 4 (1985) 301-33.

Martindale, Charles, *John Milton and the Transformation of Ancient Epic* (London: Croom Helm) 1986.

Martindale, Charles, *Ovid Renewed: Ovidian Influences on Literature and Art from the Middle Ages to the Twentieth Century* (Cambridge: Cambridge University Press) 1988.

Martindale, Charles and Michelle, *Shakespeare and the Uses of Antiquity* (London: Routledge) 1990.

Martindale, Charles, *Redeeming the Text: Latin Poetry and the Hermeneutics of Reception* (Cambridge: Cambridge University Press) 1993.

Martz, Louis L., *Poet of Exile: A Study of Milton's Poetry* (New Haven & London: Yale University Press) 1980.

Marvell, Andrew, *The Poems and Letters*, ed. H.M. Margoliouth (Oxford: Clarendon Press) 1927.

Massey, Irving, *The Gaping Pig: Literature and Metamorphosis* (Berkeley: University of California Press) 1976.

Maxwell, Catherine, 'Pygmalion and the Revenge of Galatea', *English Literary History*, vol. 60 no. 4 (1993) 985-1013.

Medcalf, Stephen, 'T.S. Eiot's *Metamorphoses*: Ovid and *The Waste Land*', in Martindale (1988) 233-46.

Meres, Francis, *Palladis Tamia: Wit's Treasury* (New York & London: Garland) 1973.

Miller, J. Hillis, 'Ariachne's Broken Woof', *Georgia Review*, vol. 31 (1977) 44-60.

Miller, J. Hillis, *Versions of Pygmalion* (Cambridge: Harvard University Press) 1990.

Miller, Jacqueline T., 'The Writing on the Wall: Authority and Authorship in Chaucer's *House of Fame*', *Chaucer Review*, vol. 17 no. 2 (1982) 95-115.

Millet, Bella, 'Chaucer, Lollius and the Medieval Theory of Authorship', *Studies in the Age of Chaucer: The Yearbook of the New Chaucer Society* 5 (1985) 93-103.

Milman, Henry Hart, 'The Belvidere Apollo', *Annals of the Fine Arts*, 5 (1820) 218-19.

Milowicki, Edward, 'Ovid through Shakespeare: the Divided Self', *Poetics Today*, vol. 16 no. 2 (1995) 217-52.

Milton, John, *Tetrachordon* (London) 1645.

Milton, John, *Paradise Lost*, ed. Alastair Fowler (Harlow: Longman) 1968.

Milton, John, *Complete Shorter Poems*, ed. John Carey (Harlow: Longman) 1968.

Minnis, A.J., 'A Note on Chaucer and the *Ovide Moralisé*', *Medium Aevum*, vol. 48 no. 2 (1979) 254-7.

Minnis, A.J., *Oxford Guides to Chaucer: The Shorter Poems* (Oxford: Clarendon Press) 1995.

Morey, James H., 'Spenser's Mythic Adaptations in Muiopotmos', *Spenser Studies: A Renaissance Poetry Annual* 9 (1988) 49-59.

Morris, Margot, 'Stifled Back Answers: The Gender Politics of Art in Joyce's "The Dead" ', *Modern Fiction Studies,* vol. 35 no. 3 (1989) 479-503.

Nagle, Betty Rose, 'Erotic Pursuit and Narrative Seduction in Ovid's Metamorphoses', *Ramus*, vol. 17, no. 1 (1988) 32-51.

Nevo, Ruth, 'Spenser's "Bower of Bliss" and a Key Metaphor from Renaissance Poetic', in Hamilton, 1972, 29-39.

Nevo, Ruth, *Comic Transformations in Shakespeare* (London & New York: Methuen) 1980.

Nevo, Ruth, *Shakespeare's Other Language* (New York: Methuen) 1987.

Newton, J.M., 'What Do We Know about Andrew Marvell', *Cambridge Quarterly*, 6 (1973) 32-42, 125-43.

Nichol, W.S.M., 'Cupid, Apollo and Daphne (Ovid *Metamorphoses* 1.452ff)' *Classical Quarterly*, vol. 30 (1980) 174-82.

Norris, Margot, 'Modernism, Myth, and Desire in "Nausicaa" ', *James Joyce Quarterly*, vol. 26 no. 1 (1988) 37-50.

Nosworthy, J.M., 'Shakespeare's Pastoral Metamorphoses' in *The Elizabethan Theatre VIII*, ed. G.R. Hibbard (Ontario: P.D. Meaney) 1982, 90-113.

Nuttall, A.D., *Two Concepts of Allegory: A Study of Shakespeare's The Tempest and the Logic of Allegorical Expression* (London: Routledge & Kegan Paul) 1967.

Bibliography

Nuttall, A.D., 'Marvell and Horace: Colour and Translucency'. in *Horace Made New*, ed. Charles Martindale & David Hopkins (Cambridge: Cambridge University Press) 1992, 86-102.

Otis, Brooks, *Virgil: A Study in Civilised Poetry* (Oxford: Oxford University Press) 1963.

Otis, Brooks, *Ovid as an Epic Poet* (Cambridge: Cambridge University Press) 1966.

Ovid, *Heroides and Amores*, trans. Grant Showerman (London: Heinemann) 1963.

Ovid, *Ovid's Metamorphoses in fifteen books translated by the most eminent hands*, ed. Sir Samuel Garth (London: Jacob Tonson) 1717.

Ovid, *Metamorphoses*, trans. by F.J. Miller (London: Heinemann) 1984.

Ovid, *Tristia, Ex Ponto*, trans. A.L. Wheeler (London: Heinemann) 1996.

Paglia, Camille, *Sexual Personae: Art and Decadence from Nefertiti to Emily Dickinson* (London: Penguin) 1991.

Patrides, C.A., *Approaches to Marvell: The New York Tercentenary Lectures* (London: Routledge) 1978.

Pigman, G.W., 'Versions of Imitation in the Renaissance', *Renaissance Quarterly*, vol. 33 (1980) 1-32.

Pitcher, John, 'A Theatre of the Future: The *Aeneid* and *The Tempest*', *Essays in Criticism*, vol. 34 no. 3 (1984) 193-215.

Pope, Alexander, *The Poems*, ed. John Butt (London: Methuen & Co) 1963.

Pope, W.B. ed., *The Diary of Benjamin Robert Haydon* (Cambridge, Mass: Harvard University Press) 1960.

Pope-Hennessy, John, *Italian High Renaissance and Baroque Sculpture* (Oxford: Phaidon) 1986.

Potkay, Adam, 'The Problem of Identity and the Grounds for Judgment in *The Ring and the Book*', *Victorian Poetry*, vol. 25 no. 2 (1987) 143-57.

Pound, Ezra, *The Literary Essays of Ezra Pound*, ed. T.S. Eliot (London: Faber & Faber) 1954.

Powell, Raymond, *Shakespeare and the Critics' Debate: A Guide for Students* (London: Macmillan) 1980.

Power, Arthur, *Conversations with James Joyce* (London: Millington) 1974.

Prior, Matthew, *The Literary Works*, 2 vols (Oxford: Clarendon Press) 1971.

Ransmayr, Christoph, *The Last World*, trans. John Woods (London: Chatto & Windus) 1990.

Ray, Robert H., 'Marvell's "To His Coy Mistress" and Sandys's translation of Ovid's *Metamorphoses*', *Review of English Studies*, vol. 45 (1993) 386-8.

Reverand, Cedric D., *Dryden's Final Poetic Mode: The Fables* (Philadelphia: University of Pennsylvania Press) 1988.

Rhys, Jean, *Wide Sargasso Sea* (London: Andre Deutsch) 1966.

Richlin, Amy, 'Reading Ovid's Rapes', in *Pornography and Representation in Greece and Rome*, ed. Amy Richlin (New York & Oxford: Oxford University Press) 1992, 158-79.

Ricks, Christopher, *Milton's Grand Style* (Oxford: Clarendon Press) 1963.

Ricks, Christopher, 'Its own Resemblance', in Patrides, 108-35.

Roche, Thomas P., *The Kindly Flame: A Study of the Faerie Queene III and IV* (Princeton: Princeton University Press) 1964.

Roche, Thomas P., 'The Challenge to Chastity: Britomart at the House of Busyrane', in Hamilton (1972) 189-98.

Rudd, Niall, 'Pyramus and Thisbe in Shakespeare and Ovid: *A Midsummer Night's Dream* and *Metamorphoses* 4 1-166', in *Creative Imitation and Latin*

Bibliography

Literature, ed. David West & Tony Woodman (Cambridge: Cambridge University Press) 1979, 173-93.

Ruffolo, Lara, 'Literary Authority and the Lists of Chaucer's *House of Fame*: Destruction and Definition through Proliferation', *Chaucer Review* vol. 27 no. 4 (1993) 325-41.

Sandys, George, *Ovid's Metamorphoses Englished* (Oxford, 1632).

Scragg, Leah, 'Shakespeare, Lyly and Ovid: the influence of *Gallathea* on *A Midsummer Night's Dream*', *Shakespeare Survey*, vol. 30 (1977) 125-34.

Sedgwick, W.B., 'The Influence of Ovid', *The Nineteenth Century*, vol. 122 (1937) 483-98.

Segal, C.P., *Landscape in Ovid's Metamorphoses: A Study in the Transformations of a Literary Symbol* (Wiesbaden: Hermes) 1969.

Segal, Charles, 'Ovid: Metamorphosis, Hero, Poet', *Helios*, vol. 12 no. 1 (1985) 49-63.

Seneca, *Controversiae*, trans. M. Winterbottom, 2 vols (London: Heinemann) 1924.

Seneca, *Epistulae Morales*, trans. R.M. Gunmere, vol. 2 (London: Heinemann) 1970.

Senn, Fritz, 'Nausicaa in James Joyce's *Ulysses*', in *Critical Essays,* ed. Clive Hart & David Hayman (Berkeley/L.A./London: University of California Press) 1974, 277-311.

Senn, Fritz, *Inductive Scrutinies: Focus on Joyce*, ed. Christine O'Neill (Dublin: Lilliput Press) 1995.

Shakespeare, *The Complete Works*, ed. Peter Alexander (London & Glasgow: Collins) 1951.

Sharrock, Alison, 'Womanufacture', *Journal of Roman Studies*, vol. 81 (1991), 36-49.

Sharrock, Alison, 'Representing Metamorphosis', in Elsner, 103-30.

Shaw, W. David, 'Browning's Murder Mystery: *The Ring and the Book* and Modern Theory', *Victorian Poetry*, vol. 27 (1989) 79-98.

Shaw Hardy, Clara, 'Ecphrasis and the Male Narrator in Ovid's Arachne', *Helios*, vol. 22, no. 2 (1995) 140-8.

Skulsky, H., *Metamorphosis: The Mind in Exile* (Cambridge, Mass.: Harvard University Press) 1981.

Slavitt, David, *The Metamorphoses of Ovid* (Baltimore & London: Johns Hopkins University Press) 1994.

Slinn, E. Warwick, 'Language and Truth in *The Ring and the Book*', *Victorian Poetry*, vol. 27 (1989) 115-33.

Sloman, Judith, *Dryden: The Poetics of Translation* (Toronto: University of Toronto Press) 1985.

Smith, A.J., 'Marvell's Metaphysical Wit', in Patrides, 56-86.

Solodow, J.B., *The World of Ovid's Metamorphoses* (Chapel Hill, NC: University of North Carolina Press) 1988.

Spenser, Edmund, *Spenser's Poetical Works*, ed. E. de Selincourt (Oxford: Clarendon Press) 1910.

Spenser, Edmund, *The Faerie Queene*, ed. A.C. Hamilton (Harlow: Longman) 1977.

Spitzer, Leo, 'Speech and Language in *Inferno* XIII', *Italica*, vol. 19 no. 3 (1942) 81-103.

Stam, Robert, *Reflexivity in Film and Literature from Don Quixote to Jean-Luc Godard* (Ann Arbor, Michigan: UMI Research Press) 1985.

Bibliography

Stanford Friedman, Susan, *Penelope's Web: Gender, Modernity and H.D.'s Fiction* (Cambridge: Cambridge University Press) 1990.

Stanford Friedman, Susan, 'Portrait of the Artist as a Young Woman', in Jones, Susan, *Writing the Woman Artist: Essays on Poetics, Politics, and Portraiture* (Philadelphia: University of Pennsylvania Press) 1991, 23-42.

Starnes, D.T. & Talbert, E.W., *Classical Myth and Legend in Renaissance Dictionaries* (Chapel Hill, NC: University of North Carolina Press) 1955.

Staton, Walter F., 'Ovidian Elements in *A Midsummer Night's Dream*', *Huntington Library Quarterly*, vol. 26, no. 2 (1962-3) 165-78.

Stoppard, Tom, *Rosencrantz and Guildenstern are Dead* (London: Faber) 1968.

Suzuki, Mihoko, 'The Dismemberment of Hippolytus', *Classical and Modern Literature, a Quarterly*, vol. 10 no. 2 (1990) 103-12.

Swift, Jonathan, *The Poems of Jonathan Swift*, ed. Harold Williams, 3 vols (Oxford: Clarendon Press) 1937.

Taylor, Anthony Brian, 'Shakespeare's Use of Golding's Ovid as a Source for *Titus Andronicus*', *Notes and Queries*, vol. 35 (1988) 449-51.

Taylor, Anthony Brian, 'Shakespeare and Golding', *Notes and Queries*, vol. 36 (1991) 492-99.

Thompson, Ann, 'Philomel in *Titus Andronicus* and *Cymbeline*', *Shakespeare Survey*, vol. 31 (1978) 23-37.

Thompson, Claud A., 'Spenser's "Many Faire Pourtraicts, and Many a Faire Feate"', *Studies in English Literature*, vol. 12 (1972) 21-32.

Thompson, James R., *Thomas Lovell Beddoes* (Boston: Twayne Publishers) 1985.

Tissol, Garth, 'Ovid's little *Aeneid* and the Thematic Integrity of the *Metamorphoses*', *Helios* 20 (1993) 69-79.

Tissol, Garth, *The Face of Nature: Wit, Narrative, and Cosmic Origins in Ovid's Metamorphoses* (Princeton, New Jersey: Princeton University Press) 1997.

Tomlinson, Charles, *Poetry and Metamorphosis* (Cambridge: Cambridge University Press) 1983.

Tooke, Andrew, *The Pantheon representing the Fabulous Histories of the Heathen Gods* (London: C. Harper) 1713.

Trousdale, Marion, 'Recurrence and Renaissance: Rhetorical Imitation in Ascham and Sturm', *English Literary Renaissance*, vol. 6 (1976) 156-79.

Vance, Norman, 'Ovid and the Nineteenth Century', in Martindale (1988) 215-31.

Vaughan, Alden T. & Virginia, *Shakespeare's Caliban: a Cultural History* (Cambridge: Cambridge University Press) 1991.

Vincent, Michael, 'Between Ovid and Barthes: *Ekphrasis*, orality, textuality in Ovid's "Arachne"', *Arethusa* vol. 27 (1994) 361-86.

Virgil, *Works*, 2 vols, trans. H. Rushton Fairclough (London: Heinemann) 1986.

Walker, William, '*Pompilia* and Pompilia', *Victorian Poetry*, vol. 22 no. 1 (1984) 47-63.

Watts, Cedric, 'Andrew Marvell and the Chameleon', *Critical Quarterly*, vol. 25 (1983) 23-33.

Weller, Barry, 'Induction and Inference: Theater, Transformation and the Construction of Identity in *The Taming of the Shrew*', in *Creative Imitation: New Essays on Renaissance Literature in Honor of Thomas M. Greene*, ed. D. Quint, M. Ferguson, G.W. Pigman & Wayne Rebhorn (New York: Medieval and Renaissance Texts and Studies) 1992.

Welles, Marcia L., *Arachne's Tapestry: The Transformation of Myth in Seventeenth-Century Spain* (San Antonio: Trinity University Press) 1986.

Bibliography

Whitby, M., Hardie, P., & Whitby, M., eds, *Homo Viator: Classical Essays for John Bramble* (Bristol: Bristol Classical Press) 1987.

Wilkinson, L.P., *Ovid Recalled* (Cambridge: Cambridge University Press) 1955.

Wimsatt, J., *Chaucer and the French Love Poets* (Chapel Hill: North Carolina University Press) 1968.

Windeatt, B.A., *Chaucer's Dream Poetry: Sources and Analogues* (Cambridge: Brewer) 1982.

Wittkower, Rudolf, *Bernini* (London, 1955).

Woolf, Virginia, *Orlando* (London: Penguin) 1993.

Wyke, Maria, 'Written Women: Propertius' *Scripta Puella*', *Journal of Roman Studies*, vol. 77 (1987) 47-61.

Yeats, W.B., *The Poems*, ed. Richard J. Finneran (London: Macmillan) 1983.

Young, David, *Something of Great Constancy: The Art of A Midsummer Night's Dream* (New Haven: Yale University Press) 1966.

Zimbardo, Rose A., 'Form and Disorder in *The Tempest*', *Shakespeare Quarterly* 14 (1963) 49-56.

Zumwalt, Nancy, 'Fama Subversa: Theme and Structure in Ovid's *Metamorphoses* 12', *California Studies in Classical Antiquity*, 10 (1977) 209-22.

Index of characters and episodes
from the *Metamorphoses*

General index

Fulton, Alice 146
Fyler, John 4, 30

Galinsky, G.K. 217
Garth, Sir Samuel 9; 'Claremont'
    138-9; *Metamorphoses* 123-39
Gawain-poet 21
Gay, John 124
Gilbert, Sandra M. 201
Goethe, Johann Wolfgang von 58, 61
Golding, Arthur 5, 58, 59, 64-6, 67,
    72, 74, 77, 101-2, 120, 124, 218,
    223
Graham, Jorie, 13-14
Greenaway, Peter 73

Hamilton, Donna 77
Hanning, Robert W. 23
Haydon, Benjamin 144
Hayward, Sir John 251
Hazlitt, William 144, 147, 149, 151
Henke, Suzette 190
Hercules 177
Hesiod 158
Hesione 177
Hinds, Stephen 17, 23, 184
Hitchcock, Alfred 217
Hofmann and Lasdun, *After Ovid* 7,
    13, 126, 128, 131, 148, 221, 223,
    225-6
Homer 2, 88, 101, 123 *Iliad* 25, 26,
    29, 37, 40, 79, 130
Horace, 85n, 125
Hughes, Ted, *Tales from Ovid* 6, 7, 9,
    12-13, 217-21, 224, 225

Ibsen, Henrik 185-6

Jack, Ian 143, 146
Johnson, Samuel 2
Jonson, Ben 84
Joseph, Lawrence 226
Joyce, James 5, 11, 167, 182, 185,
    213; 'The Dead' 186-8, 197, 199;
    Finnegans Wake 189, 194-6, 199,
    227; *A Portrait of the Artist as a
    Young Man* 188-91, 194, 199;
    Ulysses 189, 191-4, 197
Joyce, Nora 196-7

Keats, John 5, 8, 11, 139, 141-54;
    Endymion 143, 146; 'How Many

Bards Gild the Lapses of Time'
    14, 21, 155-6; 'I Stood Tip-Toe
    Upon a Little Hill 144; *Lamia*
    141-2, 145, 162, 171, 220; 'Ode on
    a Grecian Urn' 8, 142-54, 167, 219
    'Ode to a Nightingale' 149n
Koch, Kenneth 223

Langland, William 21
Lewis, C.S. 41, 48
Llewellyn, Nigel 15
Logan, William 226
Lollius 28
Longley, Michael 221
Lucretius 133, 137

Malouf, David 224n
Mann, Thomas 58, 161
Marlowe, Christopher 141, 164-5
Martindale, Charles 4
Marvell, Andrew 8, 9, 85-99, 101,
    108, 124, 125, 128, 157, 178, 202,
    203
Massie, Alan 218
Maynwaring, Arthur 126, 129-30,
    162, 185
Meres, Francis 57, 70
Miller, J. Hillis 134
Millet, Bella 28
Milman, Henry Hart 147, 148, 150,
    152
Milton 3, 8, 11, 19, 48, 85, 87, 124,
    125, 128, 130, 131, 141, 156, 183,
    201; *Comus* 103; *Paradise Lost* 8,
    10, 101-22, 124, 130, 142, 157;
    Tetrachordon 120
Monty Python 79
Moore, John 15-16, 151
Muldoon, Paul 128

Ovid, *Amores* 2, 3, 9, 135, 137; *Ars
    Amatoria* 2, 9, 135, 137; *Fasti* 3;
    Heroides 3, 12, 26, 29, 31, 79;
    Metamorphoses (for individual
    characters and episodes see
    separate index): relationship
    between art and nature in 10, 49,
    51-3, 136, 182, 184, 225; and
    Christianity 4, 8, 19, 101-11, 121,
    122, 131-3, 175, 188, 201, 217;
    detachment in 6, 8, 16-17, 42, 58,
    60-1, 63, 129-30, 141, 152-4, 204;

246